THE ARMCHAIR TRAVELLE[R]

# HUNTERS OF THE GREAT NORTH

# HUNTERS OF THE GREAT NORTH

BY

VILHJALMUR STEFANSSON

WITH ILLUSTRATIONS

PARAGON HOUSE
NEW YORK

First Paperback edition, 1990
Published in the United States by
Paragon House
90 Fifth Avenue
New York, NY 10011

Library of Congress Cataloging-in-Publication Data

Stefansson, Vilhjalmur, 1879–1962.
    Hunters of the great North / by Vilhjalmur
Stefansson. — 1st pbk. ed.
      p.    cm. — (Armchair traveller series)
    Reprint. Originally published: New York : Harcourt,
Brace, 1922.
    ISBN 1-55778-337-3
    1. Canada, Northern—Description and travel.
2. Hunting—Canada, Northern.  3. Eskimos—Canada,
Northern.  4. Stefansson, Vilhjalmur, 1879–1962—
Journeys—Canada, Northern.  I. Title.  II. Series.
F1090.5.S73   1990
917.1904′2—dc20
   [B]                              89-72109
                                    CIP

This book is printed on acid-free paper
Manufactured in the United States of America
10  9  8  7  6  5  4  3  2  1

# PREFACE

When first you leave home to travel in a foreign land you receive impressions more vivid than those of any later journey to the same country. If you at once rush your views and observations into print you are likely to have an interesting book but not so likely an accurate one. You will probably regret some parts of that book on grounds of mere regard for truth, for you will see later that you erred both in observations and conclusions.

When first I went to the polar regions I came back at the end of a year and a half full of enthusiasm for the Arctic and for the Eskimos. Luckily that enthusiasm was translated into the organization of a second expedition that left for the North in seven months, and not into a book to be published then. As I look over my diaries of that time I shudder to think how vastly I might have augmented the already great misknowledge of the Arctic had I published everything I imagined I had seen and everything I thought I knew.

At the end of my second expedition, after five winters and seven summers in the North, I published "My Life With the Eskimo" (New York and London, 1913). So far I have discovered (with the help of critics and through careful re-reading) a half dozen errors in that volume. Some of these have been eliminated as the book has been reprinted; the rest will be rectified in the next printing.

At the end of my third expedition, with a background of ten northern winters and thirteen summers, I wrote

"The Friendly Arctic" (New York and London, 1921). A comparison of that book with the earlier one will bring out few serious contradictions of fact (I hope none), although it will show a changed point of view—but only, I think, in line with a logical development founded on better understanding.

In the present book I have tried by means of diaries and memory to go back to the vivid impressions of my first year among the Eskimos for the story of what I saw and heard. I have tried to tell the story as I would have told it then, except that the mature knowledge of ten succeeding years has been used to eliminate early faults of observation and conclusion. A good many interesting stories found in the diaries of my first arctic voyage do not appear in this book because I now know them to have been based on misapprehensions. In a sense, the book is therefore less interesting than if I had published it fourteen years ago—but less interesting only to the extent in which it is more true.

The scientific collections made on the expedition described in this book are now in the Peabody Museum of Harvard University and in the Royal Ontario Museum of the University of Toronto, for those institutions joined in meeting the expense of my journey down the Mackenzie. The photographs in this volume are used by permission of the Peabody Museum, the American Museum of Natural History of New York, and the Departments of the Naval Service, Mines, and Colonization of Canada. Single pictures were furnished by personal friends of the author—Harry Anthony, Hawthorne Daniel and E. M. Kindle.

# CONTENTS

v

# LIST OF ILLUSTRATIONS

# HUNTERS OF THE GREAT NORTH

## CHAPTER I

### PREPARATIONS FOR A LIFEWORK OF EXPLORATION

My family were pioneers. In advance of the great railways that eventually came to cross the northwestern prairies, they traveled by primitive contrivance from the west end of Lake Superior across to the Red River of the North and down that river to Lake Winnipeg. Before them had been the trappers, the traders and missionaries; but they were among the earliest of the farmer colonists who in 1876 settled and began the process of transforming the pathless and romantic wilderness into the rich but commonplace agricultural community of to-day.

Those were days of stern trial. The Indians were friendly and to an extent helpful, but the settlers misunderstood and mistrusted them.

After two years of unremitting toil, our family found themselves in possession of a comfortable log cabin and the clearing of the forest had well begun, when there came a flood that drowned some of the cattle, carried away our haystacks and those of our neighbors, and left behind it destitution, which towards spring turned into famine. A brother and sister of my own are said to have died of malnutrition and some of our neighbors died of actual hunger. The terrors of smallpox epidemic were added, for epidemics and famines commonly go together.

It was partly these difficulties and tragedies and partly the pioneer spirit which leads ever farther and farther afield that took our family from the woods of Manitoba out upon the prairies of Dakota. I had been born in 1879 just before the flood and was less than two years old when we crossed the frontier into the United States.

For some ten years I grew up on a Dakota farm and walked two or three miles in winter to the little country school which in those days was in session only a small part of the year. However, there were several schools in different directions from our farm and it was sometimes possible for me, when one school closed, to get in a few extra weeks at a second school when their terms did not happen to coincide.

After the death of my father we sold the farm and I became for four years a cowboy on the "wild land," as we then called the prairies that had not yet been homesteaded. Our nearest neighbors were ten or fifteen miles away in various directions between northeast and southeast, but to the west I never knew how far our nearest neighbors were. It may have been a hundred or two hundred miles.

In boyhood I read by the dozen stories of cowboys and frontier life, and the open prairie was to me a land of romance. The buffaloes were just disappearing, but their whitening bones lay everywhere and their deep trails wound like endless serpents over hill and valley. Sitting Bull and his Indians were near enough and powerful enough so that the more sober of us feared him and the more romantic hoped that his war parties might some day come over the line of the horizon. In my imagination I could see myself as a brave scout upon whom the lives of the settlement depended, watching from afar the camp fires of the Indians. But one day we heard that Sitting Bull had been shot and that the ghost dances were over.

Although the buffalo was gone, Buffalo Bill was still with us. I never saw him but my elder brother, Joe, wore a sombrero and long hair down his back in the best frontier style and looked much like him. A number of the cowboys I worked with had known him in the early days before he started out with his Wild West show. Most of them let on they could shoot better and ride better than Buffalo Bill. Modesty is not a special virtue of the frontier nor are jealousies unknown.

In another corner of our territory was Roosevelt, gathering on the open prairie through his contact with pioneers some of the breadth and freedom and vision that characterized him later. We did not even know he was there, for in our part of the country telegraphs and telephones were still in the future and the stray copies of newspapers we saw were frequently six months old. His fame did not spread to our section until it began to spread over the whole world. That was after my cowboy days.

My first ambition, so far as I remember, was to be Buffalo Bill and to kill Indians. That was while I was still a small boy on the farm. When I became a cowboy and began to dress like Buffalo Bill and to put on my revolver in the morning as I would an article of clothing, my ambition shifted and my ideal became Robinson Crusoe. That is an ambition that never left me. Twenty years later when I discovered lands and stepped ashore on islands where human foot had never trod, I had in reality very much the thrills of my boyhood imagination when I dreamed of being a castaway on my own island or of visiting Crusoe on his.

At this time there were no indications that I was to be led eventually into the career of polar exploration. But unconsciously I was getting the best preparation for it. On the frontier farm I had hunted rabbits and grouse in the winter, ducks and geese and swans and cranes in the spring and fall. After I became a cowboy I pursued on horseback the white tail antelope. I can scarcely remember the time when I did not hunt with a shotgun, and since the age of ten I have been a fair rifle shot.

But more valuable than anything in fitting me for the life of a hunter in the polar regions was my buffeting by the Dakota climate. Dakota in summer has the same terrific heat that we find in some parts of the arctic prairies. The Dakota winter is not as long as the arctic winter but it is occasionally as cold, and some Dakota blizzards are as bad winter weather as any in the northern hemisphere. I hear the conditions are getting a little different after thirty years of cultivation. Farmhouses now stand half a mile apart where the cattle ranches once were twenty and thirty miles apart, and trees have been planted in many places to break the wind.

Things were different when I was eighteen. Four of us boys, all of about the same age, had started a ranch of our own. We had picked out a conspicuous hill that looked from a distance like the double hump of a camel. Our house stood on one hump and a hundred yards away were our saddle ponies in a barn on the other hump. That year there blew up the day before Thanksgiving a storm which is still called by the pioneers "the Thanksgiving Blizzard." The weather was warm and the sky gradually became overcast. For about six hours the snowflakes fluttered down quietly, getting more numerous hour by hour as the wind gradually increased.

The next morning it was a howling gale. Wiser men than we would have had a rope or smooth wire running from our house door to the barn door to guide us through the blizzard so we could have fed the stock. After much discussion as to whether it was safe, I decided that, as we knew the exact direction of the wind and as the barn was long and stood broadside to the house, I would probably be able to find it. I backed out of the door into the wind, holding my mittened hands over my face, for otherwise the wind takes your breath away. The protection from my hands kept my eyes from being filled with the snow as I worked my way to the barn. But the barn door was in the lee of the building and a great snowdrift had been piled up against it. Although I knew where the door was I found no sign of it, and I realized that if I dug down towards it with a shovel the drifting snow would fill the hole faster than I could dig it. Furthermore, I could not find the shovel which had been buried by the snow. I considered breaking my way into the barn through the roof, but decided that even if I made the needed aperture, I would not be able to carry hay from the stack to the barn. So I gave up and returned to the house.

We did not think much of this adventure at the time, but I now consider it one of the most foolhardy enterprises of a career that has been in considerable part devoted to similar things. When we got to the settlement months later, we heard of some twenty or thirty tragedies that had resulted from this gale. Some farmers had gone out in search of their barns, had never found them and had been frozen to death. Others found their barns and stayed there until the gale was over, not daring to return to the house. Still others found their barns, fed their stock, and lost their lives on the way back to the house. There were also stories of lightly built farm shanties that had been blown away by the wind, exposing the occupants to the blizzard or killing them in the wreck.

At that time I agreed with all our neighbors (we called each other neighbors though we were fifteen miles apart), that gales such as I have described were exceedingly dangerous to life and limb. That was because we did not know how to deal with them. I have since learned from the Eskimos how to get along in a blizzard and should feel ashamed of myself if I suffered anything as serious as a frost bite from a day out in it.

During my cowboy days our neighbors were of the regular American type, but the farming community in which I passed my earlier years came from countries in Europe where literary ambitions take the place of the money making dreams that are nowadays more common. Fully half our neighbor boys talked of going to college. Their ambitions were to become lawyers and authors and statesmen. For my part, I had decided to become a poet, and for this I considered a college education as the first requirement. Through circumstances into which I cannot go, but which hinged upon the Thanksgiving blizzard I have just described, I failed in my initial business venture (that of establishing a cattle ranch of my own) and so turned to the earlier college dreams. When I left for the State University I boarded a railway train for the first time in my life, although I had seen railway trains perhaps two dozen times before. I had fifty-three dollars, wore a seven-dollar suit of clothes, and felt no doubt of my ability to work my way through college.

This all came to pass. I attended the State University of North Dakota to the junior year, then the State University of Iowa where I got my Bachelor of Arts degree, and eventually Harvard for three years of post-graduate study.

During this college period I had changed my plans many times. My poetic ambitions lasted long enough for me to read nearly all the English poets and those of two or three other languages. I even wrote some poems that were printed in the college magazines. It may seem that this was no suitable preparation for my eventual career of hunting polar bears and exploring polar lands. I am not sure of that. The explorer is the poet of action, and a great poet in proportion as he is a great explorer. He needs a mind to see visions no less than he needs the strength to face a blizzard.

Somewhere near the middle of my college career I began to see that there is not only the poetry of words but a poetry of deeds. Magellan's voyage rounded out a magnificent conception as fully and finally as ever did a play of Shakespeare's. A law of nature is an imperishable poem.

Ideas of that sort decided me to try to win my spurs in science rather than literature.

The sciences I selected for study were those that deal with life on our earth. Darwin and Spencer took the places formerly occupied by Keats and Shelley. I dreamt of discovering some law of life comparable in significance to the doctrine of evolution. Finally I specialized in anthropology—the science that deals with man and his works in general, but pays special attention to what the thoughtless call "primitive people" or "savages."

I went to Harvard first to study comparative religions

in the theological school, but I later transferred to the graduate school to study other branches of anthropology. In that connection I became a teaching fellow.  Earlier in my career I had been a school master for portions of several years, but I did not like teaching very well so I decided to become a field investigator of anthropology in tropical Africa.  For two years I used all my spare time reading books about Africa and everything was ready for me to accompany a British commercial expedition under military escort that was going into East Central Africa.

At Harvard in my day it was usual for a number of friends to form a group and have assigned them in the dining room a special table.  At meals we used to discuss all sorts of things, including what we had read in the papers.  One day somebody asked me what I thought of the accounts then in the press about a new polar expedition being organized by an American, Leffingwell, and a Dane, Mikkelsen.  They thought I might be interested for I had written and published the year before an essay on how the Norsemen discovered Greenland about nine hundred years ago, and how they were the first Europeans who ever saw Eskimos.  But I said I had no keen personal interest in the proposed polar expedition because my thoughts for two years had been centered upon Africa.

A day or two after this discussion we were again together at dinner when a messenger boy brought me a telegram.  It was signed by Ernest de Koven Leffingwell, and said he would pay my expenses if I would come to Chicago to have a talk about going with his polar expedition to study the Eskimos in Victoria Island who had never seen a white man.

Of all the excited discussion which followed the reading

of this telegram I remember only that we guessed Leffing-well or some adviser of his had read my paper on the discovery of Greenland and that this invitation to go north was the result. The guess proved to be correct.

My decision was soon made and I took the first train west. At my talk with Leffingwell it was agreed that I should join his expedition, not at Victoria, British Columbia, where the ship was being outfitted and where all the rest of the staff were to gather, but at the mouth of the Mackenzie River. By the map, these places are far apart. But it was the plan of the expedition to sail north through the Pacific and through Bering Straits and then to follow the north coast of Alaska eastward to the whaling station at Herschel Island at the mouth of the Mackenzie River. Herschel Island was the place I selected for joining the expedition, and for several reasons.

I had already crossed the Atlantic four times and had learnt that one ocean wave looks much like another. From that point of view, at least, there is nothing to be learned from a sea voyage, and I know of nothing more tedious. If I needed a rest I should take a long voyage, but I was not feeling in need of any rest just then. So I proposed to make instead the interesting and instructive overland journey from Boston to the mouth of the Mackenzie. The road lies through a country which is even now a wilderness, although in the seventeen years since I made the journey there have been great developments. At that time you might have been a well-informed and well-traveled man without ever having seen or heard of any one who had made this trip. The Indians along the route were "unknown to science," although they had long been in contact with the Hudson's Bay Company fur traders and other wilderness travelers. Mr. Leffingwell was willing I should go by this route and meet the expedition at the mouth of the Mackenzie, providing I would find some way of paying my own expenses that far. I took this up at once with Harvard University and the University of Toronto, and the two universities agreed to share the expense of the overland and river journey. In return they were to receive the information secured, and the scientific collections.

## CHAPTER II

I LEFT New York in April, 1906, and traveled by way of
Toronto and the Canadian Pacific Railway to Winnipeg.
At that time the Canadian Northern Railway had not
been completed to the Pacific Coast but the stretch between Winnipeg and Edmonton had been opened. It
lay through virgin country where farms and towns were
springing up here and there on the prairies or in the wood-
land places. I have always had a passion for new countries and so I preferred the as yet crude service and un-
even roadbed of the Canadian Northern to the smooth
track and perfect system of the Canadian Pacific. It
took a day and a half for the nine hundred miles to Edmonton.

From Winnipeg on my journey was under the protect-
ing wing of the Hudson's Bay Company, the oldest and
most romantic commercial concern in the world and even
to-day one of the greatest in capital and financial power.
Lord Strathcona was the world head of the Company with
offices in London, but in Canada their wide empire in the
North was controlled by the Chief Commissioner, C. C.
Chipman, who welcomed me in Winnipeg. With official
courtesy and great personal kindness he gave me advice
and saw to it that the "servants" (as the employees of
this ancient organization are still called) should give me
every assistance. Through him I met the distinguished

scientist-explorer, Roderick Macfarlane, who had been to the arctic coast as early as 1867 when the Indians still lived in perpetual dread of the warlike and more powerful Eskimos to the north of them who made raids at will as much as four hundred miles into the Indian country, the Indians never thinking to make resistance and vacating large stretches of country whenever the Eskimos approached. Luckily for the Indians, the Eskimos have a prejudice against living in a forest in the winter time, thinking that a tree shade from the sun may be agreeable but having no idea that the shelter of a forest from the wind is anything to be desired. Else they might have despoiled the Indians permanently of their hunting grounds.

Macfarlane told me that the Eskimo war parties seemed to have only one object and that was to secure suitable stone in a quarry near Fort Good Hope from which to make their knives and the sharp tips of the arrows with which they hunted caribou and the harpoons with which they hunted seals and whales. They came, he said, in singing and shouting boatloads four hundred miles from their own country at the mouth of the Mackenzie River to Good Hope. The time of their arrival was so carefully gauged in advance by the increasing summer heat that the Indians had grown to know the proper fleeing time. Accordingly, they used to abandon their river bank villages in May and retreat into the forest, not returning to the Mackenzie again until autumn when they knew the Eskimos would be gone. As the villages consisted of tents that could be carried away, the Eskimos found nothing to plunder. It was only when some accident brought Indians and Eskimos together that bloodshed occurred. If the parties were anything like the same strength or if the Indians were fewer they used to flee, but occasionally it happened that a large number of Indians came upon a few Eskimos who had become separated from the main party. In those cases the Indians would kill the Eskimos. I had read stories of just this kind in the books of the early explorers, such as Sir John Richardson. It was impressive to hear them from the lips of a gentle old man like Macfarlane who had himself been in the country towards the end of this period of hostility while the fear of bloodshed still prevailed though the battles themselves no longer occurred and although the Hudson's Bay Company was now supplying the Eskimos with iron in place of their stone implements, so that they no longer had any occasion to make long journeys to the stone quarries at Good Hope. It had been one of the earliest tasks of the Company to make peace between the Indians and Eskimos. In this they had succeeded pretty well even before Macfarlane's time, and still not completely, for Macfarlane himself was once robbed by the most pugnacious of all the Eskimo "tribes," the Kupagmiut, or people of the Great River, who lived at certain seasons of year on a branch of the Mackenzie delta but who wandered far afield either in large or small groups. It was with this very group I was destined to spend the coming winter, though I did not know it when I was talking with Macfarlane.

As interesting as the scholarly Macfarlane was John Anderson, who under the title of "Chief Trader of the Mackenzie District" was in effect viceroy over a northern empire. This was a position which Macfarlane had held before him. Although younger in years, Anderson belonged to an older school of thought. He had come as a boy from the north of Scotland directly into the Company's service. This was in the days when the Company had not as yet traded away for money and for other valuable considerations the right which they once had actually to govern Canada, administering justice and having even the power of life and death, not only over their employees but over any one who penetrated the country with or without their consent. Even after these ancient powers of the Hudson's Bay Company had been surrendered, the tradition of exercising them still prevailed and Anderson could never quite understand that any one had a right to enter the north country without the consent of the Company. I learned later that his attitude towards all he met there was that of a generous and hospitable host who, nevertheless, was much on his dignity, ready to consider it an affront if anything was done without his knowledge and approval. He knew his legal rights of overlordship had been curtailed but he simply could not bring himself to realize it.

Many who knew Anderson liked him as I did; there were many others who disliked and even hated him, and chiefly because of his intense loyalty to the Company and his inability to realize that "new occasions teach new duties" and that "time makes ancient good uncouth."

I made the journey with Anderson from Winnipeg to Edmonton. In both cities and on the way between, his hospitality was so insistent as to be embarrassing. When once we passed beyond Edmonton this changed like the switching on of a light of another color and he became more penurious than can readily be imagined. This was another of his traits which caused much misunderstanding and ill feeling but which a few of us understood and sympathized with. South of Edmonton he was a private person, spending his own money as he liked; north of

Edmonton he was a servant of the Company, viceroy, indeed, of a vast empire, but handling only supplies which
belonged to the Company and not to him.  Nearly every
Hudson's Bay man of that time and many of them even
to-day have that feeling of trusteeship which makes it
unthinkable to let anything go to waste that belongs to
the Company.  But few if any carried it to such extremes
as Anderson.

To most of us it was laughable.  He would, for instance, try to impress on every one that no matter what
they paid for their transportation and daily food they
were not paying nearly as much as the bother of carrying
them was worth.  For that reason he insisted we were all
guests of the Company and not ordinary passengers and
we owed to the Company the courtesy of a guest towards
a host.  One thing he felt we should not do was to commence eating before he started or to continue after he
stopped.  He ate frugally and rapidly but in his opinion
the quantity he ate was enough and the time was sufficient
for any one to eat all that was good for him.  He expected us to stop eating when he did and I for one always
did so, but there were six or eight other passengers
(missionaries, Government officials, etc.) who felt they
were paying enough for their food and that they were
entitled to gorge themselves if they chose.  Anderson
spoke of them with bitterness as lacking in courtesy, as
gluttonous and as unable to appreciate how precious
food is and how many people there are in the world who
have not enough of it.  That was a point of view little
comprehensible then but one which we understand better
now since the Great War put us on rations and since we
have come into more intimate contact with famines in
Russia, China and elsewhere.

A few years before Edmonton had been but a fur trading outpost, but by 1906 it was a city of six or eight thousand people and since then it has grown to sixty thousand (in 1922). The railways did extend west beyond it, but not north beyond it, and so we had to drive by a horse stage chiefly through sandy land covered with jack pine, a hundred miles to the head of river navigation at Athabasca Landing on Athabasca River. This was then a town of some five or six hundred, half the people either pure or part Indian. In Edmonton the northern fur trade had been an important topic of conversation but in Athabasca Landing it was the only topic.

Below Athabasca Landing two methods of river travel were in use. There was a steamer, the *Midnight Sun*, and there were flat-bottomed boats called scows, each carrying about eight tons of freight and manned by crews of Cree Indians. The method of travel by scow was more picturesque and in reality more rapid, as our experience showed. I used that method on my second journey down the Mackenzie with great satisfaction. On this first journey I chose the steamer, not having the northern point of view and being prejudiced in favor of steamers, believing in their greater speed and comfort.

A floating log would have outdistanced the *Midnight Sun* several times over, for it took us thirteen days to navigate 165 miles down stream. This may be the slow record for down river steamboat navigation. There were many reasons. For one thing, we used to get shipwrecked every so often. Being shipwrecked sounds rather exciting but was a tame performance on the *Midnight Sun*. She was used to it and knew exactly how to do it. Because of her aptitude in sinking, Lee, an expert canoe-

man of our party, and also our leading humorist, gave
her the nickname by which we always called her—the
Rockbound Limited.

One of our fellow-passengers was a clergyman new out
of England on his way to a mission station at Fort Nor-
man just south of the arctic circle. His was a restless
curiosity about all things indigenous to the country, but
he admitted that the more he investigated the more depressed he became. He told me that he would have
turned south before ever he reached his subarctic station,
oppressed with the depravity of the "civilized" Indians
whom he already more than half-suspected of inability
to see the superiority of the Anglican over the Catholic
Church, but for two things which kept him to his job—
the encouragement of Bishop Reeve, who had seen much
improvement among the Indians in his time and was
therefore optimistic, and his own pride which forbade
turning back from work once undertaken.

And if his missionary ardors were somewhat cooled
by the unromantic aspect of lazy-looking, gambling Indians dressed in cheap ready-made city clothes, they were
no less affected by the mosquitoes. In England he had
vaguely anticipated the possibility of being tomahawked
by savages and he modestly doubted whether he could
have met such a death with fortitude. Martyrdom before lions or howling savages could perhaps be met cour-
ageously in an instant of spiritual exaltation. But martyrdom through being tortured for days and weeks by
insect pests was a wholly different thing. In the stifling
afternoon heat when (on one occasion) the temperature
on our boat rose to 103° in the shade, he had to wear
heavy clothing and even then the mosquitoes crawled
down the gauntlet of his glove and bit him on the wrist

if nowhere else. At other times if he took off his face net to get a breath of free air, they stung him on ears and nose and cheek. So they stung all the rest of us, and we itched no less than he. But we had been inoculated in other years with the virus of the mosquito and had developed antitoxins that prevented inflammation, while he was almost fresh from mosquitoless England. Wherever an insect bit he became flecked and bloated. Then he scratched and rubbed the swellings till they were raw and began to smart more than they itched.

But if he was depressed by the appearance of his prospective converts and tortured by the heat and the insects, he still felt a mild craving for adventure. He looked on the map to see that he was veritably hundreds of miles from railway and telegraph, and thereby succeeded in half-convincing himself that the country could not be in reality as tame as it looked. Somewhere romance must be lurking concealed by the tangled underbrush. A few times we had seen from our steamer black bears hunched up in the tops of trees, and once or twice our Indian deckhands had been allowed to go ashore and murder these defenseless animals that had been scared into climbing a tree by the noise of our steamer. Our missionary had no real thirst for blood so he never joined in these expeditions. But when the steamer tied up to the bank either because night was about to fall or else because they needed wood for engine fuel, he used to go in search of mild adventure—to discover and report new flowers, strange birds or the tracks of moose.

One evening at twilight he met in the bush a pretty animal of black and white stripes, slow-moving and approachable. In fact, it was standing still in the path before him, so he killed it with a club. Upon the unanimous request of the passengers and crew of our steamer he had to change his clothes at once when he came back from this adventure. I believe there is a way of getting rid of skunk odor from clothing; but our clergyman was so mortified that he took no advice from any one on that point, put all his garments in a bundle and dropped them overboard into the river when no one was looking. I think this was his clerical suit, and that it was his only clerical suit. However, the Indians of the lower Mackenzie were not at that time sticklers for form, and probably did not know whether they belonged to the High or Low Church, so that his being without clerical garments may not have proved a serious handicap when he got to his field of work.

One of the great sights as we went down the river in 1906 was the burning gas well at Pelican Rapids. The whole Mackenzie valley, of which the Athabasca is a part, has since been shown to be a country of many oil prospects, and oil wells are now actually flowing in some places. At that time we had indications of this by getting our boots smeared with what we called mineral tar when we walked along the river bank.

The Pelican Rapids gas well was a spectacular demonstration of the power and wealth that may lie under the surface. Some years before, a party had been there drilling for oil and had struck natural gas instead. The gas has been flowing ever since. Some one had set fire to it and it was now burning as a torch, with flames shooting some ten or fifteen feet into the air. At night it illumined with a flickering light the broad Athabasca on one side and the forest on the other. I was poetical in those days and wrote in my diary that this was the torch of science lighting the way to the Far North for explorers and engineers and captains of industry.

At Grand Rapids Island, 165 miles down stream from Athabasca Landing, we came on the thirteenth day to the end of our steamboat navigation. There is here an island in the middle of the river. The rapids between it and the west bank are spectacular and so dangerous that we heard of no attempt to run them by boat. They will doubtless sometime give water power to a city and to factories built in that vicinity.

The rapids to the east of the island are spectacular enough but they are occasionally run by expert canoemen and sometimes by the scows of the fur traders. The scows are unloaded at the upper end of the island, which is about half a mile long. Sometimes they are carried on a tramway across the island, and the freight always is so carried. Some of the scows run the rapids. Serious accidents do not often happen but danger is always imminent and whoever is within reach always goes out to a vantage point and watches breathlessly as the rapids are being run.

It is common that Indians have a contempt for the rivercraft, woodcraft and plainscraft of white men. This is partly because many white men who go beyond the frontier are unbelievably helpless and partly because the white men themselves have an exaggerated respect for the ability of the Indians and tell the Indians that no white man can do certain things which to an Indian are easy. It is human to believe that we excel in one way or another, and so the Indian readily puts on himself the white man's valuation.

But it is a fact that there are few such canoemen in the world as are developed in certain parts of Ontario. Our humorist Lee was one of these. He had never seen the Grand Rapids of the Athabasca and everybody knew he had never seen them. But both Indians and whites had told him much about how dangerous they were. By watching Indians farther up river, he had formed a contempt for their boatmanship, and when he heard that some Indians had run the rapids in canoes he went to Anderson and succeeded in borrowing a small new Peterborough that we were carrying to sell to some wealthy Indian down the river. Getting into this canoe he paddled towards the rapids. To the astonishment of those of us who knew little about rivercraft, he turned his canoe around as he was approaching the rapids and ran the half mile of seething water backward. This impressed the local Indians even more than it did the white men, especially as they knew that he had not seen the rapids before.

Below the Grand Rapids we took to the scows and navigated the rest of the distance to Fort McMurray more rapidly and far more pleasantly. We had several exciting rapids to run, and once a scow was thrown against a boulder and broken so badly that it sank just at the foot of the rapids and as the crew were approaching the bank. The sugar it carried and similar trade goods were entirely spoilt. A rather amusing circumstance was that a bale containing ribbons of all colors became soaking wet. The colors were not fast, and when the ribbons were taken out to dry, each was found to have upon it a little of the color of all the others. I imagined this would ruin the ribbons, but was told that the consignment was for one of the remote posts on the Liard branch of the Mackenzie and that the Indians up there would not mind. One of the traders said that you never could tell exactly how those things would strike the Indians. It was even possible that this lot would prove more popular than any other and might set a fashion so the Indians would demand similar multicolored ribbons next year.

There were three things I did not like about our journey down stream. The first was the increasing heat. After the middle of June we began to suffer from it a good deal. One day the temperature was 103° in the shade. It was a humid heat and therefore difficult to stand. A temperature of 110° or 115° in a desert like Arizona would be far less unpleasant.

Our second trouble was that the mosquitoes were getting worse day by day. Towards the 20th of June they were so bad that they annoyed us even in midriver. When we landed they came about us in swarms. If the weather had been cool it might not have been unpleasant to dress heavily enough so that mosquitoes could not sting through, but in the extreme heat it is exceedingly unpleasant to wear thick clothes all over your body, heavy buckskin gauntlet gloves on your hands, a big sombrero on your head, and a mosquito net that is gathered around the crown of the hat, comes out over the brim and has to be tucked under the collar of your coat so as to prevent insects from exploring your back. When it is hot you want every breath of air and a veil of heavy mosquito netting keeps a good deal of the air away.

Luckily I do not smoke. It was amusing to see the bother the smokers had. They would get long-stemmed pipes, make small round holes in the mosquito netting, and thrust the stems of the pipes through so they could puff at them. Occasionally a mosquito would get on the stem of a pipe and crawl in that way. This was not so likely to happen, however; but when the smoker was through there was a hole in his netting through which a few mosquitoes would be sure to find their way.

It is difficult to describe adequately the unbelievable plague of mosquitoes in the North. As you go nearer and nearer to the arctic circle they become worse and worse. I have found by experience that people will never believe the truth about the northern mosquitoes and so, instead of trying to describe them myself, I am quoting Ernest Thompson Seton's "The Arctic Prairies," pp. 63-64:

"Each day they got worse: soon it became clear that mere adjectives could not convey any idea of their terrors. Therefore I devised a mosquito gauge. I held up a bare hand for 5 seconds by the watch, then counted the number of borers on the back; there were 5 to 10. Each day added to the number, and when we got out to the buffalo country, there were 15 to 25 on the one side of the hand and elsewhere in proportion. On the Hyarling, in early July, the number was increased, being 20 to 40. On Great Slave Lake, later that month, there were 50 to 60. But when we reached the Barren Grounds, the land of open breezy plains and cold water lakes, the pests were so bad that the hand held up for 5 seconds often showed from 100 to 125 long-billed mosquitoes boring away into the flesh. It was possible to number them only by killing them and counting the corpses. What wonder that all men should avoid the open plains, that are the kingdom of such a scourge."

Of the three things I did not like on our northward journey, I mention last the unforgettable cruelty towards their dogs shown by most of the Indians and by some of the white trappers and traders.

There are various apparently incongruous things about how an Indian treats his team. To begin with, he likes to have them fine in appearance, fat, with a glossy fur and a proud carriage of the head and tail. This is not easy to reconcile with his insistence that the dogs shall jump every time he makes a noise or a move and especially when he cracks a whip. To this end he beats them unmercifully. I have often seen Indians hitch up their dog teams in the early morning, tie them to a tree and with a whip that cracks like pistol shots beat one dog after the other as they lie tied and helpless in the harness until each one of them is mad with fear and pain. Then they untie them and the sleigh dashes off at full speed.

The mind of a dog has the same power over his body that our minds have over our bodies. Most Indian dogs, therefore, have a cringing attitude which the Indian does not really like, for he wants a proud appearance. To gain that, he lavishes all his ingenuity and a large part of his money upon decorations. There are ribbons and all sorts of adornments, and there are bells of every size and liquid note that tinkle and chime with the slightest movement of the dogs. The bells are on the collars of the harness and sometimes on vertical rods that stand high above the collars and wag from side to side as the dogs move. Then there are bells along the backs of the dogs and in whatever place is most likely to tremble or shake as the animals move.

If the Indian is particular about what he considers good form in starting out in the morning, he is far more particular about the style in which he arrives at a village. For that reason it has been the custom, in the lower Mackenzie at least, that the Indians who are coming into the fur trading posts will camp the evening before five or ten miles away, so as to give their dogs a good night's rest. In the morning they are hitched up, beaten and otherwise thrown into a high excitement, and then the cavalcade dashes at top speed into the trading post just at the psychological moment—commonly the middle of the fore-noon when the daylight is already clear and when the factor and all the inhabitants of the post have had their breakfast and are ready to come out and watch and welcome the arriving sledges.

This is a partial picture of the dog's winter life as I was told about in 1906 and as I have seen it since. During winter he has the advantage of being well fed, for his master needs his strength and wants him to appear well. But the Indians have found that a few weeks of ample feeding will put a dog into good condition. During the summer they do no driving and can make no ostentatious use of their dogs. It is, accordingly, the custom to stop feeding them in the spring and let them rustle for themselves during the summer. The result was that by the time we began our journey down the Athabasca (early June) the dogs had already been starved into skeletons. They were skulking about everywhere, looking for any scrap they might eat. Sometimes they would find a greasy rag, swallow it because it smelt like food, and die in agony because a rag is indigestible and sticks in the intestines.

Every one has to protect his property, and for that reason a dog is occasionally killed when caught stealing or attempting to steal. So far as dogs are concerned, cruelty is in the air. A maimed dog is a great joke. I remember particularly a white man who had been in the country only three or four years but whose disposition was such that he had taken naturally to the ways of the Indian. It is frequently the case and was so here, that this man was worse than almost any Indian. I have forgotten now what it was that he had in front of his camp but it was something tempting to dogs. He kept the tent door open and by his side he had two or three hatchets. When he saw a strange and starving dog approaching his property outside he would watch till the animal was about to take a bite, and then throw a hatchet at him. I never knew him actually to kill a dog, but I saw one case of a broken shoulder and heard of other serious injuries. Some of the Indians made claims upon this man for maiming their dogs and even charged him with cruelty. Judging by how they themselves behaved, I should say that this was pretended sympathy for the dogs and was put on merely in an attempt to recover damages from the well-to-do white man.

Some of the Indians who were our boatmen owned one or several of these starving dogs. It is difficult to see how dogs could have affection for such owners, but still that appeared to be the case, in some instances at least. Or it may have been merely that the wretched things knew no other hope than to follow their masters around. Twenty or thirty of them kept abreast of us on the river bank as we proceeded down stream. The current is now along one bank and now along the other, and a boat keeps to the current. When we shifted with the current to the far side of the stream the poor dogs knew no better than to jump in and swim the quarter or half mile of turbulent water to climb up on the bank nearest us. The forest was thick along the river and heaps of drift logs were piled in certain places. This made difficult traveling for dogs already weak with hunger, and one by one they dropped behind. I did not know whether their destiny was to die of starvation or whether they would return to some village and perhaps live through the summer. I asked the Indians about it but they did not seem either to know or care.

It seems unbelievable but appears to be the fact that even with this treatment a majority of the dogs do live through the summer somehow. I was told that Indians whose dogs are left behind as the boats go down stream, will later in the summer when they are journeying back up stream inquire for their dogs from village to village, and that they usually manage to pick up most of them before they get to their home settlements.

At McMurray the steamer *Grahame* was waiting for us. She was so much like an ordinary river steamer of the Mississippi or Ohio that she is not worth describing. We made our journey in her rapidly and comfortably down the rest of the Athabasca, then across Athabasca Lake and down to the head of the sixteen-mile series of rapids known as the Smith Portage.

At the head of Smith Rapids is a fur trading post which was then called Smith's Landing after a man who has left his impression upon Canadian history and upon Canada partly in the form of place names. These place names in turn preserve his history by the way they change. He used to be plain Donald Smith and at that stage Smith's Landing and a good many other places were named after him. Then he became Sir Donald Smith and many places bear that name, among them none so famous at present as Mount Sir Donald in the Rockies that is each year admired through the windows of moving trains by about two hundred and fifty thousand travelers over the Canadian Pacific Railway. When his power was at the greatest and when he had become one of the leading figures in the British Empire and in the world, this same man was Lord Strathcona, after whom are named hotels and parks, villages and cities, rivers and mountains and lakes all over Canada and in many other countries.

In the terrific humid midsummer heat I walked the sandy road across rolling hills and occasionally waded through small patches of swamp from the head of Smith Rapids to Fort Smith which stands at the lower end. The roar of the rapids could be heard through the forest which hid the river. I should have liked to see the whirl-pools and waterfalls and especially the pelican rookery on a little island, for this is said to be the most northerly rookery of that bird in the world. But I had not as yet become acclimated enough to the North to have the cour-age to fight the mosquitoes through as long and tedious a battle as would have been necessary had I clambered my way among the boulders and through the brush along the river's brink for fifteen miles. Just then nothing ap-peared to me so desirable as getting quickly into a house at Fort Smith where mosquito netting and closed doors would shut out the insect world.

At the Rapids we left behind our humorist, the same Lee who had astounded the natives as a canoeman. His job was to build the sawmill which was to produce the lumber needed for the construction of a more modern river steamer for service on the lower Mackenzie. In his main purpose Lee succeeded well, for two years later on my second journey through this country I photographed the launching of the *Mackenzie River*, which had been built in the intervening two years from the lumber cut by Lee's sawmill. She has been plying regularly since then up and down the magnificent 1300 mile waterway that lies between the Smith Rapids and the head of the Mackenzie delta well within the arctic circle.

The *Wrigley* awaited us at Fort Smith. The *Mid-*

STR. *Mackenzie River* BELOW SMITH RAPIDS

THE SMITH RAPIDS

*night Sun* and the *Grahame* had both been typical river steamers, flat-bottomed with shallow draft and with paddle wheels at the stern. The *Wrigley* was smaller, was built much like an ocean-going ship and had a screw propeller. It was then believed by many that only a specially seaworthy ship with a screw propeller could safely cross Slave Lake, a great body of water subject occasionally to violent gales. There is probably some truth in this view. The *Wrigley* could cross the lake almost at will but I have heard that the more modern *Mackenzie River* now watches for a fair opportunity and dodges timorously from shelter to shelter in her dealings with the lake. Flat-bottomed stern wheel steamers that look above water more like a house than a ship are well enough on rivers but difficult to deal with on a lake or on the ocean.

The *Wrigley* had berths for six passengers only. Some of our fellow-travelers, such as Bishop Reeve (the Right Reverend William Day Reeve) had to have stateroom accommodation because of their dignity—not that the Bishop himself insisted on it but merely because the rest of us felt the impropriety of anything else. Others had to be in the cabins for other reasons. But I was a youngster without dignity and more anxious for experiences than for what is called comfort. So I used to sleep on deck wherever I could and whenever I felt like it.

The *Wrigley* traveled rapidly and was so well managed that nothing special happened to us. In crossing Slave Lake we were out of sight of land for some hours. This gave us an impression of the vast extent of that lake, which is intermediate in its size between Lake Huron and Lake Erie. If the large lakes of North America are arranged in order of size, I believe they are as follows:

Superior, Michigan, Huron, Great Bear, Great Slave, Erie, and Ontario.

Although we had no adventures strictly on our own account, we nearly had some because a small steamer belonging to the Hudson's Bay Company's chief trading rival, Hislop and Nagle, had run on a sandbar. Far out in the lake we met a launch which told us the news. To help this ship in distress we turned in the direction of a locality known to be infested with sandbars. All of us were keenly on the lookout for the stranded steamer. Presently we saw her, changed our course slightly and steamed directly towards her, until all of a sudden we realized that what we had taken for a steamer was only a small log lying on a bar.

It was my first experience with an atmospheric condition which is common in the North although not peculiar to it. There is a certain lucidity and shimmer in the air which makes it especially difficult to judge distance. If you are looking for a ship far away and see a small piece of driftwood near you, the bit of stick is likely to be mistaken for a ship. On certain occasions since then I have mistaken for a grizzly bear a spermophile (an animal something like a prairie dog or a hedgehog). I have known of other travelers who have mistaken a white fox, not much bigger than a cat, for a polar bear. Nordenskjöld tells of seeing a dark mountain with glacier-filled valleys on either side and of steering his boat towards it until fortunately it dived as he was just about to collide with it, for it had been a walrus and the two glaciers had been the tusks.

We nearly ran aground on the sandbar towards which we had been led by the piece of wood we took for a steamer. We did run aground several times later and had a special way of dealing with that situation. Ordinarily a ship such as the *Wrigley* will run on a level keel, drawing slightly less water forward than aft. But we kept the *Wrigley* down by the bow with a cargo of shot in 200 pound bags. When we ran aground her nose would stick solidly in the sand or mud. Thereupon all the crew and some of the passengers would turn to and carry the shot from the bow to the stern. This lifted the nose of our boat a foot or two and released her from the grip of the mud.

Having been once deceived by a log that looked like a ship, we were more on our guard. Thereafter ships that were plain ships in the eyes of some of us were logs in the eyes of others. Eventually we really found the *Eva*. She had not had the forethought to carry a cargo of shot in her bow to keep it down, and consequently she was hard aground along the full length of her keel. We passed over to her a long hawser and pulled her off.

It must have been difficult for Mackenzie, the original explorer of a hundred years before, to find the place where the river leaves Slave Lake. Even with an Indian pilot of some experience, we had a good deal of difficulty. Where it heads in the lake, the river is so wide that it really is a lake and you cannot say exactly where lake ends and river begins.

Especially where the Mackenzie River leaves Slave Lake, but also elsewhere in the lake and at many places in the river, there is danger of running on sandbars. Eventually when commerce develops, the channel will be buoyed and even an indifferent pilot will have no trouble in finding the way. It is a matter of great difficulty now. Memory will scarcely serve the pilot, for land and landmarks are too far away.

In rivers of developed commerce, such as the Mississippi or Yukon, shoals and sandbars are indicated by buoys, and pilot launches patrol the channels continually to keep account of their rapid shifting. For a sandbar that is here this week may be elsewhere next week. But in 1906 a pilot passed down the Mackenzie in July, returned in August, and did not see the stream again till next summer, by which time many shifts of shoals and channels had taken place. Consequently, the pilots then did not try to rely much on memory but kept their eyes upon the river ahead trying to tell by the color and the character of the ripples made by the wind or current whether the water ahead was deep or shallow. It is one of the consequences of this condition that when one praises a Mackenzie River pilot it is by calling him a good judge of water. One day when we had been running aground rather frequently, the Captain remarked to Anderson that our pilot might be a good judge of water but that he must be a pretty poor judge of land.

Where Hay River empties into Slave Lake we had passed a mission of the Church of England that had a fine garden and an especially large potato field. I find people commonly surprised when they are told about how well vegetables grow so far north, but they would not be surprised if they traveled through the country. When you are puffing and perspiring at a temperature above 90° in the shade, the rapid growth of potatoes seems no more remarkable than the thickness of the mosquito swarms. You rejoice at the one a good deal more than you do at the other, but either ceases to be mysterious in the sweltering heat.

On the Mackenzie River proper north of Great Slave Lake, we found flourishing gardens at every trading post.

The Roman Catholics at Providence showed us strawberries and various garden flowers in front of the buildings, and to one side of them waving fields of wheat and barley. Potatoes are cultivated with great success as far north as Fort Good Hope, just south of the arctic circle. They could be raised farther north, but under present conditions it pays the down river traders better to buy their potatoes from Good Hope and have them brought in by boat.

The trading posts of the Mackenzie River are on the average about two hundred miles apart. Every one of them has a series of buildings belonging to the Hudson's Bay Company. Some of them have churches or other mission buildings and many of them have the stores and residences of the so-called Free Traders.

The name Free Trader comes from the old days when the country was not free to trade in by any one except the Hudson's Bay Company, and when adventurers used to brave the penalty of what was then law and defy the Company by trading within its domain. When the Company in 1869 sold its sovereignty to the Dominion of Canada, these Free Traders made a rush for the deeper interior. At first they fared rather badly, for the Indians of that time had been born and brought up under the guardianship of the Great Company and were not easy to alienate. By the time of my journey this stage was over and some of the Free Traders did as extensive a business as the Company itself.

Up to 1906 it had been the policy of the Company not to help the Free Traders in any way—they would not carry them as passengers on the Company's ships nor carry their freight at any recognized tariff. This was a shortsighted policy, for it compelled the Free Traders to

build their own steamers. It would have been better business for the Company to secure a share of the Free Traders' profits by carrying their freight for them at a figure
that would have been remunerative to the Company and
still not so high as to make it pay better for the small
traders to build their own ships. Now when it was in a
sense too late, the Company's policy was being changed
by orders from Winnipeg. Anderson was no man to
carry out such orders. They were a complete reversal
of the policy under which he had risen from the lowest
rank in the service to the highest rank. He spoke with
suppressed fury of the recreant officers in Winnipeg who
had so far forgotten the dignity and glory of the Company
as to truckle and trade with the enemy.

This was a situation I did not fully understand until
at Arctic Red River when a young man by the name of
Jaquot came aboard the *Wrigley* and paid his fare to
ride with us to the last outpost of the Company, Fort
Macpherson. He was a personable, well-spoken young
man whose blood was obviously mainly Indian. Anderson received him with surly looks. Indeed, he could
hardly be said to receive him at all, for he avoided him
as much as was possible on so small a craft. At first I
took this for a prejudice against Jaquot's Indian blood,
but a little thought showed that this was not possible, for
I had already observed through a month of close association that Anderson treated Indians and white men with
an even hand. I think it was Bishop Reeve who made
the situation clear to me. Anderson had nothing against
Jaquot except that he was a Free Trader.

From Red River, we went a few miles north and came
to the Mackenzie delta, but were still perhaps a hundred
miles from the ocean proper. Here we steamed west

across the head of the delta and up the Peel River eighteen or twenty miles to Fort Macpherson and the northern limits of the Hudson's Bay Company's domain at that
time.  For many years this post had been under the
charge of John Firth, an old Orkneyman with a grey
beard halfway to his waist.  Some years before he had
reached the age for pensioning and retirement, and had
gone out to live in Winnipeg.  But Winnipeg was not
far enough north for him, and after a year of unhappiness
he begged to be allowed back into the Company's service
and had come north to Macpherson to take charge again.
I am writing this in 1922 and have just learned that Mr.
Firth has retired a second time, but now to live in a little
house near the post that has been under his charge for
the better part of half a century.  Like most of the northern men of the Hudson's Bay Company, he wants to
spend his last days where he has spent his best days.  A
few of the retired officers live in some southerly land,
such as Ontario or Scotland, but nearly always through
family reasons.  They have children to educate.  I have
never known one kept south by family duties who is not
unhappy there and longing for the North.

I said good-bye at Macpherson to the Bishop and to
John Anderson, and the *Wrigley* steamed back south.  My
only connection with the outside world now was Elihu
Stewart, the Chief Forester of Canada, who was going
to walk eighty miles west across the mountains to the
Bell River where canoes would meet him to take him
south to the Yukon River.  There he would get a steamer
upstream to Dawson and White Horse and a railway to
carry him south from there to the north Pacific Ocean at
Skagway.  Partly because he needed help and partly because I was reluctant to cut the last threads that bound

me to civilization, I accompanied Stewart along the old Indian trail through the thick brush on the first lap of his journey. In a warm, drizzling rain and among mosquitoes almost as numerous as the raindrops, we said good-bye at his first camp, which was pitched in the spruce woods four or five miles west from Macpherson. He would continue west and south, but I turned back toward Fort Macpherson and the North.

# CHAPTER III

My head was full of booklearning about the North. This proved to be mostly wrong and consequently I met a surprise at every turn. A whole series of surprises came when I met the Eskimos. I have said nothing about them before, but there had been some of them at Red River and there were three or four dozen of them on the bank as the *Wrigley* steamed up to Fort Macpherson. There were white men standing among the Eskimos, and the Eskimos and whites were about the same height. I had been expecting the Eskimos to be small and was thinking to myself that it was a curious thing that the Hudson's Bay traders, Mounted Police and missionary at this place should be of such small stature. When I went ashore and shook hands with them, I found some of them were taller than I, and I am half an inch under six feet. This meant that some of the Eskimos were big men. I have found since that while Eskimo women strike you generally as being smaller than white women the Eskimo men of the Mackenzie and Alaska are little if at all under the average size of Europeans. Possibly the women appear small because they do not walk on their toes as do white women in their high-heeled shoes.

My very first day among the Eskimos I noted the free swing of their walk and their independence of bearing as compared with the Athabasca Indians they were walking and talking with. This brought to mind what Macfarlane

had told me in Winnipeg and what I had read in Sir
John Richardson's books about their formerly aggressive
attitude towards the Indians and their feeling of superiority over them.   This was now confirmed by Firth,
who told me many stories of the early days when peace
had been but recently established by the Hudson's Bay
Company between the Eskimos and Indians.   Both people
felt secure enough so that they met every summer both at
Fort Macpherson and Fort Red River, but neither trusted
the other completely and the two kept their separate
camps.   At that time it had taken diplomacy to enable
Firth to prevent acts of violence.

In one sense Firth was prejudiced in favor of the Indians.   His own wife was half-Indian and he spoke the
Indian language fluently but could not speak the Eskimo
at all.   The mode of thought of the Indians was, therefore, familiar to him.   He knew enough about certain of
their characteristics to distrust them in one sense; but he
trusted them in another sense, for he knew just what
weaknesses to figure upon.   The Eskimos were a much
more enterprising and reliable people but, in spite of that,
he had for them the distrust that comes from only partial
understanding.   For certain individuals among the Eskimos he had unstinted praise.

Firth told me especially about a "chief" by the name of
Ovayuak, who for enterprise, reliability and a generally
attractive character was unexcelled by any white man
or Indian he knew.   There was another Eskimo of whom
he also spoke highly, although in a different sense.   This
was a sophisticated middle-aged man known as Roxy.
The whalers had given him this nickname when they first
came to Herschel Island in 1889, at which time Roxy,
then a youngster, had secured a job from one of them as

cabin boy. Firth advised me to engage passage with Roxy from Macpherson the 250 mile journey to Herschel Island. A party of Mounted Police were going down also, but they, like me, would be passengers in Roxy's boat, for the Hudson's Bay Company had taken a contract to transfer certain freight for the Police to Herschel Island and they had sublet the job to Roxy. The evening of July 30th we left Macpherson in Roxy's whaleboat.

I now know that Eskimos have no family names. If a man's name is John you call him John, and if his wife's name is Mary you call her Mary. I did not know this at the time and so I noted in my diary that our party consisted of the following: Captain Roxy, Mrs. Roxy and their daughter Navalluk, about ten years old. Roxy was a tall man, with a roman nose, skin not darker than the average Italian, with black Chinese hair like all Eskimos, and no beard. Few Eskimos have beards, but there was working with Roxy a short and stout man named Oblutok with a full but straggling black beard. He had with him his wife, whom I called Mrs. Oblutok, and their daughter about fourteen years old. As passengers there were Constable Walker of the Mounted Police, who was in charge of the freight we carried, and two Indians who were in effect his servants. Besides them there were two miners and I.

The miners were named Sullivan and Waugh. Sullivan was a big, aggressive-looking, black bearded man; Waugh was smaller and more retiring. They had turned up at Macpherson a few days after I got there with a story that they had left the gold country in the Yukon with pack horses, had spent the whole spring and midsummer coming slowly across the mountains looking for gold, had eaten up all the provisions carried by the horses, had eventually turned the horses loose and built a canoe on the head waters of one of the branches of the Peel River, and had drifted and paddled down to Macpherson. They said they had found no gold nor signs of any.

Everything went well for 150 miles or more down one of the branches of the Mackenzie delta. For a hundred miles the trees were still large; then suddenly we came to trees markedly smaller. After a few miles there were no trees, but only low willow-covered and grass-covered islands among which the Mackenzie winds in its innumerable sluggish channels. Where the branch we were on came out into the ocean we stopped because the weather was bad and a heavy sea was running with waves breaking threateningly over the mud-flats. We were towing a boat loaded with freight belonging to the Police. Our only motive power was the sail on the whaleboat. Even in the best weather it is somewhat dangerous to undertake a 60-mile journey as this would be from the river to Herschel Island, towing a big and heavy boat loaded down with freight behind a small whaleboat with only its sail for power. In bad weather it was unthinkable. We remained in camp, accordingly, for two or three days and then we decided that Constable Walker would stay behind with the Police freight and his two Indians, while Roxy took the rest of us to Herschel Island. Walker favored this plan for the sake of the safety of his freight, for we were to send back more seaworthy boats from Herschel Island to fetch it. The miners and I were eager to proceed, for I had promised Leffingwell to be at Herschel Island on or before August 10th. The miners had come with us, hoping to overtake whaling ships at Herschel Island and to secure passage with them for Nome and San Francisco.

CONSERVATIVE OLD MAN WEARING LABRETS

AN UP-TO-DATE YOUNG MAN

It had been known to us at Fort Macpherson that between ten and fifteen whaling ships had wintered at Herschel Island or various points east of there and would now be about ready to sail west. It was believed that none of them intended to winter, for they had been there two or three years, most of them. Some had even tried to leave the previous fall and had been caught by an early freeze-up and compelled to winter.

With the freight left behind, we at first made good progress towards Herschel Island. This was later interrupted by a head gale and we were so delayed that, although we left Walker behind on August 4th and although the distance was less than sixty miles, we did not sail into the Herschel Island harbor until 12:30 (just after midnight) on the morning of August 9th.

There were a number of whaling ships in the harbor and to them we brought tragic news. The terrible calamity of the San Francisco earthquake had occurred before I left Boston and I had read a good deal about it in the newspapers. Never having been in San Francisco, my ideas were vague as to which parts of the town had been destroyed. I did not realize the deficiency of my information until we told the whaling captains and officers about the earthquake, when I was immediately besieged with questions of details as to which streets had suffered most in the fire, and the like. They were anxious for just the facts I could not give regarding the fortunes of their families and friends. The season was getting late, from the point of view of sailing west, and this tragic uncertainty in the news made the ships all the more restive. It was, therefore, only a day or two until the first of them began to leave.

A stranger in the Arctic is met by so many new things on every hand that his impressions are at first confused. Some changes come so gradually that they are not noticed; others, while they come suddenly, come so many together that the impression is not clear.

One of the changes that comes too slowly to be noticed is the gradual disappearance of the night. When we left the railway at Edmonton, there were fourteen or fifteen hours of daylight. On Slave Lake there were seventeen or eighteen, and not far north of that we reached a point where at midnight there is still a glimmer of light in the northern sky. If we had been traveling with railway rapidity straight north, the next night down the river would have been bright enough for reading at midnight. But our steamer's speed was only eight or ten miles an hour, which the river current accelerated to twelve or fourteen. Then the Mackenzie runs northwest instead of north, which slows up the advance of the midnight light, and we stopped a day or two at a post every two hundred miles to do the business of the fur trade. I did not notice the increasing light enough to make any entries in my diary about it until we came to the head of the Mackenzie delta. We had thought we might see the midnight sun there, and all of us were on deck watching for it. The daylight at midnight was as broad as it is in ordinary latitudes five minutes after sundown, but the sun itself was below the northern horizon. Then we stopped at Fort Macpherson long enough so that even on the later journey to Herschel Island the sun did not rise above the horizon, and we never saw it at midnight that year. Still, we had several weeks of such bright light that for all purposes of travel we got along as well as if the sun had been shining all night.

Next to the sun, we had been looking forward to the polar ice with the keenest expectation. The feeling was somewhat different, for the reading of many books had taught me to dread it. On the way from the river mouth to Herschel Island we were in a gale when Roxy said to us, "There is ice ahead." The announcement brought to me almost a thrill of horror, for I had seen so many paintings of ships and boats being buffeted among ice floes that I thought it was something like a canoe running a rapid or a ship being tossed among rocks. I soon saw, however, that the Eskimos were speaking with rejoicing about the ice. When I asked Roxy why that was, he said there were several reasons.

Having lived with white men on whaling ships for something like twenty years, he knew what my fears would be, and so he explained to me that while white men dreaded the ice the Eskimos had been living among it so long that they were fond of it and not happy when long out of sight of it. He and his party had now been several weeks up on the Mackenzie River and were beginning to be hungry for the sight of ice. He explained further that it is a great convenience when you are sailing. If you want drinking water or water for tea, go up to an ice cake and dip fresh water off the surface of it. This is much less bother than going ashore, and furthermore the water is fresher and better.

At first this astounded me, but I have found since through long experience that it is correct. If you find an ice floe so big that the spray that dashes over it in a gale can not quite reach the middle, then you may be sure that by going to the middle you will find a pond of the freshest of fresh water. Of course, the polar ocean is about as salty as any other ocean, and just after forming the young ice (as we call it) is bitterly salt. But during the first winter it gradually freshens and by the time it starts floating around in the form of isolated cakes the following summer, it is so fresh that the palate can detect no salt.

But Roxy told me the main reason for his rejoicing was that the waves were running pretty high and his little girl was seasick, and that when we got in among the ice we would have no more trouble with the waves. This turned out to be so. The ice floes were scattered. Few of them were bigger than a city block in area and there were between them half-mile open patches where we sailed through smooth water though the wind was blowing stiffly.

This was my first introduction to the sea ice. Through many years I gradually became more and more fond of it, until I now regard it as the Eskimos do. When I come back to it after an absence, I feel like a forest dweller who comes in sight of trees after a long journey over the prairie.

Another new thing to me in the Arctic was the whaling industry, but it took me a long time to get that straight in my head. From many long narratives I eventually became able to condense the story into a brief statement. The first whaling ship had come to Herschel Island in 1889. At that time some of the Eskimos in this district had never seen a white man, although most of them had been to Fort Macpherson once or oftener to trade. The next year (1890) there was a large fleet of whaling ships and they brought in considerable numbers of Alaska Eskimos who had been on and around ships for many years. Learning from people of their own kind was much easier for the Mackenzie Eskimos than it would have been to learn from white men, and it was, therefore, only a few years until they changed in many ways.

When the first ships came, these Eskimos had no white men's food and their trading at Macpherson had been in tobacco, arms and ammunition, knives and other iron goods, cooking utensils, tents and clothing, etc. The whaling ships came laden with all sorts of civilized food and all sorts of trade goods, and the one thing they lacked was fresh meat. At that time the Eskimos considered meat and fish about the only things fit to eat, and it was at first difficult for the whalers, no matter what price they offered, to secure fresh meat or fresh fish. It became one of their chief purposes, therefore, to teach the Eskimos quickly to like sugar, bread, fruit, bacon, and other things which could be purchased cheaply in San Francisco and easily carried north.

When I arrived at Herschel Island sixteen years later this sort of thing had already passed and the Eskimos had become so far acquainted with American foods that they were willing to consider them approximately one-quarter as good as fresh meat or fresh fish. By this I mean that in 1906 they used to trade fifty pounds of fresh caribou meat for about two hundred pounds of flour and other groceries. Some of them still confined themselves largely to a meat and fish diet but there were others who ate considerable quantities of bread, sugar, dried fruit, etc., and nearly all of them had become passionately fond of tea and coffee.

In ordinary years the whalers had groceries in plenty to sell, whether for meat or for money. But in 1903 they had come to the Arctic outfitted for two years and had now been compelled to spend three because of being frozen in prematurely the autumn of 1905. They had

enough to eat for the time being but it was impera-
tive for all of them to get out of the Arctic within two
or three weeks if they wanted to avoid putting their crews
on short rations.

# CHAPTER IV

ALTHOUGH I was now myself an arctic explorer, I was ill grounded in the craft, whether theoretically or practically. As I have said, my plan for two years had been to go to Africa, and for those two years I had been immersed in books about the tropics. I did not even know the names of some of the most famous arctic explorers, and it is, therefore, not particularly strange that I had never heard of Captain Roald Amundsen, though he is now famous. I found him and his ship, the *Gjoa*, in the harbor at Herschel Island.

Although the Northwest Passage had been discovered in 1847 by Sir John Franklin and re-discovered by Mc-Clure in 1850, and although ships had navigated the entire distance, no ship had yet gone the whole way in the same direction. Sir John Franklin's ships had come from the Atlantic side, had attained a certain point on the north coast of North America, and had been wrecked there. A few years later Captain Collinson's ship had come from the Pacific around Alaska and had proceeded far enough east to overlap handsomely Franklin's track. Had Collinson wanted to proceed east to England that year, he could doubtless have done so, for where Franklin had preceded him with ships drawing over twenty feet of water, Collinson could have won through with the same type of ship. He was, however, bent on an errand of a different sort and his purpose took him back west again.

Amundsen had conceived the plan of being the first to make this voyage traveling consistently in one direction. He had approximately followed Franklin's route to where it overlapped Collinson's, and then he had followed Collinson's route until he reached King Point, thirty-five miles east of Herschel Island, the summer of 1905. Here he was overtaken by the same unfavorable ice conditions and early freeze-up which prevented the whaling fleet from sailing out, and like them he had been imprisoned for the winter. Now he had come as far as Herschel Island and would already have sailed out had not the spring been as unfavorable as the preceding fall. Like the whalers he had been restrained by a pressure of ice that hung heavy upon the west side of Herschel Island.

Captain Amundsen invited me to be his guest aboard the *Gjoa*. I had a delightful time learning from the Captain and crew, but especially from the first officer, Lieutenant Godfred Hansen, about the Eskimos of King William Island and about various conditions to the east. This was of great interest to me, but an event of still greater interest came about through circumstances as dramatic as those invented by authors who write books of adventure for boys.

One of the whaling captains was James McKenna. Once upon a time he had been wealthy. Some said he made his money through whaling and others that he had made it selling liquor to the natives of Siberia and western Alaska. However that may be, he attained prosperity and was said to have owned ten or fifteen ships. Perhaps because the activities of the United States Revenue cutters in Alaskan waters made trading in rum more difficult, his fortunes had gradually dwindled until in 1905 he had left of his whole fleet only the schooners

*Charles Hanson* and *Olga*. The *Olga* was commanded by an officer whom McKenna did not trust, so he decided to promote to the command Charlie Klinkenberg, a Dane who had come to the country originally as a cook. Before this time Klinkenberg had acquired at least two kinds of reputation; one for enterprise, energy and fearlessness, and the other for a character not very different from that of the buccaneers of old, or the Sea Wolf of Jack London's story.

McKenna, accordingly, did not trust Klinkenberg much better than he did the deposed officer. In that connection he got the bright idea of removing from the *Olga* all provisions except food enough for about two weeks, thinking that Klinkenberg would not try to run away with the ship if he had no food in it. This showed how little he knew Klinkenberg.

It was not long till a fog came, for fogs are numerous in the polar ocean. The *Olga* had instructions to stay near the *Charles Hanson,* but when the fog lifted she was gone and was not seen thereafter up to the time, more than a year later, when I arrived at Herschel Island. There was a good deal of speculation among the whalers as to what had happened. Some pointed out that Klinkenberg, being a better cook than he was a navigator, might have gotten lost unintentionally in the fog and might have wrecked his ship and drowned himself and the crew. Others thought he had sailed a circle around Captain McKenna, had probably reached the Pacific and had sold the *Olga,* possibly in China or in the South Seas somewhere, and disappeared with the money. Others told that Klinkenberg had for years had an ambition to sail farther northeast into the arctic archipelago and visit some of the islands beyond the ordinary range of the

whalers.  He had dreams of finding gold and hopes of
meeting Eskimos who did not know the present high
prices of fox skins, from whom he could buy at a great
profit.  Some thought accordingly that Klinkenberg was
now in Victoria Island or Banks Island and would turn
up either this year or next.

I had barely assimilated all these speculations when
one day there was great excitement at Herschel Island,
for a ship was coming in from the northeast.  The keen
eyes at the mastheads of the various whalers were not
long in recognizing the *Olga*.  When she came into our
harbor she had indeed a tale to tell.  I was at the police
barracks when the *Olga* dropped anchor.  Captain Klinkenberg came ashore at once with some members of his
crew, went to the police and requested that a statement by
himself and certain testimony of his crew should immediately be taken under oath and placed on record.  The
statements amounted roughly to this:

Klinkenberg admitted having run off with the *Olga* the
previous year.  He had known of an unguarded store-
house at Langton Bay, some three hundred miles east
of Herschel Island, where one of the whaling companies
had a considerable amount of food.  He went there, took
the stores, broke up the house and put it on board his
ship.  To the police he explained that his intention had
been to pay for all these things.  He had then sailed to
Victoria Island.  In the fall he had been off on a caribou
hunting trip and on returning to his ship he had found
that some of his men had commenced to make alcohol
out of flour and sugar.  This he could not tolerate for
two reasons: he wanted no drunkenness on the ship, and
he did not have the flour and sugar to spare.  They were
needed for food.  The ringleader in the distilling was

the ship's engineer. When told he must stop making alcohol, he had received the Captain's orders with defiance and had reached for a gun, whereupon the Captain, to forestall him, had shot him with a rifle. An old man, a member of the crew, had died of illness during the winter; two sailors had lost their lives by traveling over ice that was too thin. This was the first version we heard of the tragedies that had cut down the *Olga's* crew from nine to five men.

The Captain's witnesses substantiated his story in every detail.

McKenna's ship was at this time not at Herschel although expected momentarily from a whaling cruise. Some of the other captains wanted the police to arrest Klinkenberg for having stolen the *Olga*. This the police did not see their way clear to do, but they told the captains they would restrain Klinkenberg if he tried to take the *Olga* away from Herschel Island before Captain McKenna arrived. This Klinkenberg probably had no intention of trying. He had a whaleboat which was said to be his own property. Into that he loaded his Eskimo wife and large family of children, and sailed west.

After Klinkenberg got away, the Island and fleet began to buzz like a beehive. The story now unanimously told by the crew of the *Olga* differed entirely from the one they had sworn to in Klinkenberg's presence and became one of murder. The Captain was said to have killed the engineer without provocation, and there were various dramatic and blood-curdling details. The old man, whom Klinkenberg had reported as dying from illness, was said to have died in chains in the forehold, either from freezing or starvation or a combination of both. It was said that the two sailors who lost their lives had been the only eye witnesses to the killing of the engineer by the captain and that the captain had deliberately planned their death. The sailors explained their former testimony by saying that when the *Olga* had come in sight of Herschel Island, Klinkenberg had called all hands on deck and had made them a brief speech to this effect: "Boys, you know the penalty for killing five men is the same as for killing four. You know what has happened to the four of you who are not here to-day. The same thing will happen to the first man who tells on me, and maybe to the second and third." Then he outlined to them briefly what his own testimony to the police would be, and advised them to make their testimony similar. They had done so, and while Klinkenberg was still at Herschel Island none of them had dared to say a word. All this and more the crew testified under oath after Klinkenberg had sailed west from Herschel in his little boat.

When the new story got about there was great excitement at the island and much talk of pursuing Klinkenberg, but it was soon agreed that by now he must have crossed the international boundary, only forty miles west of Herschel Island. There a Canadian police would have no jurisdiction, Alaska being U. S. territory. Furthermore, it was clear that if the American authorities wanted to arrest Klinkenberg, they could do so whenever they liked in Alaska.

People who do not know the frontier, imagine that criminals can hide in such places as the polar regions. Nothing is more nearly impossible. People who live two or three hundred miles away are in effect near neighbors. News does not spread rapidly but it does spread. If one Hudson's Bay trader stubs his toe in January, the trader down river may not hear about it till March, but he will hear some time and will not only hear but will remember for years. That a man you have never seen and who lives a thousand miles away has a wart on his nose is well known to you and to every one in your post. In this respect the whaling fleet does not differ. When you are living in a big city, it seems reasonable to be told in the movies or in a novel that criminals go into "the northern wilderness" to hide, but if you know the North yourself you will know that that is one place where hiding is impossible. Klinkenberg's arrest, then, would come whenever the authorities desired, unless, indeed, he might be able to get "outside" and lose himself in the really impenetrable jungle of some big city.

The Klinkenberg story of romance and horror was impressed upon me more strongly because there was at the island a United States Commissioner by the name of Judge Marsh. He consulted with me about various things. His theory was that an American ship was American territory and that it was, therefore, his business to investigate the charges against Klinkenberg. He wanted somebody to act as clerk to copy down testimony and, accordingly, asked me to come aboard the *Olga*. He took testimony from all the crew. It is the gist of this testimony which I have given above. Judge Marsh later took this testimony to San Francisco. A warrant was eventually issued for Klinkenberg. He was arrested by a United States Revenue cutter, tried in San Francisco and acquitted. He may have been guilty or innocent. If he was guilty, he may have been guilty of only a part of the charges made against him. But the stories which center about this affair have continued since then to multiply in the North, until now they form a whole cycle of legend. Klinkenberg himself still lives in the Arctic.

The last I heard of him he was in Coronation Gulf.

But a story that interested me more was one that bore every earmark of being true. The only suspicious thing about it was that it seemed too romantic to be true.

The *Olga* was said to have met in Victoria Island a people who dressed and behaved like Eskimos but who did not look like Eskimos. Some said they looked like Europeans; others said they looked like Jews; some said that the majority of them looked like any other Eskimos but that there were among them a few persons with light hair and blue eyes.

When I discussed this story with the whaling captains, I found they paid little attention to it. It was, however, in the line of my profession as an anthropologist and so I pressed the inquiry, whereupon the captains all told me that I had better forget whatever I had heard from the white sailors of the *Olga* and depend entirely on what I could learn from those Mackenzie Eskimos who had been on Klinkenberg's ship. I went to these and found that they confirmed in substance the story which originally came from the white sailors.

The Mackenzie Eskimos who had been with Klinkenberg told me that the Victoria Island Eskimos had a language differing from theirs only in accent and in a few words. After a little intercourse, they could converse together easily. These strange people had knives and other implements of native copper, which of itself marked them off from the western Eskimos. They were remarkably skilful at winter seal hunting and had for that reason the great admiration of the westerners. The most striking thing was, however, that several of the Victoria Islanders looked to the Mackenzie Eskimos as if they were white men in Eskimo clothing.

TENDING FISH NETS BY KAYAK

KLINKENBERG AND HIS FAMILY

The reason for my having come north on a polar expedition was that I had once written a paper upon the history of Greenland. From my studies of that history I knew that something like three or five thousand Norsemen had been lost from Greenland about the time of Columbus or a little before. No man knew what had become of them. Some thought they had died; some thought they had intermingled with the Greenland Eskimos and disappeared; and some thought they had moved from Greenland to the islands to the west of Greenland. It was not impossible that some of these might have penetrated to Victoria Island. Neither was it impossible that a few survivors of Franklin's last expedition of sixty years ago might have escaped starvation by settling among the Eskimos. No matter how unlikely it might be, it was not impossible that the *Olga* had discovered the descendants of one group or another of these lost Europeans. All this was fascinating to ponder upon and made me watch all the more eagerly for the arrival of our schooner, *Duchess of Bedford,* to pick me up and carry me east to where Klinkenberg had seen these strange people.

When Klinkenberg had met these Eskimos with blond complexions and with copper knives, he had noted the blondness; but what had interested him was the copper and he had tried hard to find out where they got it. About that he had learned a good deal more than the truth. One of his stories was of a mountain of solid copper in Victoria Island. This apparently fabulous tale really has some foundation, for there has been located since in Victoria Island a hill that has a boulder of copper in the side of it as big as a piano. There is of course a good deal of difference in size between a piano and a mountain.

Still, there are many large tales that develop from less.

The Copper Mountain and the rest of Klinkenberg's fabulous tales did not rob me of much sleep. But the problem of the blond people never left my mind until several years later when I had the chance to visit Victoria Island and see them for myself.

# CHAPTER V

## THE WHALING FLEET SAILS AWAY

A WEEK after I got to Herschel Island Captain Amundsen sailed west, and the whaling ships began to follow. They were pessimistic about the ice conditions and left me with gloomy forebodings as to the *Duchess of Bedford*.

Captain McKenna had come in to Herschel Island harbor from his whaling cruise shortly after Klinkenberg got away. On August 26th he, the last of the whalers in the harbor, was about to sail. We thought he was not only the last in the harbor but also the last in this part of the ocean, for we had seen all but one of the whaling ships start west. The only ship we had not seen, the *Alexander*, was supposed by the other whalers to have passed outside the island and to have preceded them to the westward. The early morning had been decided on by McKenna for weighing anchor, but shortly after midnight a whaleboat came in from the east bringing Markley, the second mate of the *Alexander*, and the story that the *Alexander* had been wrecked several days before by running ashore on the rocks of Cape Parry, three hundred miles to the eastward. A few hours later a second boat came in, bringing Captain Tilton and a number of the crew. Captain McKenna now waited for the rest of the crew of the *Alexander*. They arrived during the next two days and on August the 28th the *Charles Hanson* and *Olga* set sail, thus cutting off from the world for a year the little arctic colony of Herschel Island.

After the ships were gone, the Herschel Island community continued shrinking. There is a beautiful harbor, so it is the logical wintering place for ships. This year no ships were going to winter and there was no reason for any white men to stay there except one or two policemen to keep the barracks. Inspector Howard had the notion himself that Macpherson, up in the spruce forest, would be a pleasanter wintering place than wind-swept Herschel Island. The other policemen encouraged him in this view on various ostensible grounds but, as they told me, really because of the well-known principle that when the cat is away the mice may play. Inspector Howard was called by his friends a good disciplinarian and by the rest a martinet. There was covert rejoicing in police quarters when he sailed away, leaving the island for the winter in charge of Sergeant Fitzgerald.

Apart from the police and myself, there were only two white men on the island. One was a picturesque character called Chris Stein, whom I judged from his name to be a German. I found later that his real name was Sten and that he was a Norwegian, a seafaring man who had had adventures in many seas and could relate them so that they lost no interest in the telling. Aboard ship he had held nearly every position from cook to mate, and by his own telling he had been in the navies of various countries, as well as in the merchant marine and in whalers. He was married to a native woman, whose two brothers, Kunak and Kakotok, were among the wealthiest of Eskimos. Some years before, these brothers in partnership with two others, Ilavinirk (called by the whalers Anderson) and Tulugak, had purchased from a whaling captain the schooner *Penelope*, which had once upon a time been one of the finest pleasure yachts on the Pacific Coast.

She was built for speed, had ten tons of lead on her keel, and with a good wind could sail faster than any of the arctic whaling fleet could go under combined steam and sail—or so Sten told me. Through his influence over his brothers-in-law and the other owners of the *Penelope*, Sten was now practically master of this craft.

When the *Charles Hanson* was gone, carrying away Captain Tilton and the crew of the wrecked *Alexander*, Sten began to tell stories that had not been heard while his former captain was still in port. Those were to the effect that when the *Alexander* ran on the rocks at Cape Parry, she did so bow on, under full pressure of sail and steam. The shock lifted her so high out of the water that, while she drew sixteen feet regularly, she was now drawing only nine feet forward and thirteen at the stern. In other words, as Sten said, she was as solid as a lighthouse perched on the rocks of Cape Parry.

Sten's account ran that the *Alexander* had sailed on the rocks in a fog so thick that the man at the lookout did not have half a minute's warning from the sighting of the breakers until the ship was high and dry. The excitement had been so great and the fear of not overtaking the whalers at Herschel Island had been so keen, that no time had been lost by the Captain in getting everybody off the ship. I think Sten said it was only fifteen or twenty minutes from the actual wreck until the whaleboats were launched and under way.

Another point is that the whaling ships carry insurance that covers not only the ship but also all the whalebone, fur, etc., that have been captured or purchased and entered into the ship's records. In case of wreck it is necessary only to save the ship's papers and the insurance company in San Francisco will be compelled to return full value for every fox skin and every slab of whale-bone lost. From the point of view of the owner of the ship, there is, accordingly, no motive for saving anything out of a wreck. By these insurance conditions and the excitement of the shipwreck, Sten explained his statement that the Captain's cabin was full of silver fox skins and other items of priceless value, while all the ship's gear, including chronometers, was still on board. There were even said to be gold watches hanging on the walls of the cabins of the various officers.

Sten came to me with this story, wanting me to join him on the *Penelope* to sail east and plunder the wrecked *Alexander*. But I was still hoping for the arrival of my own ship, the *Duchess of Bedford,* and although plundering a wreck on the most remote cape of arctic Canada would have been a great adventure, I felt still keener interest in the unknown Eskimos of Victoria Island beyond, especially now that I had heard from Captain Klinkenberg that some of them looked like Europeans. I accordingly declined Sten's offer, saying I would have to wait near Herschel until the actual freezing of the ocean made it certain that my own ship could not come. I told him I would then go with him by sled. He said that would be too late, for a trapper by the name of Fritz Wolki was living only about a hundred miles from Cape Parry and would be sure to get to the *Alexander* ahead of any sled party we could organize. Wolki was the only white man living on the north coast of Canada that winter, except Sten and the rest of us at Herschel Island.

Sten told me he would try to get Eskimos enough to man the *Penelope.* Of his success in that we shall learn later.

The other white man at Herschel Island was Alfred H.

CABINS OF WHITE TRAPPERS, MACKENZIE DELTA

THE VILLAGE AND HARBOR OF HERSCHEL ISLAND

Harrison, who has since written a book called "In Search of an Arctic Continent."  He was really in search of this continent but had not been getting along very well, and through no fault of his own.  He had a theory, which would have seemed tame enough to Admiral Peary or to any one used to reading the books of polar exploration. But to the whalers and Eskimos around Herschel Island, it was exactly what they called it, "a harebrained scheme."  The Canadian and Alaskan Eskimos are in great fear of the ocean ice.  In winter they make their living upon it in the vicinity of land, but seldom venture more than five miles from shore, and never willingly more than ten.  The whalers had little book knowledge of polar exploration, but had been for twenty years in Alaska where sledge travel on moving ice is little understood, and they were greatly impressed with the danger and impracticability of it.

With no first-hand knowledge of sea ice, but filled with the lore of books, Harrison had come down the Mackenzie intending to go from there to Cape Bathurst and across by sled to Banks Island.  Fifteen years later, this had become such a commonplace that an old Eskimo employee of mine, accompanied only by his wife who was rather sickly, made the journey between Banks Island and Cape Bathurst without difficulty.  Harrison, however, was fifteen years ahead of his time, and when he proposed to the whalers and the Cape Bathurst Eskimos that they should sell him an outfit and some of them accompany him on this journey, they thought him crazy.

Harrison had come North accompanied by Hubert Darrell, a man who had made a good pioneer journey with David Hanbury from Chesterfield Inlet to the arctic coast of Canada, then west to the Coppermine River, up that river and across to Bear Lake and the Mackenzie.

Darrell was one of the best winter travelers that ever came to the North, but he knew overland travel only and was convinced by the whalers and Eskimos that attempting to accompany Harrison over the ice to Banks Island would be suicidal. From this and from other causes the partnership between Harrison and Darrell had broken up the winter before I arrived in the Arctic. Darrell was now trapping in the forest country some two hundred miles south, but Harrison was still on the coast trying to get Eskimos to go with him to Banks Island. By August, 1906, when I met him, he had given up hope of doing anything that year beyond exploring the mainland east of the Mackenzie River and mapping the great bodies of water known as the Eskimo Lakes. Eventually he accomplished this, and you will find notable differences between the maps of that section if you compare those that preceded Harrison with the ones he made.

Harrison had engaged for the winter the family of Kakotok, Sten's brother-in-law and part owner of the *Penelope*. At first there had been some thought of using the *Penelope*, but when Captain Tilton came to Herschel Island with the whaleboats saved from the wreck of the *Alexander*, Harrison bought one of these and decided to use it to carry him to the Eskimo Lake country. He invited me to take passage in this boat with him as far east as I cared to go, and to spend the winter with him if I liked. I did not dare to go beyond Shingle Point, however, but took the chance to go that far. I left a memorandum with the police at Herschel Island to give to the *Duchess of Bedford*, should she come, telling her to pick me up at Shingle Point if she was going to proceed farther east that year.

My journey with Harrison from Herschel Island to Shingle Point was merely a fifty-mile boat voyage without adventure. He pitched camp for a few days on the sandspit there for fishing purposes, and partly also with a friendly desire to wait around to see if I would not change my mind about taking a chance with the Eskimos. He argued that the season was now so late that the *Duchess* was not likely to come and that I had better go with him east. He had half a dozen sacks of flour and several other items of white men's fare, and his offer to share these with me was a generous one from the point of view of any ordinary white man, for no one who has not lived with the Eskimos in their houses and on their food is likely to think in advance that it is going to be pleasant. I did not think that it was going to be exactly pleasant, but I told Harrison that in case my ship did not come I had made up my mind to live as an Eskimo with the Eskimos for the purpose of learning their language and customs and becoming as intimate with them as possible. You can never live in your own house as a neighbor to people of a strange race and expect to get an intimate view of their lives through visiting them no matter how frequently.

On September 3rd Harrison's whaleboat and five others owned by Eskimos sailed east from Shingle Point, and I began my apprenticeship at living as an Eskimo among the Eskimos.

## CHAPTER VI

LEARNING TO LIVE AS AN ESKIMO—ON A DIET OF FISH
WITHOUT SALT

OUR village at Shingle Point that fall was never for long
of any one size. It was a tent village. Sometimes there
were only three or four tents and sometimes there were
thirteen or fourteen, for people kept going and coming.
Mostly the Eskimos were on their way from Herschel
Island to some point east of us on the coast or on some
branch of the Mackenzie delta where they intended to
spend the winter. Those who chose the coast would be
for that winter fishermen exclusively, for seals are not
found in any number so near the Mackenzie on account
of the fresh water.

The Mackenzie is almost as large a river as the Mississippi and brings down so much fresh water that ships at
sea, even out of sight of land, can drop their buckets
overboard and dip up good drinking water. We estimate
that Shingle Point is about twenty miles west of the
Mackenzie (there is no certain line where a river delta
ends and the ocean proper begins) and still the water in
the ocean outside our camp was commonly as fresh as
in a mountain brook. At King Point, fifteen miles west
of us, it was fresh about half the time, and even at
Herschel Island, more than sixty miles west of the Mackenzie, it was likely to be fresh or nearly so whenever
there was a protracted calm or when the wind blew from
the east.

The Eskimos going up the Mackenzie expected to live partly by fishing and partly by hunting moose, rabbits and ptarmigan. Those who left their boats on the coast and traveled inland by pack dog towards the mountains expected to live mainly on caribou, with an occasional mountain sheep in some places and ptarmigan everywhere. No matter where they lived, these hunters were also going to trap for the skins of various animals. In the Mackenzie delta they would get beaver, marten, mink, lynx and the various foxes—silver, cross, red, blue and white.

Most valuable of all these skins is that of the silver fox, worth at that time as much as five hundred dollars even to the Eskimos and a great deal more than that to the traders who dealt with them. The cross and red foxes are more numerous and therefore less valuable members of the same family. There may be cross, red and silver foxes in one litter. But the white and blue foxes are only distant cousins of the others and are little more than half the size. Just as red, cross and silver may belong to one litter, so the blue and white may belong to one litter. On the arctic coast there are about a hundred white foxes for one blue fox. Among the dark foxes, the silver are the rarest and the reds the most common. There are perhaps four or five silver foxes to a hundred reds. Of course, the silver foxes are of varying grades, approaching more and more closely to cross fox, and it may be that the ratio of perfect silver foxes (which are called black foxes) to the red is not far from the one to a hundred ratio which applies to blue and white.

We were all going to trap foxes later in the year, but just after Harrison left us our energies were bent on fishing. Some years earlier caribou had been in the habit of coming down to the coast frequently, but the Eskimos told

me that during the last few years they had been so much
hunted by natives in the employ of the whalers that none
were to be expected now north of the mountains, which
were twenty or thirty miles inland.

At Shingle Point we were looking forward to a winter
of nothing to eat but fish.  In recent years the Eskimos
had been able to buy from the ships all the groceries
they wanted, but they had never wanted very much.  In
fact, the whalers had been coaxing and almost forcing
the Eskimos to eat groceries so as to get from them in
exchange more fresh meat and fish to use on shipboard.
This year the condition was entirely different.  The
whalers had been compelled by the accident of an early
freeze-up to spend the previous winter in the Arctic.  The
summer of 1906 they were so short of groceries that none
of the Eskimos had been able to buy any appreciable
quantity.

There had been the expectation that one or two ships
would come in from the west, and we had all been hoping
to buy from them.  Mr. Harrison had had the forethought
to wheedle some groceries out of one of the whalers before
they had given up hope of a western ship coming in.
That is how he came to have the flour and other things
I have mentioned.  I did not try to buy anything, for I
was at first expecting my own ship any day.  The
Eskimos had tried their best to buy, but had been able
to get nothing except tea and a little flour.  The flour
they had secured from Captain McKenna and that only
because some gasoline had been spilt upon two or three
dozen sacks and they were fairly soaked and reeking with
it.  The Eskimos I was living with had secured a few of
these sacks and occasionally they used to make some
pancakes or doughnuts fried in seal oil.  I had as yet a

strong prejudice against seal oil. Although that prejudice was strong, I found the gasoline taste even more disagreeable. And for a special reason the fish, which was the main item of diet, was to me most distasteful of all.

I grew up with two main food prejudices. I cannot remember the time when I did not hear my mother explain to the neighbor women that I could neither drink chocolate nor eat fish. I do not remember what reason she assigned for my inability to drink chocolate, but I remember well how she used to explain that my unwillingness to eat fish had its reason in the famine which came on our frontier community when I was in my first year. The cows had died and there had been no milk, and she had been compelled to feed me on boiled fish made into a sort of mush. She used to say, and the neighbor women used to agree with her, that it was no wonder I had acquired a prejudice against fish. It was taken for granted by them, by my mother and by me that this inability to eat fish would mark me throughout life. In school and college, at boarding houses and private dinners, I always omitted the fish course and always used to explain that I differed from ordinary people in my inability to eat fish. Similarly, I avoided chocolate until I was something like twenty. I cannot remember now how it came about, but either inadvertently or as an experiment I tasted chocolate and found to my surprise that it was not bad. Gradually I got to like chocolate but the abhorrence of fish persisted. I used to taste fish gingerly once or twice a year. This was usually done in connection with the stories I was telling of how disagreeable it was; it gave effective emphasis to my stories if I grimaced at the difficulty of swallowing even the tiniest bit of fish.

But now I was face to face with a winter of nothing but fish—fish without salt or tea or anything else. The gasoline flour would soon give out if we ate any of it. The Eskimos had about half enough tea to last the winter. They were exceedingly fond of tea and I did not care for it, so that from the first I voluntarily left that all to them and lived on fish and water. There are no more hospitable people in the world than the Eskimos, and they never allowed a meal to pass without trying to coax me into drinking tea. But as the taste had no attraction for me, I was easily able to resist. I always did prefer water to any concocted drink.

As to the absence of salt, that was due to an oversight. Had I thought of asking for it, Harrison would have given me some before he left. One reason why I did not ask him may have been my subconscious idea that I could secure salt by boiling down sea water. At Shingle Point this was ordinarily not possible, because the ocean was not salty. However, there was an occasional westerly gale which brought the salt ocean to Shingle Point. On such occasions I took potfuls of brine and boiled it down to a thick scum on the bottom of the pot. Thereby I learned some chemistry, for the taste was not particularly salty. It was rather bitter, for (as the chemists tell us) the sea contains a great many strong tasting substances besides ordinary table salt.

I used to write pages in my diary about my troubles with the fish diet, and a continual refrain was that it would not be so bad if I only had salt. I used to get up early in the morning and go hunting inland. To meet a caribou that had wandered down from the mountains was less than one chance in a hundred; although I hunted day after day I never saw a caribou or sign of any. But that was not why I was hunting. I was trying to get up an appetite. I would commonly start, without breakfast, at any time from five to nine in the morning and would walk until from four to six in the afternoon. When the Eskimos saw me coming across the hills towards camp, it was the regular job of Navalluk, the little ten-year-old daughter of Roxy, to pick out a salmon trout just fresh from the water and weighing about a pound and a half. She would clean it and put it on a spit beside the camp fire and have it beautifully roasted against my arrival. Had I been a normal person fond of fish I should have found it delicious. As a matter of fact I used to nibble chiefly at those parts that had been burnt nearly to a crisp in the roasting, leaving untasted what another would have eaten by preference.

But gradually and almost without noticing it, I began to eat more and more of the fish, until at the end of ten days or so I was eating square meals. For a while it was only the best fish specially prepared, but in another week or two I began to join the Eskimos at their potfuls of boiled fish. They told me that fish heads were best of all, but this I could not believe, and it was not until midwinter that I finally decided to try. I found then that they were right and have since agreed that the heads are the best parts of most fishes. Later I came to find that this applies to caribou no less, and I am now of the opinion that heads generally are the best parts of animals, or at least seem so to people who are living on an exclusively meat diet. The northern meat-eating Indians all agree with the Eskimos in this, and so do all those white men I know who have ever lived for long periods on a hundred per cent. meat diet.

Our fishing methods at Shingle Point were peculiar.

The fish that were running in the largest numbers are called by the whalers "white fish," though they do not resemble closely our commercial whitefish. The Eskimos call them *kaktat*. The water was clear and the fish were wary. They could not be netted in daytime unless there was a heavy surf rolling in from the sea that muddied up the water so they could not see the nets.

As I remember them, the nets we used were about three feet wide and about thirty feet long. Sometimes they were set out by Eskimos in kayaks, but ordinarily we used a long stick to shove them out. The Eskimos would find a straight-grained log of driftwood on the beach. This they would split and adze into rods each the full length of the log and two or three inches in diameter. They would then splice several of the rods together, end on end, making a pole perhaps sixty and even a hundred feet long and so weak that it could not stand its own weight. If you picked it up by the middle the two ends would remain on the ground, and if you raised the middle high enough the rod would break. These rods were dragged about the beach rope-fashion, and when we came to places where nets were to be set we would slip upon the tip of the pole a loop that was fast to one end of the net and shove it out upon the surface of the water. In that way the net was set so that the outer end was perhaps sixty or seventy feet from the beach and the near end thirty or forty feet away.

The catch varied on different nights. When the run was good, two or three men could be kept busy tending two or three nets. You would pull in a net and find the fish stuck in it almost as thick as they could be. There was not a fish in every mesh, but a person seeing the quivering mass pulled in would have said that there was.

We would pull the fish out as quickly as we could and throw them in a pile inland, then shove out the net and walk to the second net. We would similarly empty that and then pull in the third net. By the time that was done we would go back to the first net, pull it in and find it just as full as it was the time before. We never counted the fish but I should say that on a good night three or four of us caught between one and two thousand, giving from fifteen hundred to three thousand pounds of food.

The hardest work of the women came during the day. With half-moon-shaped steel knives as sharp as razors they cut open the fish, cleaned them, removed the backbone and hung up the rest to dry. This was done when the run of fish was not very rapid. When large quantities were being caught, the women did not have time to remove the backbones, but merely cleaned the fish and threw them into enclosures made log cabin fashion out of pieces of driftwood. When the fish in each of these boxes were three or four feet deep, the whole thing would be roofed over with a pile of logs, thus furnishing adequate protection from dogs and foxes and indeed from any animal except a polar bear. Even from bears these caches were safe so long as the fish were perfectly fresh, for a polar bear does not hunt fish and does not seem to recognize the smell of fresh fish as the smell of food. But caches containing "high" fish will be broken into by bears—probably because all rotten meats and rotten fishes smell much alike.

I had read in books that the Eskimos eat their food raw, but found little of this. The Mackenzie people are no more likely to eat a fresh fish raw than we are to eat a beefsteak raw. I have seen butchers and cooks eat small pieces of raw steak and similarly I have seen Eskimos on rare occasions take a mouthful of raw fresh fish.

But fish in another condition they do eat raw. On account of the difficulty of netting in daylight in clear weather, there is little fishing on Shingle Point during the midsummer while the sun never sets. The natives, therefore, look forward eagerly to the coming of the dark nights. A few fish are summer-caught, however, and they are put in bins and protected from the sun by piles of logs. Although it is extremely hot in summer when you are twenty or thirty miles inland (perhaps 80° or 90° in the shade), the temperature on a sandspit surrounded by ocean water as Shingle Point was, is seldom above 60° or 70°, and frequently around 40° or 50°. Therefore, the fish did not decay rapidly, but became high, somewhat in the sense in which venison and game are allowed to become high in our markets. Fish that has a high or gamey taste is seldom cooked and indeed seldom eaten at all during the summer. But when winter comes and the fish are frozen, they are sometimes brought into the house in that condition. An armful of them is thrown upon the floor and allowed to lie there until they are half-thawed, so that they are about of the consistency of ice cream—they are still frozen, but nevertheless are so soft you can easily cut them with a knife or bite chunks out of them. At that stage the skin is stripped off and they are eaten by the Eskimos very much as we eat corn on the cob. The backbone and ribs form the core and are thrown away or given to the dogs, as we reject the cob after eating the corn.

At first I was horrified at seeing people eating high, raw fish. But when I came to think of it, it did not seem any more remarkable that some people should like high fish than that some people should like "strong" cheeses or high venison and pheasants.  Neither is it any more remarkable that the Eskimos eat raw fish than that the Japanese and Norwegians do so.  Furthermore, there is no essential difference between eating raw fish and raw oysters.  After all, what is the difference between eating a thing raw and eating a thing "rare?"  When you order a big steak "underdone" you get a little meat on the outside that is cooked and a lot of meat on the inside that is raw.  If you try on your friends the experiment of just calling raw meat rare, you will see that it helps a lot in making it easier to swallow.

At least it helped with me.  By the time I had gone through all the above reasoning (which it did not occur to me to do for several weeks) I one day tried the frozen fish and found it not so bad.  Each time I tried it I liked it a little better, and eventually I got so fond of it that I agreed with the Eskimos in preferring it to cooked fish "for a change."

I had not yet been thoroughly broken in to the fish diet nor had I become completely used to many other strange features of my life with the Eskimos, when one day a schooner was seen coming along from the west.  At first I thought it was the *Duchess of Bedford* but the Eskimos presently recognized her as the *Penelope*.  She dropped anchor half a mile outside of our camp and a boat came ashore, bringing Sten and two of the part-owners of the *Penelope,* his brother-in-law Kunak and the junior partner Tulugak.  Sten said they were on their way at last toward Cape Parry to make their fortunes plundering the wreck of the *Alexander.*

The visitors received a jolly welcome from us, as all

traveling parties did. A part of this welcome always was a meal. To me this particular one was an especial feast, for Sten had brought ashore with him some flour that had no gasoline in it, and some molasses. We had doughnuts of exceptional quality. I eventually got so that I liked the taste of things fried in seal oil as well as I like similar things fried in lard, but with doughnuts properly made this is hardly a question. If the oil or lard is kept so hot that it is almost burning, you can cook doughnuts in either without leaving an appreciable taste. This is especially true if porousness is avoided by leaving out the baking powder, thus getting greaseproof glazing on the outside—like that of pretzels.

At the end of the feast Sten arose to go aboard ship, whereupon it developed that there was a hitch in his plans. His Eskimo crew had decided that Fritz Wolki, two hundred miles to the east of us, must surely have reached the wrecked ship by now and that there was no point in anybody else going there. Sten was of a different opinion. The Eskimos, with the greatest good nature, replied that it would be all right for him to go but that they personally were inclined to stay. Some would camp right here at Shingle Point, and the rest of his crew would go inland to the mountains to hunt caribou. Sten became angry and threatened and blustered a good deal, but without any effect either in making the Eskimos angry or in changing their course.

Sten was of a naturally equable disposition and, furthermore, knew the Eskimos well by now. He soon saw the case was hopeless, and made them a new proposition. This was that a few of them should go back with him on the *Penelope* fifteen miles up the coast to King Point, where Captain Amundsen had left a cabin and where

A Fishing Camp—Sun-drying the Fish

A Summer Camp Near Arctic Mountains

Sten himself had another cabin from the previous winter, for he had that year been shipwrecked near King Point in a schooner, the *Bonanza*. The wreck had been partly salvaged, and there was a good deal of valuable property ashore. The *Penelope* was now to fetch this property to Shingle Point where Sten would spend the winter with us.

This would not take more than three or four days and a sufficient number agreed to help. Sten asked me to join in the enterprise and we sailed to King Point, tore down his house but not Amundsen's, and loaded the ship with whatever seemed valuable—lumber, carpenter tools, ropes and the like. The whole was landed at Shingle Point inside the week and with the help of several Eskimos and myself Sten soon had a comfortable house built. In this he invited me to spend the winter with him, but I declined again for the same reason as I had declined Harrison's previous invitation. Learning all about the Eskimos was my object in coming North, so I decided I would live with them and occasionally visit Sten, instead of living with Sten and occasionally visiting the Eskimos.

From the time Harrison left me at Shingle Point till the freeze-up several weeks later, we had visitors nearly every day. Some of them stayed with us a few days; others would arrive in the morning and leave towards evening, or arrive in the evening and leave in the morning. This brought to my notice the remarkable ability of Eskimo children to stay awake for long periods.

In the summer time with perpetual daylight, the sleeping habits of every one in the North are as irregular as can be. At Macpherson, and in the interior generally, it is common to go to sleep in the morning and get up

in the evening.  This is because the days are extremely
hot and outdoors work is much more pleasant in the
slightly cooler night hours.  On the coast, however, the
days are never unpleasantly hot, so we had no motive
for going to sleep in the morning, and went to sleep
instead whenever we liked.  With the southern idea that
there is a certain merit in regularity I used to try to
sleep eight hours a day, but soon gave that up and fell
into the native way of sleeping when I felt like it, sometimes for an hour, sometimes for five hours and sometimes for ten.  Not infrequently I would sleep for five
hours to be awakened by the announcement that there
was something especially good to eat, whereupon I would
join the others in the eating and then go to sleep again.
All this is ordinary custom and perfectly good manners
among the Eskimos.

If the sleeping of the grown people is irregular, that
of the children is still more so.  This is especially the
case because of the arrival and departure of visitors.
All the Eskimos for hundreds of miles around knew each
other well enough so that when a boat arrived there
always came with it children that were at least familiar
by name to some of the children that were in our camp.
There would be great rejoicing and great excitement.
Before this had time to quiet down some family would
leave or perhaps another family would arrive, bringing
the further excitement of parting with old playmates or
greeting new ones.  One of the Eskimo mothers told me
in this connection that her eight-year-old daughter had
been awake continuously for five days and nights, playing all the time.  This interested me so much that I
inquired from a number of other people in the village
as well as from Sten, and ascertained with reasonable

certainty that several of the children had been awake
continuously from three to five days. I have never since
been at a village similarly situated, but I have frequently
known Eskimos, both older people and youngsters, to
stay awake as long as two and three days. Indeed, I
am so used to doing this myself that I am not likely
even to note it in my diaries.

One day a boat came from the west bringing us news
of importance. The whaling ship *Narwhal* had arrived
at Herschel Island with messages from the *Duchess of
Bedford*. This news had been so ill understood by the
Eskimos that I became very anxious to go to Herschel
Island to learn the whole truth. The Eskimos said the
*Narwhal* had gone off on a short whaling cruise but
would probably be back at Herschel Island harbor by
now. It was said she did not have any considerable
amount of trade goods, but I thought I should be able
to buy from her some flour and other groceries. It was
accordingly arranged that I should take Sten's whale-
boat and make a trip in it to Herschel Island to get for
him and me jointly a boatload of supplies. Roxy and
Oblutok, my companions of the summer journey from
Macpherson to Herschel, decided they would go with me,
Mrs. Roxy coming along too. We sailed for Herschel
Island and got there without incident.

# CHAPTER VII

### HOW AN ESKIMO SAILED THROUGH THE STORM

At Herschel Island we found the *Narwhal* and on board of her the warmest sort of welcome from Captain George Leavitt and from his officers and men. The Captain told me that his ship and all the others, including Captain Amundsen's *Gjoa,* had reached Point Barrow without much trouble. From this point all the other ships continued west to the Pacific and south to San Francisco. But as Captain Leavitt found himself able to half-stock his ship with provisions for another winter, he decided to come back to Herschel Island, for doing so would give him a fine chance to catch a lot of whales next spring. He had hitherto been compelled to compete with twelve and fifteen ships but now he could have the whole western Arctic to himself at the price of merely the slight hardship of wintering with a less variety of supplies than he was used to. He would have to put his men on rations, but felt no doubt of getting through the winter all right, especially as he hoped to engage a number of Eskimo hunters to go south into the mountains and secure for him a large amount of caribou meat.

Captain Leavitt's news of the *Duchess of Bedford* was that she had rounded Point Barrow safely. She had started east ahead of the *Narwhal,* but coming east the *Narwhal* had passed her somewhere without seeing her (probably in a fog), and the Captain could not say where she would now be. He thought it unlikely that she would get through to us at Herschel Island, for the season was so late (September 23rd) that any ship going out into the ocean would run the danger of having ice form all around her, preventing her from getting back again to the safety of a harbor. The best guess was that the *Duchess* was wintering somewhere near Flaxman Island, about halfway between Herschel Island and Point Barrow and two hundred miles west of Herschel Island.

Captain Leavitt thought the thing for me to do was to spend the winter where I liked, waiting for news. Shortly after the freeze-up Eskimo sled travel up and down the coast would commence and it would not be more than a month or two until news would get to Herschel Island about any ship that was wintering between there and Point Barrow.

My main errand at Herschel was to buy on behalf of Sten and myself as much as I could of certain things, chiefly groceries. Captain Leavitt told me at once that he had nothing to spare of most articles but a little of some staples. Of what he had, he would give me as much as I wanted.

I was at the police barracks on shore when our purchases were being loaded into the whaleboat. On coming down to the ship I noticed that one thing missing from the list I had requisitioned was a barrel of molasses. Captain Leavitt had gone off somewhere and I asked the Mate whether they were short of molasses. He said that on the contrary it was one thing they had in unlimited quantity, and he felt sure the Captain would not mind if he gave me a barrel of it. The barrel was, accordingly, put in the boat. It was not until many months later that I found out why Captain Leavitt had not given me the molasses in the first place. He had intended to do so, but had found that when the boat was loaded with the rest of my purchases it already had as much cargo as it could safely carry. He had stopped the men at the last moment when they were about to lower the molasses barrel, saying that in case of a gale we were liable to be swamped through overloading.

Not being much of a sailor myself and having full confidence in Roxy, who had a great reputation in that regard both with Eskimos and whalers, I did not even suspect we were already overloaded as we rowed ashore from the *Narwhal* a hundred yards to the beach where some Eskimo friends of Roxy's had in waiting for us two or three huge tubs filled with what is known as "blackskin." This is a favorite food not only of the Eskimos but of many northern white men. It consists of slabs of whale skin and attached a certain amount of blubber. The skin varies in thickness according to the age of the whale and according to the part of the body it has been taken from, but generally it is from one-sixth to one-third of an inch thick and there may be anything from half an inch to several inches of blubber attached. I do not know exactly how much each tub of blackskin weighed, but I estimated later that between it and the molasses we must have been nearly a thousand pounds overweight—carrying three thousand pounds in a boat that was not really seaworthy with much more than two thousand.

We started September 26th. There was a light breeze when we sailed which carried us a few miles away from the harbor. Then it fell a dead calm and Kay Point to the east was still twelve or fifteen miles away, too far, we thought, for rowing. Accordingly, we put in at Flanders Point, which is the landward end of Herschel Island and a good fishing place.

The next morning Roxy awoke me, saying that there was a fair wind blowing but that the weather later in the day would probably be bad. To me it seemed rather bad already. There were periods of calm and between them squalls of strong wind with flurries of snow. Along the coast just east of us there were several harbors, and Roxy and I agreed that on so threatening a day we would not proceed beyond Kay Point, for on the thirty-five-mile stretch from there to Shingle Point there is no shelter or any possibility of landing in case of a gale.

Had we jumped into the boat promptly on waking up, I think all might have gone well. The Eskimos were eating a breakfast of dried fish and whale blubber. Had I been a good Eskimo also, I should have shared that with them and we might have been on the road in a few minutes. Thinking, however, that we could not proceed beyond Kay Point in any case, I took an hour to fry a small piece of pork that Captain Leavitt had given me and made a meal of that. When we finally started the gusts of wind had become so strong that had we been wise we would not have started at all.

Everything was plane sailing for a few miles. When we were about halfway to Kay Point, Mrs. Roxy suggested that we had better turn into shelter by Stokes Point, but Roxy answered that this would not be necessary for we would find shelter behind Kay Point. This seemed reasonable. We were sailing northeast straight before a southwest wind. At Kay Point we were going to round a corner of the coast, turning southeast. A southwest wind would then be blowing off the land, giving us quiet water to beach the boat.

Before we got to Kay Point it was a real gale. In all his experience Roxy had never sailed this sea in such a high wind.  He knew the bay to be shallow but did not know how shallow it was.  He had never seen breakers on it, but now when we came to the vicinity of Kay Point we found ahead of us a long line of breakers stretching far to the northwest from the tip of the Point. We saw this so late that there was nothing for it but to run through the breakers.  We thought the boat would not touch bottom for Roxy assured me the depth of water would not be less than ten feet.  But there was danger of the boat filling and sinking.

Roxy now lived up to all the things I had heard about him as a wonderful sailor.  He had to sit low at the tiller to do the steering but his wife stood on a pile of bedding at the mast and chose the road, for she had more sea-craft than I.  The line of breakers was perhaps not more than fifty yards wide and we were through them in a moment.  But it was an exciting moment.

Now the time had almost come to make a ninety degree turn to the right, and Roxy warned all of us to stand by as the sail came over.  But the sail did not come over; for just as we rounded the cape the wind changed.  Evidently it was blowing parallel to the hills, and when we turned the corner of the land we had also turned a corner of the wind.  That meant that we had before us a straight and steep coastline thirty-five miles to Shingle Point and never a place to land, for we had based our supposition of shelter behind Kay Point on the theory that the wind would be blowing from the southwest when we got there, and now it was blowing from the northwest.

There was only one other hope.  The wrecked schooner, *Bonanza*, was lying up on the beach at King Point and behind her there ought to be shelter as behind a pier.

This thought encouraged us a good deal, for it meant that the run for our lives would be eighteen miles only instead of thirty-five.

Just after starting out in the morning we had changed the large regular sail of the whaleboat for the smaller storm sail. Later we had close reefed this, and we were now running straight before the wind with the smallest sail possible. Every now and then we took water on both sides of our bow, and every now and then we took water on both sides of our stern. We had cleared a place in the middle of the boat to do some bailing and had to bail steadily.

There were two kinds of trouble with our cargo. One was that certain goods which would soak up water were in the bottom of the boat. It was not possible, therefore, to bail out all the water that came in, for some soaked into the baggage. Another trouble was that we had certain bulky things on top of the load. Roxy and I agreed we ought to throw overboard about half the cargo, but we were every moment in such imminent danger of being swamped that we never dared try to shift the bulky and heavy things so as to get them overboard.

It was a tense time as we approached King Point. We saw the masts of the *Bonanza* clearly all the time but for some reason her hull appeared and disappeared. At first we thought she had been moved away from the beach and was floating, lifted up and down by the waves. But when we got nearer we saw that the situation was entirely otherwise. She was still fast on the beach, but the water was so steadily breaking over her that she was for that reason hidden two-thirds of the time. Half a mile before we got abreast we had decided that there would be no shelter behind her, and when we ran by we saw the water pouring over her lee side like a great river over a precipice. What had been a peaceful little eddy behind a sort of pier when we sailed west, was now about as much of a shelter as a whirlpool under a waterfall.

In the beginning of the gale it had been Oblutok's job to do the bailing, but shortly after we passed Kay Point he had become so paralyzed with fright as to be entirely useless. Mrs. Roxy was a better sailor than I and understood more clearly how to do what she was told, so it was she who stood by for any emergency help, while I took the job of bailing, which required no orders but only incessant work.

From King Point to Shingle Point we felt each mile as if we should never stay afloat another mile. Roxy remarked that speculating upon so doleful a possibility was unwise, that when the choice was between cheerfulness and gloom, good cheer was always to be preferred, and that the best way to keep your spirits up was to sing. I was too busy for singing and am not sure that I felt like it. Roxy tried first to sing various ragtime songs and hymns he had learned from whalers and missionaries, but when he found I did not join in he said that he might as well then sing Eskimo songs which had more spirit to them. This also had the advantage of enabling his wife to join in.

I have not described Shingle Point and I had never until now made for myself a complete mental picture of it. But with our lives depending on its shape and position, I was able to build up from various memories a diagram of it and of the safe harbor behind. Thousands of years ago there must have been here a high cape and no sandspit. Then in the lee of the cape the currents began to build up a finger of sand, pointing straight east from the cape while the land runs southeast. This finger of sand had gradually lengthened and lengthened until now it was nearly two miles long with a good-sized triangular bay behind it. A quarter of a mile beyond the finger tip of this sandspit was a little island and between it and the spit was a channel about nine feet deep for a hundred yards of its width.

The village, consisting of Sten's house, some old Eskimo houses, and some tents, stood at the landward end of the sandspit not far from the mainland cliff. The sandspit itself is here probably some eight or twelve feet above sea level, and Sten's house was twelve feet high on top of that. We were still several miles away when we began to see the top of Sten's house as we were again and again lifted to the crests of the waves. When we went down into the troughs between them, the house went out of sight. Not only that, but even the land along which we were running was occasionally hidden. We were about a quarter of a mile from the beach and the land was two or three hundred feet high. Even so, the waves between us and the land were frequently high enough to hide the cliff completely.

When we came near the village we could see all the people outside, and among them Sten standing at the beach and waving to us. We could not hear what he was shouting but his signals meant clearly that we were to run the boat ashore right where he stood and he and the Eskimos would stand by and try to rescue us from the undertow of the surf. Roxy and I discussed this and decided that if we landed we would be sure to wreck the boat, that most or all of the cargo would be lost, and that the chances were that we should all be drowned. He pointed out we had already run more than thirty miles safely and suggested that we risk another two miles and try for the end of the spit. The difficulty was that in rounding the spit into the shelter of the harbor we would come broadside to the sea and would probably sink. However, we would have land on both sides and a good chance of swimming or floating ashore, while there was at least a possibility that we might make it and save our cargo.

Sten told us later that as he ran along the beach parallel to us, our boat was frequently out of sight, mast and all, in the trough between the towering waves, and that each time we disappeared he fully expected we would never rise again. Long before we got to the end of the sandspit we had left him and the Eskimos far behind although they did their best to keep up. We were going pretty fast, and then the running is never the best in the loose gravel on a beach.

When we came to the end of the spit and had to turn we eased the sail over gently and all leaned to the windward side of the boat to try to keep her on an even keel. It was rare luck that no big wave struck us just then and we barely rounded the point. We had everything ready, dropped the sail as we came to and got in two or three good pulls at the oars before our boat actually began to sink. By then we were in such shallow water that we saved complete sinking by jumping out, thus relieving the boat of our weight and giving her a little more freeboard. Three of the Eskimos got to the tip of the spit just at that moment and rushed into the water to meet us. Between us we almost carried the boat to the beach.

Sten, who was a little fat, came puffing up just then and scolded us for not beaching the boat by the village

ROXY AND HIS WIFE

and making sure of our lives even at the cost of losing the boat and her cargo. He admitted later, however, that we would not have been sure of our lives even had we made this attempt. Roxy always maintained that in addition to the other advantages of actually rounding the point in safety, we had by saving the boat escaped a whole winter of being told by Sten how valuable his boat had been and what a sacrifice it had been to him to encourage us to beach and smash it. Roxy's saying this was mainly Eskimo humor, for Sten really was a very generous man.

For a landsman this was something of an adventure and, indeed, all the adventure I cared for in that line. It gave me one more reason to be glad when the freeze-up came a few days later to give us a safe bridge over what had previously been treacherous water.

The *Penelope* might have been able to get into the harbor behind Shingle Point, although that is debatable as she drew about as much as the estimated depth of the channel. However that may be, Sten had not tried to take her into the harbor. Through the great gale that nearly drowned us she had ridden at anchor safely, although the people ashore had been in continual fear of her breaking loose. Now the freeze-up came unexpectedly (October 2nd), and she was fast in the ice nearly half a mile from shore. This looked bad. But Sten and Roxy told of several instances where ships had lain for a whole winter in such exposed situations safely. I had a friendly interest by now in her Eskimo owners, and a personal interest in the ship for she might carry me on some adventure next summer if our own *Duchess* failed to come. So I hoped the optimists were right and that the *Penelope* was safe in her berth in the ice.

# CHAPTER VIII

SHORTLY after the freeze-up Roxy repaired one of the old Eskimo houses for us to live in. It had been built of sod and earth over a frame of driftwood and the floor of it was about a foot lower than the ground outside. In April of the previous spring another Eskimo family had been living in this house. When the sun became warm the snow on the roof began to melt, causing dripping within doors. The family then moved out and when I first saw the house I looked in through a skylight upon a stagnant lake covering much of the floor. Now this had frozen into solid ice and we went in with axes, adzes and picks and hacked up the ice and a good deal of mud from the earth floor under the ice and shoveled the whole thing out. We then split a large number of driftwood logs, each along the middle, hewed the surfaces flat and thus made a floor over about three-quarters of the house, the flat sides of the split logs being up and the round sides resting on the ground. Had the house been intended for more permanent occupation, we should have made real planks by adzing both sides of the logs flat.

That part of the earth floor not covered by logs was covered deep with a layer of chips so that the ice underneath should not thaw, no matter how hot the interior of the house might become. Here was one of the many instances of the usefulness of frost. What had been sloppy and malodorous mud in the summer was now odorless and almost as hard as concrete, making a sanitary and pleasant foundation for our floor, whether for the planking or for the shavings and chips.

Roxy told me that twenty years ago such a house would have been heated with a number of lamps burning seal or whale oil. But we had instead a galvanized iron stove and lived much as prospectors and other pioneers do in the forests of the northwest—only our house stood on a sandspit running out into the sea and the land back of us was a rolling prairie stretching in higher and higher hills back towards the mountains one or two days' journey away.

Not long after the freeze-up a party of Eskimos came from the interior to fetch the sledges and other belongings which they had left behind with us in September when they had journeyed inland, carrying their belongings on their own backs and on the backs of their dogs. Nothing heavy or bulky can readily be transported in that way. They had, therefore, left with us not only their sledges, but also their sheet-iron stoves and many other things they needed, among them spare ammunition and the traps which they were going to use during the winter.

The season for trapping had now almost arrived. On or near the arctic coast it is considered to begin about the middle of November and to last until early April. Our visitors reported that they had their winter homes just beyond the mountain range, and, as I understood, thirty or forty miles inland. They had killed a number of caribou and expected to kill some more. Half the hunters of that particular village were now at home hunting while the rest had come down to fetch the sleds.

Roxy and Sten became greatly interested in the stories

of caribou hunting inland, and I think that I was more interested than either of them. Roxy was used to living on fish alone and did not mind it. And Sten had in his house a little flour and other provisions. When I purchased the groceries from Captain Leavitt in the fall, I had thought I was getting about half enough to live on all winter. This could easily have been eked out with fish to last the whole winter. To do that seemed reasonable at first, but when we actually got the goods ashore at Shingle Point both Roxy and Sten explained to me that nothing could be saved or rationed which was kept in the house of an Eskimo. They were communists and, furthermore, great believers in the doctrine that sufficient unto the day is the evil thereof and that the morrow is well able to take care of itself. The only way I could save the groceries would be to keep them in Sten's house. The Eskimos understood the peculiar prejudice the white men have for private property and would not mind it at all if white men had in their own homes any delectable things unobtainable by Eskimos. But anything left in the home of an Eskimo would be eaten up just as quickly as suited all the Eskimos. Roxy explained that I would never be able to make friends with the people if I lived among them and still tried to have my own food in private. I would either have to go and live with Sten on groceries or else live with them on fish.

I had, accordingly, given Sten all my groceries. Occasionally, however, I got back from him five or ten pounds of flour and we had in Roxy's house a little feast of doughnuts shared by all. These doughnut banquets had been less than a tenth of my diet and I was hungry for a change from the fish that had been nine-tenths of the diet. I was no less eager to see the country inland

and to learn how the caribou-hunting Eskimos lived. This suited all parties. Roxy would go inland with his own dog team to fetch caribou meat and I would accompany him with Sten's dogs.

We started October 18th, Roxy and I each with a team and the other hunters with four teams. A boy of about eighteen, named Sitsak, accompanied Roxy. As a favor which we expected them to repay later in deer meat, we helped them carry their gear. This sharing of the loads made all our sledges light.

We traveled slowly, however, and for many reasons. One was that we were in no hurry and there was much to talk about. We enjoyed the camp life, sat up joking and telling stories till after midnight, and slept till the middle of the day. The days, too, were exceedingly short. When they were cloudy there were not more than four or five hours of traveling light. For another thing, the snow was not deep and, as we came into the mountains, the ground became rockier, necessitating many detours. Even the light sledges dragged heavily when the runners cut through the snow to the ground or rock beneath. Then we seemed to be traveling a sort of diagonal course across valleys. We did not follow any one valley for long but would leave it and climb over a steep ridge, descending sometimes with considerable difficulty into the next valley. Altogether, it took us five days to climb to the crest of the mountains, although I do not think the distance can have been over thirty miles. Beyond that it was down hill and easier.

On the way up the mountains we traveled at first through a river valley that had clumps of willows here and there five or eight feet high. As we climbed higher we saw continually fewer willows standing, but my companions knew exactly where to look on the gravel bars in the river bed to pick up little willow roots and stems that had been left there as driftwood by the high water of last spring. This gave us enough to burn.

One day it was anticipated that the evening's camp site would be nearly destitute of fuel, and that day we kept watch as we traveled across the gravel bars, picking up here and there a little piece of stick and thrusting it under the rope lashings that held the loads in place on our sleds. The crest of the mountains was, of course, bare of any willows big enough to show above the snow. But going down we soon came to bushes, for we were now on the southward slope where the heat of the sun in summer is more effective. It was about five or eight miles till we got into willows that were higher than a man's head and presently we came to the homes of our caribou-hunting friends.

Nowadays the Mackenzie Eskimos purchase from the whalers and traders tents of the ordinary white men's style. In the old days there used to be two kinds of Eskimo tents. The Mackenzie River people preferred conical shapes, much like the Indian wigwams you see in pictures; the Alaska Eskimos generally had hemispherical tents. The framework of these reminds one very much of a round basket lying bottom side up— except, of course, that the bent willows which form the frame of the tent are not a fraction of an inch apart, as they would be in a basket, but two or three feet apart. Over this frame they nowadays throw a canvas covering. In the old days this covering was made of skins, commonly caribou. Even now caribou skins are sometimes used for winter tents, for they are much warmer than canvas.

The village at which we had arrived was made of houses built on the general plan of the dome tent. First they had made a hemispherical framework of pliant willows with a floor space perhaps ten feet across, and a dome-shaped roof, so high that a tall man could stand erect in the center. Sometimes the height of the house was determined by the height of the man that built it. One of our hosts, Ningaksik, was about six feet tall and his house was the loftiest.

When the preliminary framework had been made of strong willows, they had woven in among them smaller willows until the frame really resembled a basket. Into the spaces between the willows they had then stuffed wads of moss and over them had been laid a layer of moss. On top of the whole had been sifted soft snow. This made a house so warm that, although there was fairly good ventilation through a pipe in the roof, it was still not necessary to do any more than barely keep a fire in the stove to maintain the house at as high a temperature as we consider comfortable in American houses. When cooking was going on, the houses became uncomfortable to me from the heat, although the Eskimos did not mind it. In general the Mackenzie River and Alaska Eskimos keep their winter houses anything from ten to twenty degrees warmer than the typical steam-heated houses of our cities.

There were only three real houses in this village, for two of the families were still living in tents. Up to our arrival they had been using fireplaces but now all but one of them installed stoves which we had brought from the coast. I found especial interest in watching the cooking in the house where they still used a fireplace. There was nothing in the way of a chimney nor was the fireplace at the side, as our pioneers used to have them. Instead, the fire is built in the middle of the floor. The fireplace is made of huge stones, not to hold in the fire nor yet to rest the pots on, but merely for the purpose of absorbing heat from the fire so that the stones shall give it out slowly after the fire has died. When the cooking is about to begin, the fireplace is filled with specially inflammable material—dry bark, twigs with resin on them, and the like. Directly above the fireplace is a square opening in the roof covered by deer skin parchment or some other translucent material. This skylight is the main window of the house.

Just before the fire is lighted the window covering is removed and when the match is applied the flames rise almost to the roof of the house. This conflagration is for the purpose of creating a draft suddenly and thus preventing any smoke from spreading through the house. While the fire is going a crevice is kept open at the bottom of the door on a level with the ground. In some houses there is a second opening along the ground just opposite to the door, and I have heard of houses that had still two more openings, these at right angles to the first two. Through these apertures the fresh air enters to supply the strong current that rises through the skylight, thus keeping the house free of smoke.

When the cooking is finished the fire is allowed to die down until there are only a few coals left. By that time the great boulders around the fireplace have become hot. The last coals are gathered in a pan, carried outdoors and thrown away, so that there shall be no smoke in the house when the parchment is again put over the skylight.

I have found by actual experience that even on a very cold day the stones of the fireplace will usually retain enough heat so that a fire every six hours is ample to keep the house comfortable. The cooking of the three regular meals a day, therefore, gives enough incidental heat to last until nearly midnight when people go to sleep. Like us, the Eskimos prefer to have their houses cooler at night than in the daytime, and houses of the inland type may get almost cold. I do not, however, recall ever having been in one where it froze even towards morning.

On our way over the mountains Roxy and I had talked about spending a week or two at the caribou camp hunting, but the weather continued unpropitious. It was foggy or snowing nearly every day and there was consequently little chance of finding game. The hunters who had been at the camp all the time said also that for the last two or three weeks caribou had been very scarce. Just ahead was the period of mid-winter darkness when hunting is difficult, and the meat already in camp was, therefore, precious. Between us, Roxy and I had fifteen dogs. On the coast, where fish by the ton were piled up under heaps of driftwood, feeding the dogs did not make noticeable inroads into the winter provisions. But here in the mountain camp we could daily see the little store of caribou meat growing smaller.

It is always one of the most difficult problems of the caribou-hunting Eskimos to decide how many dogs to keep. You must have enough to follow the herds around and to fetch home the meat of the animals that have been killed. On the other hand, if you have too many they will eat you out of house and home. In the present case there was no lack of hospitality on the part of our hosts and they urged us to stay till the weather became better so we could do some hunting, but Roxy finally decided that doing so would be unfair to our hosts and even unsafe, for our dogs were eating the meat that might be needed to keep our hosts from shortage during the absence of the sun when hunting is difficult. Accordingly, we loaded up our sledges with the meat we had come to fetch and started for the coast.

The journey back was on the whole no more difficult than coming south had been. Our sledges were now loaded where they had been light, but there was more snow on the ground and the going was better. Also it was down hill most of the time. Coming up we had cut across the river courses a good deal, scrambling up and down steep places. Going back we took a longer way, following the windings of a river that comes out about five miles east of Shingle Point.

On the way down the river Roxy walked ahead of the leading sled with an ice spear which had been made by fastening a big file at the end of a staff seven or eight feet long and then sharpening the point of the file. He jabbed this through the snow into the ice ahead of him, raising the spear methodically and bringing it down again every three or four steps. Evidently he was testing the ice to see if it was strong enough to bear us. At first this appeared ridiculous, for we had now had continuous frosts for more than a month and the temperature was twenty or thirty degrees below zero. But, like everything else, the explanation of the danger was simple when you once understood it.

Roxy explained the situation to me in detail. Early in the fall while the river is still open the falling snow melts in the running water and disappears. Later you may have a sharp frost for two or three days when there is no snow falling, and ice two or three inches thick or even a foot thick may form on the river. Then comes a

Winter Travel—Arctic Mountains South of Herschel Island

heavy fall of snow, blanketing the ice with a foot or more of light flakes. This snow blanket keeps the winter cold away from the river ice better than an eiderdown quilt or a fur robe. It now makes little difference how cold the air is above the snow, if the water running under the ice is a little bit above the freezing point. If that is the case, the current will gradually eat away the ice that was formed until there remains only a scum of ice to support the snow above it. In some cases even this scum of ice is eaten away by the current and then the snow drops down into the open water, leaving a gaping hole which can be seen from a distance and which can, therefore, be avoided. However, when an actual hole appears the frost gets another chance, so that it will not be many hours until clear ice perfectly safe to walk upon forms over that particular patch. The danger places, therefore, are not where any danger sign is visible, but where the snow in front of you lies white and apparently safe.

In later years of travel in the North I have heard story after story of the most experienced Indians being drowned in the northern rivers and in those northern lakes where there are currents. In big lakes, such as Great Bear or Great Slave, strong currents are occasionally developed, possibly through tidal influence. Far from shore these are not dangerous, but in the vicinity of a point of land the traveler on the northern lakes should be exceedingly careful. Though the ice of Great Bear Lake, for instance, may be ten feet thick in places, there are other places where men and sleds will disappear suddenly through the snow because the ice that formed before the snow fell has since been eaten away. This is a type of danger to which the Eskimos are far less exposed than the Indians, for the Eskimos mainly keep to the seacoast. When they are on the inland rivers they appear to be on the average more careful than the Indians.

On our river there was little danger of drowning, for it was shallow, but there was the danger of getting your feet wet, not only in the way I have described but also in another way that is more common and more difficult to avoid. A shallow river will quickly freeze to the bottom in some rapid. The water above the frozen place will then be held back until finally it will burst through the ice somewhere above the obstruction and flood the surface. Now there are places where snowdrifts lie clean across the river in ridges, forming obstructions that dam the water back so that you may have ten or even fifteen inches of water on top of the previous ice. If this flooding has taken place only a few hours before you come to that stretch of the river, there are only two courses open. Either you must scramble up into the hillside and travel parallel to the river till you get below the flooded place, or else you must camp and wait till the surface water has frozen over. In winter this is seldom a long wait. The general rule is that if you come to a bad place in the forenoon you try to get around it, but if you come to one in the afternoon you camp over night and expect the ice to carry you next morning.

On the last day of our homeward journey we were in a hurry so as not to have to make camp. We had made up our minds to sleep that night at Shingle Point. For that reason we took more risk than ordinary, traveling over thin flood ice. We all broke through several times. Roxy, being ahead, was the first to break through and I saw how he jumped instantly out of the water into a deep snowbank and rubbed the snow all over his wet feet. This was because dry snow at low temperatures acts like the best kind of blotter, soaking up all moisture. If you have on several thicknesses of woolen socks, for instance, you may slip to your ankle into water and get your foot out of the water into the snow so quickly that this blotter sucks the moisture out before it gets through all the different layers in to your skin. If you know in advance you are going to get into the water anyway, it is a fine idea to go to some place where you can stand firmly on one foot while you stick the other quickly into water and then into a snowbank. This will form a coating of frost in your outer stockings which will later on be water-proof and keep out further wettings almost as well as a rubber boot.

The Eskimos make admirable water boots out of seal skin. These are always used in summer, but in winter they are too cold and are put on only when you know for certain that you are going to have a good deal of wading during the day. This day we had not put on our water-proofs and, as I was inexpert in waterproofing my foot-gear by dampening and freezing it, I got wet through my deer skin boots and socks. That evening when we got home and when I removed my footgear, I found that my heel was frozen slightly. Since then I have spent ten winters in the North and this is the only time that I have had a foot even touched by frost. I have already given part of the reason—my inexperience. Another part was that we were still wearing autumn clothing and were not as admirably prepared for meeting the cold as we would have been had the journey been made a month later.

# CHAPTER IX

### THE SUN GOES AWAY FOR THE WINTER

A NEWCOMER in the Arctic spends much time watching the sun as it sinks lower and lower each day until at last it ceases to appear above the horizon and the "Long Night" begins. With us, the sun disappeared behind the mountains to the south about the middle of November.

Towards Christmas I became dissatisfied with my stay at Shingle Point, but for no other reason than that the Eskimos there were too sophisticated. Roxy, for instance, had worked on whaling ships for more than twenty years and spoke English fluently although it was, of course, the kind of broken English which whalers and traders always use in dealing with Indians or Eskimos. If the white men who come in contact with the Eskimos would only speak good English to them, the Eskimos would have some chance of learning good English. This is never the case, however, except in those parts of Alaska where Government schools have been established or in some part of Canada where a missionary maintains a school. The captain who is talking to an Eskimo will never say, "He traveled rapidly." Instead he says "Him go plenty quick," or something of that sort. This, then, was the kind of English that Roxy spoke and he used it in our dealings continually.

The rest of Roxy's family were his wife, his adopted son about fourteen years old, and adopted daughter (whom I have called his daughter) aged ten. By the time winter actually set in, all our fellow villagers of the autumn had moved away except the same bearded Ob-lutok whom I have described, his wife, daughter and son-in-law, Sitsak. None of these spoke English to any extent but they used instead a sort of "pidgin" which has grown up among the Eskimos for a peculiar reason.

There are probably few languages in the world more difficult to learn than Eskimo. If you want to get along well, you have to use every day a vocabulary of ten or twelve thousand words. This is a vocabulary three or four times as large as that used by the average European when speaking a European language. In addition, the inflections are so complicated that Greek or German would be easy in comparison. The white men who come in contact with the Eskimos are ordinarily not of the scholarly type. They may try when first they come to the country to learn Eskimo but they soon give it up as being hopelessly difficult and drop into the general habit of using "jargon" or "pidgin."

This jargon itself has been developed because of the difficulty of learning the real language. It is an artificial tongue, comparable to the pidgin English that is used by Europeans in dealing with Chinamen. The Mackenzie River jargon consists of three or four hundred words, according to which whaler or which Eskimo you talk with. In addition to the regular jargon nearly every individual invents a few special words of his own which are known to him and those he deals with. Where the real Eskimo is highly inflected, this jargon is not inflected at all.

It is a curious thing that many white men, even those who have lived for long periods with the Eskimos, have mistaken the jargon for the real Eskimo language. Examples of that were all the police who were in the vicinity

of Herschel Island during my first year. These policemen had come to the country only a year or two before
and had found the jargon in daily use between Eskimos
and white men (such white men, for instance, as Captain Klinkenberg) who had been married to Eskimo
women so long that they had large families already partly
grown. I think Klinkenberg's oldest daughter was about
twelve or fourteen when I heard him talking to his wife
fluently in some language I did not understand. I wrote
in my diary at the time that he talked with her in Eskimo. The same had been the impression of the police
when they came to the country. Then month by month
they had learned this language which the whalers were
talking to the Eskimos until they knew nearly or quite
every word of it and could speak it as fluently as the
whalers. They then thought they could speak Eskimo,
and when I came they told me so.

Constable Walker gave me a three-hundred-word vocabulary of what he considered pure Eskimo. I found
out later that the stems of about ten of the words came
from the languages of the South Sea Islands. These were
apparently words used by the whalers in talking with
Hawaiians and later incorporated by them into the speech
they used with the Eskimos. There were a few words de-
rived from Spanish and from English, as in the case of
the phrase "me savvy" where the "me" comes from English and the "savvy" from Spanish by way of southern
California where some of the whalers had lived. Other
whalers had been in Greenland waters before they came to
Herschel Island and had brought with them Greenland
jargon words which came ultimately from the Danish—
such as "coonie" (so written by Constable Walker when
he gave me his vocabulary). Although I can read Danish,

I did not at the time recognize this word as the Danish word *kona*, meaning woman. In the Herschel Island jargon it is used to mean either woman or wife.

It did not take me long to find out that the jargon was not the real Eskimo, for I had brought with me an excellent grammar of Greenland Eskimo made by a German scholar who had lived nearly all his life in Greenland. I used to beg Roxy and the rest of the people to talk to me in real Eskimo and they would sometimes do it for a while, but they always relapsed, Roxy into the broken English and the others into the jargon which they spoke to Sten and which they had been using with the white men since 1889. Indeed, there had been a similar jargon in use between the Eskimos and the Indians to the south of them even before the whites came, so that the habit of talking pidgin to any kind of foreigner was ingrained in all the Mackenzie Eskimos.

I understood from Roxy, however, that the people who lived to the east of the Mackenzie delta were far less sophisticated. One peculiar thing Roxy told me about his cousin Ovayuak (whom Mr. Firth had recommended to me as the best of all the Eskimos) was that he was proud of the Eskimo ways and Eskimo tongue and did his best to keep them pure. This Roxy considered an amiable eccentricity, but he understood that the eccentricity would serve my purpose, so he suggested that if I wanted to learn real Eskimo and find out as nearly as possible what the Eskimos were like before the white men came, I had better go to visit Ovayuak. The idea struck me favorably at once. It had the further advantage of bringing me near to Harrison's camp, and being a little lonesome I thought of the possibility of spending Christmas with him.

Roxy now agreed that he and Sitsak would take me to Tuktuyaktok, the place where Ovayuak lived, a journey of about a hundred and fifty miles by the devious channels between the islands, although no more than half of that as the crow flies. The arrangement was that when we got there I should purchase from Ovayuak a chest of Hudson's Bay Company's tea and a Hudson's Bay Company's four-point blanket to pay him for the trip. He insisted that these things and none other should be the pay for the journey and through his insistence I learned one more way in which the Eskimos are similar to ourselves.

Before the whalers came to Herschel Island, the Eskimos had been in the habit of purchasing from the Hudson's Bay Company four or five main items—tobacco, tea, guns and ammunition, traps and cloths of various kinds—silk, velvet, canvas, blankets, etc. For all of these they had to pay fabulous prices because the Company's difficulty in getting goods to Fort Macpherson overland was great, and of course the trade of the country was small. That there was in the early days no competition may have had something to do also with keeping up the price.

When the whalers came to Herschel Island in 1889 they were so eager to get fresh meat and fresh fish from the Eskimos (things for which there had been no sale until then) that they heaped upon the Eskimos far more than they knew what to do with of all the different things the Hudson's Bay Company had been in the habit of selling them, and a great many other things besides. Now the whaler goods differed from the Hudson's Bay Company's goods. The eagerness of the whalers to exchange their wares for things which had previously had no market value gave the Eskimos the impression that the whaler goods must be inferior in quality. In some cases this may really have been true, as with the velvets, blankets, etc. But in other cases the opposite was obviously true. Take, for instance, shotguns. The whaling officers frequently brought in double-barreled guns of Greener and other well-known English types. These they used to present to the Eskimos in return for special favors or as mere acts of friendliness. In other cases they sold them to the Eskimos for small quantities of fresh meat. The Hudson's Bay Company had been bringing in only single- or double-barreled muzzle loaders. In the world markets the muzzle loaders would probably have cost less than ten dollars each while the breech loaders of the whalers were in some cases worth over a hundred dollars.

But the Hudson's Bay Company had never given away any muzzle loaders and had instead insisted on a fabulous price for them. The impression then grew up among the Eskimos that the muzzle loaders were much better guns than the breech loaders. When I tried to argue them out of this, it was like trying to convince a woman that silk and lace are less valuable than woolens because they give less warmth and wear out more easily. The Eskimos I met said to me quite plainly: "It is true that the breech loaders shoot as well and are much more convenient." "But," they added, "they are, nevertheless, inferior guns"—just as women might admit that a lace gown is neither strong nor warm but is, nevertheless, a better dress than a stronger, warmer one made out of a cheap fabric.

For a similar reason Roxy wanted Hudson's Bay Company's tea. I knew the price of that tea in Winnipeg to be eighteen cents a pound and I knew that some of the tea we had at Shingle Point would have cost in Winnipeg at least forty cents a pound. However, the forty-cent tea was whaler tea which the Eskimos were accustomed to get cheaply, while the Hudson's Bay Company's tea had never been sold for less than two dollars a pound. The Mackenzie Eskimos, accordingly, considered Hudson's Bay tea as the only tea any man would drink who could afford it.

I readily promised Roxy the tea and blanket, for I thought I would be able to secure them from the Hudson's Bay Company's goods which Ovayuak was selling as their agent. Later Roxy made a second condition, that I was to buy from Sten two good dogs and lend them to him to use along with his own team on the way east. When we got to Ovayuak's I would keep those dogs there and he and Sitsak would return to Shingle Point with the diminished team.

# CHAPTER X

WE started on December first. This was my initial winter journey and on it I learned a good many things about winter travel. The first was how to dress. In this I had been well coached both by Roxy and by Sten, and the women had made me up a suitable outfit of clothing.

The ideal clothing for winter travel is made entirely of caribou skin. We speak of it as being tanned because we have no better word, but really it is not tanned at all—only scraped.

When I lived among the Dogrib and Yellowknife Indians of Great Bear Lake (1910-11), I found they had an elaborate system of tanning. First they dried the skin thoroughly, next they rubbed all over the surface a paste made out of decayed caribou liver or decayed caribou brains. Then they rolled the hide up and allowed it to remain for a day or two. This was only one of several processes through which they put the skin. At the end it was soft, had a yellowish color on the flesh side, and a pungent odor. The entire process took a week or more.

A Mackenzie Eskimo woman gets better results with one-fifth of the labor and in one-tenth of the time. She just scrapes the skin with a blunt scraper, then dampens it, dries it, and scrapes it a second time. This makes the skin if anything softer than the Indian tan, a beautiful pure white on the flesh side and without any odor. Furthermore, the Indian process fills the pores of the skin with some material which stiffens on freezing, so that even though the Indian tanned skin may be just as soft as the Eskimo tanned in a warm room, it will be appreciably stiffer out of doors.

The Eskimo "tanning" also makes the skin exceedingly light so that a complete set of winter garments weighs rather less than the average man's business suit in winter in such places as New York or London. The best suit I ever had weighed a little less than ten pounds, and that included every stitch I had on from my toes to the top of my head.

Our winter undergarments have the fur in all the way from socks to mittens. You may think this would tickle, but it does not any more than a sealskin collar tickles your cheek. We arrange our clothes so that we seldom perspire even with fairly violent exercise, but if they do get damp, they dry much more quickly than woolen garments. The outer clothes have the fur out everywhere except the palms of the outer mittens and the soles of the boots.

Both the undershirt and the coat that goes over it have a hood which covers the head so as to protect the ears but leaves the cheeks and forehead exposed. I have known white men who wore knitted woolen caps inside the hood and I think if I were bald I might do the same. For a man who is not bald (and Eskimos seldom are) using a knitted cap is no advantage. I used to think it would be better to have the hood come far forward, something like a sunbonnet, so as to shelter the nose and cheeks from a cold wind. I have found this the opposite of an advantage, for your breath catches in the hood if it sticks too far forward and forms a mass of ice that rubs against your cheek and eventually freezes you.

Regulation of temperature is obtained by adjusting your belt. Both the shirt and outer coat are made so that they hang loosely outside of the trousers and come down halfway to the knee. If the day is, say, around zero or 20° below, you would very likely wear nothing but your shirt (or, as we frequently call it, undercoat) hanging loose like a cloak. If that proves chilly, you put on a belt which keeps the warmth in a bit more. If you begin to perspire, you take off your belt again. If it is still too warm, you open up the neck of the shirt a little under the chin and allow a cold current of air to circulate up around your body and come out at your neck. When you are overheated this feels very pleasant, and if it begins to feel unpleasantly cool you tighten up the neck of your undercoat again.

If the undercoat with a belt is not warm enough, you put on over it the outer coat, which you have been carrying on top of the sled. The two coats with the belt on the undercoat may now be too warm so you remove the belt. If it is extremely cold, you take the belt off the inner and put it outside the outer coat so as to hold both of them against you.

With the trousers the same general principles apply except that I have found it even better than two pairs of fur trousers to have the inner trousers of fur and over them several pairs of light outer trousers made Chinese-fashion of some thin cloth, such as drilling. You would carry three or four pairs of them on top of the sled. If the single under trousers are not enough, you put on one pair of loose drill trousers over them. If that is not enough, you put on a second pair, and if that is not enough still a third, and so on till you have enough. When it gets warmer you take them off one by one and put them on top of the sled to be ready for the next emergency.

These are ideal clothes to use in winter in such places as Russia, the Adirondacks, Minnesota, or Montana, and generally everywhere in Canada except on the Pacific Coast. Or, rather, they would be ideal if people knew how to take care of them, but that is a delicate matter. Should they become damp you must not hang them up near a stove, for in that case they would not last you many weeks. The same heat that would not affect our ordinary "civilized" furs at all will spoil caribou skin clothes. If they become damp they shrink when they dry, but a little scraping makes them soft again. There are many other tricks of taking care of caribou skin clothes after they get wet or when something goes wrong.

But the main thing is to see that nothing does go wrong. To begin with, you should not let them get damp. Before going North, I had read some polar books and had learned how the arctic explorers suffered from wet clothing. Hoar frost would gather in them in the day time. This cannot be prevented, for even when you are not perspiring there is a certain amount of invisible vapor coming out all over your body. I found on this winter journey across the Mackenzie delta that on a calm morning if I held my bare hand in front of me there would be columns of steam rising from every finger although the hand appeared perfectly dry. This steam is always rising from the body no matter what the temperature, and indeed it rises the more rapidly the warmer the temperature. But it is not visible to the human eye except when it is condensed into a kind of fog by a temperature of thirty or forty below zero. It is this ordinarily invisible vapor that the explorers tell about condensing in their clothing and making them damp.

When the explorers I had read about came into camp in the evening, there was a little rime along every seam, and perhaps in other parts of their clothes. As the camp became warm this melted and made the clothes damp. They did not dry over night. Next day more rime gathered and next night they became more wet. Some explorers have described how their clothes became soaking wet in a week or two of travel. They would sleep at night with everything on inside the sleeping bags. The frost in the garments then melted and the explorers slept in a cold bath all night. Next morning when they got up they would have to take hold of their sleeves with their fingers to keep them tight while they were freezing, so that they should not wrinkle up and leave the wrist bare. The sleeves were now as stiff as boards. One explorer tells how his sleeves were so hard that the edge of one cut a gash into his wrist just above the thumb so deep that the scar remained for years after.

With all this book knowledge in my head, I was a good deal worried setting out on my first trip with Roxy, but he explained to me how all these troubles could be easily avoided. On this particular trip we would have a stove and a roaring fire every night, so wet things could be dried. However, the trick was to take off before going into camp the garments with hoar frost in them. If you are wearing only one coat the hoar frost will not gather inside of it because of the warmth of your body, and it is found only on the outside. This is the smooth skin side and you can scrape the rime off with a knife or shake it off. But if you are wearing two coats, the hoar frost will probably gather on the inner side of the outer coat.

Before going into camp you will, accordingly, take off your outer coat, turn it inside out and scrape off the frost. Or else you may just pull it off as you go in and leave it outside the door so that the hoar frost will never have a chance to thaw. Next morning you slip it on as you go out and, although there may be hoar frost in it, it does not annoy you, for it is in the form of dry powder.

The only kind of hoar frost that becomes disagreeable is what you allow to melt either in the house or else on your body when the weather gets warm. Warm weather is, therefore, something to watch and guard against carefully. Changes of temperature are occasionally rapid. You may have forty below zero when you start out in the morning and hoar frost will gather on the inside of your outer coat during the forenoon. In the afternoon it may cloud up, the temperature rising to twenty above zero. Just as soon as you notice the increasing warmth of the air, you must take off your outer coat and either put it on the sled where it will remain unthawed, or else turn it inside out, shake it and carefully remove all hoar frost.

When you describe this technique of keeping skin clothes dry, it sounds a little complicated, but in actual practice you get so used to it that it is no more bother than brushing a dark "business" suit to keep dust and fuzz from showing.

I had heard and read about Eskimo snowhouses and was eager to see one. On this trip, however, Roxy never built a real snowhouse, for he considered it more convenient to carry a square piece of canvas to use along with a snow wall. We built each evening a circular wall about six feet high and then spread over it our piece of canvas.

It had a hole in it for a stovepipe. There was plenty of driftwood everywhere and we kept a roaring fire in a sheet-iron stove every evening until bed time. When we went to sleep the camp became exceedingly cold. While the fire was going, sparks used to drop on our canvas roof and burn holes in it, so that before the trip was over it looked a good deal like a sieve. By shifting my head a little I used to be able to lie in bed and follow for an hour through one of the holes the motion of some good-sized star. When it was forty below outside, I think the night temperature inside of the camp must have been about twenty below. This is an easily avoidable hardship, as I discovered later. However, I was expecting hardships and was rather pleased to find that at last I had to endure something disagreeable. We had plenty of bedding and were not actually cold, but I had to cover up my head in sleeping, and that is unpleasant.

As a boy I had read James Fenimore Cooper and many other stories about Indians and Eskimos. One of the ideas I got from all these books was that an Indian never gets lost. Traveling down the Mackenzie River I had been told by some of the Hudson's Bay traders that this was correct and that an Indian is almost infallible in finding his way. Other traders told me that an Indian gets lost as easily as anybody, and those called me to notice that the other traders who had told me that an Indian never loses his way were stay-at-homes. This I verified. Perhaps two-thirds of the northern fur traders are traders primarily and remain in or near their cabins the whole time, no matter how many years they live in the North. A few are of an adventurous disposition and travel and hunt with Indians. These latter were usually if not always of the opinion that a white man with the same amount of experience can find his way about better than an Indian.

However, it is difficult to shake off the ideas we have held for a lifetime, and when on the third day of travel through the Mackenzie delta, Roxy and Sitsak stopped frequently to climb upon little hummocks and look around and talk with each other, I did not guess what it was all about. Finally I asked Roxy and he told me that "maybe they were lost." Little by little the doubt on this point was removed. They were lost sure enough. For two days we wandered aimlessly up one river channel and down another, never finding out exactly where we were until the morning of the third day when we came upon a sled trail and soon after that a camp site. This was our old trail and our own camp of two days before. We had been traveling in various curves among the islands and had finally happened upon our own trail. Roxy and Sitsak now agreed that at the time when we made this camp we had not yet been lost and that we must have lost the way a little beyond that. We watched carefully, accordingly, and sure enough after following our old trail four or five miles we came to a point where it turned to one side and where it should have turned to the other.

A river delta is the easiest of all places in which to lose your way. A little farther south the Mackenzie delta is thickly forested with spruce but, where we were, the islands were all covered with willow. The spruce islands can be traversed by sled, although with difficulty, but the willow islands are impassable, for the vegetation is so tangled that even in summer it is almost impossible to force your way through. The shrubbery commonly varies in height from four to eight feet. In winter this brush retains and holds up such masses of soft snow that there

is no thoroughfare for men or sledges. You must, therefore, thread your way through the devious channels between the islands, and no man need be ashamed of getting lost, especially if the light conditions are bad.

It was now the time when the sun did not rise at all.
Writers of arctic romance have given this period the name
of "The Great Night" but that is really a misnomer, con-
veying a wrong impression. We were only about a hundred miles north of the arctic circle and at that distance
you have something like six or seven hours of daylight
clear enough for reading large print out of doors. The
sun never actually rises, but at noon you can see the glow
of it in the south where it lies about as far below the horizon as a tropical sun would be ten or twenty minutes
after sundown. The Mackenzie Eskimos when traveling
at this time of year (and it is their favorite time for
traveling) ordinarily get up about one or two o'clock in
the morning and spend three or four hours in cooking and
in their usual talkative breakfasts. They then hitch up
the dogs any time between five and seven o'clock and are
on the road sometime before the faintest dawning. About
noon they stop so as to have plenty of daylight for making camp and feeding the dogs, and everything is snug
and comfortable before it is yet dark. On cloudy days
we sometimes camp as early as ten or eleven o'clock in the
morning, for on overcast days there are only three or
four hours of good working light. Pitch darkness such
as we have in the tropics or "temperate" lands is unknown
in the Arctic, for even on a cloudy midwinter night there
is enough light from the stars behind the clouds reflected
by the snow on the ground so you can see a man in dark
clothes ten to fifty feet away.

In many later years in the North I have had hundreds

of different Eskimo traveling companions but never one with such contradictory qualities as Roxy. To begin with, he was about the cleverest Eskimo I ever saw. In some respects he was not far from being a confidence man. As he had shown when we nearly lost our lives in the autumn gale, he had unlimited courage. I have never known any one upon whose quick wit and decisive action I would have been so willing to rely in an emergency of life and death. He was cheerful under misfortune but sulky and morose if he imagined himself to have a grievance. In some ways he had the white man's point of view perfectly after his long association with the whalers. In other respects his Eskimo mental attitude was still unmodified.

I had a good example of the Eskimo point of view when we had been on the road seven days, which was as long as the entire journey to Tuktuyaktok had been estimated to take. On account of having lost our way we had made only half the distance. The snow was deeper and softer than had been expected and we were moving slowly. I noticed that the two dogs I had bought from Sten were not pulling as well as Roxy's dogs. When I remarked upon this, Roxy said rather sulkily that it was no wonder, for the poor dogs had had nothing to eat for several days. This astounded me, for I knew that there was still some fish on our sled, nor did I know any reason why there should be nothing to eat for my dogs when his were well fed. I had understood it to be a part of our bargain that he would provide all the dog feed. He said, however, that his bargain had been that he would supply a certain number of dogs and I a certain number and that it was always the Eskimo custom that when two men traveled together each supplied food for his own dogs. This was all the more confusing because he had explained to me earlier in the year the Eskimo communistic idea of food, where what belongs to you belongs to me equally. He now told me that this form of food communism applied only when you were at home. He said (and I found it later to be true) that you can arrive at a man's house with any number of dogs and feed them and your party out of his fish pile. But when you leave you are not entitled to take with you any of his fish for your men or your dogs, but must buy what you want. My two dogs could have eaten at his fish pile all winter if we had remained at Shingle Point, but on a journey it was an entirely different thing.

Roxy now seemed to be angry at me for not having brought along fish for my own dogs and also apparently at Sten for not having explained to me that it was necessary. He said that he had fed my dogs for two or three days at the beginning of the journey but that each day he had done so he had become more angry at the injustice of being compelled to do it, until finally, when he found we were lost and that the journey was going to be longer than we expected, he had stopped feeding them. No arguments of mine would induce him to feed them now. I argued the less because he said it was his intention to stop feeding his own dogs either to-night or to-morrow night. "For," he said, "dogs are more used than men to going without food. They can stand it better, and anyway we have the upper hand and must look after ourselves."

Being new in the Arctic, I was greatly worried by the situation and began to picture myself heroically starving to death. Of course, there was no real fear of this, for it was only seventy-five miles or so to Tuktuyaktok. Roxy now told me that he thought there might be two or three settlements this side of Tuktuyaktok, in which case we could secure food that much sooner.

It was not long after I noticed the slack traces of my dogs until they stopped pulling entirely. Roxy then unhitched them and let them follow behind the sled. From my experience with the Indians up the river and from the fact also that Roxy seemed to be angry not only at me for not providing dog feed but also at my dogs for pulling so badly, I wondered why he did not cut a willow switch from the river bank and try to whip them into pulling. When I asked him about it he said that whipping tired dogs was one of the white man's customs which he had not yet learned. The Eskimo idea was that a dog should be treated with great consideration, and his opinion was that a good dog would pull about as long as he had any strength without being whipped. Whipping, he said, would not help our speed much, if any, but would hurt his reputation and lower his standing in the community. He told me that the only approved Eskimo method of inducing dogs to work is either by shouting to them and trying to cheer them up by the voice, or else by having some person walk ahead of the team of whom the dogs are fond so that they will pull hard to try to keep up.

I regret to say that during the twelve years following 1906 the Mackenzie River Eskimos adopted the custom of whipping dogs, so that when I was among them last (1918) it was only a few of the old men who did not do so.

Something like forty miles from Tuktuyaktok we began to look for people at well-known camp sites, but all the camps turned out to be deserted. We were thirty miles away when our dogs had become so weak that it was necessary to leave behind most of our belongings.

REPAIRING A BROKEN SLED WHILE THE DOGS LIE COMFORTABLY STRETCHED OUT ENJOYING THE WINTER SUNSHINE

For several days all of us had been taking turns pulling on the sleds. After stopping feeding the dogs, we still had fish enough for three or four days for ourselves at a little more than half rations.

Some fifteen miles from Tuktuyaktok we came upon a new sled trail. When the dogs got the strong smell from the fresh tracks of the men and dogs, they interpreted it to mean food and began to pull with such energy that we were able to let go our hauling straps. When at last the houses came in sight the people there soon saw us and began to shout, and upon hearing this the dogs speeded up so that we had to run to keep up with them.

When we got within about half a mile of the house ten or fifteen people came running out to meet us. At their head was Ovayuak who welcomed all of us cordially and me even more effusively than the others. He was especially cordial when Roxy told him that I had come to spend the rest of the winter with him because his people still lived in the old Eskimo fashion.

# CHAPTER XI

AN ARCTIC CHRISTMAS WITH AN ENGLISH COUNTRY
GENTLEMAN

WHEN we started from Shingle Point it had been the understanding that after a few days' visit with Ovayuak, Roxy would take me to Harrison's camp on the Eskimo Lakes, two or three days' journey south, for I planned to spend Christmas with Harrison and then come back to the coast to live the rest of the winter at Tuktuyaktok. But shortly after we arrived Roxy suggested to me that Ovayuak had plenty of dogs and could easily take me across to Harrison's, while his own dogs were tired out and weakened by having gone several days without food. I said that this would be all right if he would arrange with Ovayuak for doing it. Roxy replied that he had already spoken to Ovayuak and that it was nothing but fun for Ovayuak or one of his men to make the trip and that it had been agreed between them that I was to pay him (Roxy) both for bringing me to Tuktuyaktok and also for taking me south to Harrison's. Accordingly, I secured from Ovayuak the sixty-pound chest of tea and the two Hudson's Bay blankets. The day after receiving this pay Roxy and Sitsak started back for the camp at Shingle Point.

The week before Christmas, I asked Ovayuak one day when he would take me over to Harrison's, whereupon he was greatly surprised and said that he had not considered making any such trip. When I told him about the arrangements which Roxy said he had made, Ovayuak laughed uproariously and said that his cousin had evidently been up to his old tricks. It seemed Roxy had told Ovayuak that I wanted to stay there until a sled came from Harrison's camp to fetch me or until I could get some other Eskimo to take me there. Ovayuak said I was welcome to stay as long as I liked but that he had such a big household and one so difficult to provide for, that he would have to fish industriously all winter and could not make any trips until after the sun had come back. Then he was going to Herschel Island to see his married daughter and his new-born grand-daughter. He did not think any of the people now living at Tuktuyaktok would care to make the trip to Harrison's, but added that there were others traveling up and down the coast every week or so and probably one of these would take me there. "Some people," he said, "are always traveling and there are many who don't care just whom they visit or in what direction they travel. Some of these will turn up soon and we will get them to take you to Harrison's."

It was not many days later when there arrived my acquaintance from Shingle Point, Ilavinirk with his wife, Mamayauk, and their four-year-old daughter, Noashak. Ovayuak suggested at once that here was one of the traveling type. I was glad to see Ilavinirk for this reason and also because I had liked him the first time I met him. A further reason was that he brought with him a can of salt and I was getting exceedingly salt hungry.

As I have mentioned earlier, I had to go without salt from the time Harrison left us at Shingle Point until Sten arrived. Sten had plenty of salt and I borrowed what I wanted from him, but when we left Shingle Point we had forgotten to take any along. I began to miss it pretty badly on the way down, and Roxy consoled me by saying that Ovayuak would be sure to have some. But when we got to Tuktuyaktok we found that Ovayuak hadn't any. He said that ordinarily Mr. Firth supplied him with some as a part of his trade goods, but as the Eskimos never cared to eat salt and as he himself never thought of asking for it, it happened some years that Mr. Firth did not give him any. This was one of those years.

In that connection Ovayuak raised the question of whether a white man really needs salt or whether the salt habit with some people is like the tobacco habit with others. He said that since he could remember, most of the Mackenzie River Eskimos had used tobacco, both men and women. Mothers frequently teach tobacco chewing to their children before they are one year old, and they grow up to be exceedingly fond of it. In fact, many Eskimos now imagine that they cannot live without it. Ovayuak had heard, however, from the men who were old when he was a boy, that in their childhood no one used tobacco and that when tobacco was first brought in (which I estimate to have been about 1850) everybody disliked it. Even now he said there were two or three Eskimos who did not use tobacco and seemed to get along just as well as the others who did.

On the other hand there were only two or three Eskimos who did use salt and the great majority abhorred it. The common Eskimo belief was that the desire for salt was peculiar to white men, but he himself thought it was only a habit almost any Eskimo might acquire. Conversely, he thought that it was a habit which any white man who tried could probably break, and he suggested that in a little while I would cease craving it.

However, I had not stopped worrying when Ilavinirk

came, and when Ovayuak told him about my hankering for salt he immediately went out to his sled and brought in half a baking powder tin of it. At this I was overjoyed and sprinkled salt liberally on my fish the next meal. I was a bit disappointed to find the fish not as much improved by the salt as I had expected. That did not lessen my gratitude to Ilavinirk, and I thought that for me this would prove the beginning of better times, for used by me alone the pound or two of salt ought to last for months.

When the next meal came I was interested in something that was going on and absentmindedly ate the whole meal without recalling till the end that I had put no salt on my fish. This made me realize that my hankering for salt had been in a sense imaginary. I had really been without it long enough already to break myself of the habit but had been longing for it because I imagined I needed it. From that time on I never opened the salt can, although I kept it with me in case I should want it. A month or two later I lost it, nor did I worry at all over the loss.

It turned out that Ilavinirk was more than willing to take me inland. He had just come from the Eskimo Lakes country himself where he had been living less than a day's journey away from Harrison's camp. He told me that his camp was a fine fishing location if you got there early enough in the fall. He had arrived too late, however, and the fish run had been nearly over. He caught a few fish and hunted caribou without success. He had snared a few ptarmigan, but altogether it had proved a difficult place to make a living and he had now just abandoned his house to come down to Ovayuak's to live on fish until the sun came back. He had, however, left some gear at his camp and this he would be able to fetch back with him on his return after delivering me to Harrison's. Some of his best friends also lived on the Eskimo Lakes and he would be glad to visit them and introduce me to them.

The territory we traveled through going south from the seacoast towards the Eskimo Lakes reminded me of the North Dakota prairies where we used to have our cattle ranch. There was snow on the ground, of course, but rather less than there would have been in North Dakota at the corresponding time of year, and the grass was sticking up here and there through the snow. It was evident that if the winter resemblance between an arctic and a Dakota prairie was close, the summer resemblance would be equally great, and this I have since found to be the case.

Our first day was a short one, only about ten or twelve miles, and we came to the trapping camp of a single family that lived in a creek bed well stocked with willows. Although few of these were more than six or eight feet high, they gave an adequate fuel supply. As for shelter from winter blizzards, that is something the Eskimos cannot imagine to be necessary. If they need a shelter for the house they can always build a semi-circular wind-break wall of snow blocks in an hour or two that gives not only protection but also directs the snow so that the blizzard piles it into drifts at some distance from the house where it will be in nobody's way.

The next day we reached the first camp in the Eskimo Lakes country where we found Sten's brother-in-law Kunak with his family occupying half of a big house, and another Alaska family occupying the other half. Their house was not the regular beehive type used by the hunters in the mountains, from whom we had fetched the caribou meat in October. It stood just within the fringe of spruce trees that surround the Eskimo Lakes. Well formed trees thirty and forty feet in height are not rare. From these white men could easily build log cabins of the type we have all seen either in pictures or otherwise. That sort of cabin, as I know from ample experience, takes a long time to erect and is difficult to build so well that it keeps out the cold adequately. Three or four Eskimos can build in a day or two as big a house as three or four white men could build in a week or two and the Eskimo house will be much warmer.

The chief reason for the ease of making the Eskimo house is that the walls instead of being vertical, slant in just a little. If a house has a vertical wall and if you try to make it warmer by building a sod wall outside of it, then it takes great skill as well as good sods to build in such a way that there is not an open space between the frame and the sod. But if the wall of the framework leans in a little, you can heap sods and earth up against it any old way and the sods will hug the frame. Kunak told me that it had taken him and the other man three days to build this house. It was hexagonal in outline, about twenty-two feet in length, and fifteen in width. The frame of the walls was of spruce and the roof was of split spruce logs. Outside this the walls were of earth, with a roof covering of moss and a layer of earth over that. There was a great stone fireplace in the center of the house directly under the parchment skylight.

This was the first Eskimo house I had seen that had windows also in the walls. Each was made of a single pane of ice about an inch thick, two feet wide and four feet high, with the lower edge level with the floor. Although the house temperature seldom fell below 70° these windows did not melt, for they were kept hard by the outdoors frost which now averaged about 30° Fahrenheit below zero. On an occasional warm day it was necessary, Kunak told me, to curtain them off with a blanket to protect them from being thawed by the heat of the interior.

After a pleasant visit at Kunak's house, we traveled next day something like twelve miles across one of the Eskimo Lakes to the journey's end. Our arrival seemed both to surprise and delight Harrison, who was having rather a lonesome time, for Kakotok, with whose family he was living, knew scarcely a word of English and Harrison had not mastered even the Eskimo jargon. It may have been because of his bringing up as an English country gentleman or because of a naturally aloof disposition that he was living in one house with his Eskimo servants in another, on terms about as intimate as if they were neighbors in a suburb. Getting some one to talk with was a relief to Harrison. It was added good luck that both of us were fond of chess, which helped pass the time. He was a very good chess player.

Ilavinirk had told me that he had had to abandon the idea of spending the winter on the Eskimo Lakes because of the poor fishing. I now asked Kakotok about the fishing at Harrison's camp and found that, although it had been much better than Ilavinirk's, still it was getting worse every day, and he much feared that they also would have to leave the lakes and come down to the coast. He felt sure they would either have to do this or else go with the dog teams on a journey to the coast, spending a month or so and leaving only some of the family to keep the camp in the forest. The feeding of the dogs through the midwinter is the chief worry of the Eskimos in those seasons when food is scarce. Kakotok said that their shortage of food was due to late arrival at the Eskimo Lakes in the fall. Had they come two or three weeks earlier, he considered that they would have had no trouble in getting all the food that they could possibly have needed for the winter.

Ilavinirk and Kakotok agreed, and my whole observation since has confirmed it, that to make a living in the Mackenzie district you should follow the well-known principle of making hay while the sun shines—which here means fishing in the fishing season. But throughout the preceding winter they had been accumulating fox skins and other things which they wanted to sell during the summer. The cargoes of trade goods from Edmonton ordinarily arrive at Macpherson early in July, and the traders that come in through Bering Straits arrive at Herschel Island late in July or sometime in August. In some places, such as Shingle Point, you cannot fish very well until the nights turn dark. But there are many other places where the water is muddy and the fishing good even during the summer of perpetual daylight. That is the logical harvest season, but the Eskimos are then off on their trading journeys to Fort Macpherson or Herschel Island. Many of them want to visit both places. If the season happens to be late, as it was my first summer there, the Eskimos hang around Herschel Island until the end of August. Harrison and I had hung around there with them, and so we did not leave for the fishing grounds until it was too late for either the Eskimos or Harrison to lay up a suitable supply.

I used to go with Kakotok to see how he fished. There were two methods in use on the Eskimo Lakes. One was very simple and depended on a little open patch where the water flows out of the lake into the river that takes it to the sea.  Here the rapid current prevents the formation of ice in even the coldest weather, and nets can be set exactly as in summer.  In other places the nets had to be set through the ice.

In getting ready to fish through ice you fasten your floats to one edge of the net and your sinkers to the other, so that one edge of the net shall be held at the surface of the water and the other down vertically.  Then you cut two holes in the ice about forty feet apart (for that is a common length for Eskimo nets) and each a foot or eighteen inches in diameter.  Between these two holes you cut a series of smaller holes just big enough to stick your arm into the water, and perhaps six or eight feet apart.  Next you take a stick of dry, buoyant wood that is eight or ten feet long.  You shove it down through one of the end holes until it is all in the water, when it floats up and rises against the ice.  You have a string tied to the stick and this string you fasten to one end of the net.  Then you lay the stick so that, while one end is still visible at your hole, the other end is visible below the next hole six or eight feet away.  You now go to the second hole, put your hand into the water and slide the stick along under the ice until you can see it through the third hole.  The stick, of course, pulls the string in after it and by the time you have worked the stick along to the furthest hole your net is set.  You now take a rope that is about ten feet longer than the net and tie each end of the rope to one end of the net so as to make an "endless chain," the net being under the water and the rope on top of the ice.

During the night the holes all freeze over.  You allow

the small holes to remain frozen permanently but each time you go out to tend the net you open the two end holes and pull the net out of one of them. As you pull the net out the rope part of your endless chain is pulled into the water. When you have picked all the fish out of the net, you pull on your rope and thus drag the net back into the water.

I am lucky in having hands that stand cold pretty well, but when I came to help Kakotok pick fish out of a net at forty below zero I found it the coldest job I had ever tried. We dragged the whole net up on the ice and the wriggling fish soon got themselves all covered with snow. This turned into slush on their wet bodies. A fish feels cold enough at best but these felt particularly chilly.

It does not make any difference if the net all freezes into lumps while you are getting the fish out. Our net got so balled up with snow and slush which turned into ice that if it had remained in that condition it would have caught no fish after being put back into the water. Kakotok told me, however, that the water in the lake was warm enough to melt the ice off the net, whereupon the strain between the floats and the sinkers compelled the net to take its proper vertical position in the water.

Kakotok was setting three nets and he got from twenty to fifty fish a day, ranging in weight from one to four or five pounds. This was about as much as the men and dogs of the household were eating, and when visitors came the camp ran behind to the amount eaten by the visiting men and dogs. This made evident the validity of what Kakotok had told me, that they would either have to abandon the camp entirely or else some of the family would have to go off on a visit, taking away the dogs and leaving only one to two persons to tend the nets. That way several hundred fish could be accumulated against the return of the party from the coast.

In the books I had read about the Eskimos I had always been impressed with how lonesome and depressing it must be to spend the several weeks of midwinter without one ray of sunlight. This had been worrying me a great deal even before the sun disappeared, but Roxy had told me that he had never heard of any Eskimos who minded the absence of the sun, and had added that all white men got used to it after a year or two. Sten had confirmed this and, altogether, I had gathered from him and the Eskimos that in the Arctic the period of the sun's absence is looked forward to by everybody and is the jolliest time of the year.

It is not that the whites and Eskimos that live in the Far North prefer darkness to daylight; neither do we in the big cities prefer stifling August to the moderate days of May or September. Still, there are many of us who look forward to August because, although it is disagreeable in weather, it is agreeable in being the vacation time. That seems to be about the Eskimo point of view. In midwinter it is almost impossible to hunt caribou or mountain sheep and less pleasant than usual to fish or to trap. Accordingly, they make it the vacation time and utilize it for taking long journeys and for dancing, singing, and general rejoicing.

I understood already that this was the attitude of the Eskimos and of such white men as Sten who had lived there for many years. For myself I was so impressed with the idea that I would find the winter depressing that I really found it so—at least occasionally when I had time to think about it. Harrison was a good mathe-

Eskimo Log Cache to Protect Meat from Predatory Animals

matician and enjoyed calculations and plottings. He had
it estimated that in our particular location the hills to
the south were just so high and the hills at our camp
were of just such another height, and accordingly the
sun would appear above the horizon the 15th of January,
if the temperature was about zero, and probably a day
or even two days earlier if the temperature should be
thirty or forty below zero. I accordingly climbed to the
top of the highest nearby hill on the 15th, and sure
enough, saw half the sun above the horizon. I then
went home and wrote a long entry in my diary, telling
how glad I was to have the sun back. My joy was real,
but I now think that the preceding depression and the
consequent relief when the sun came back were largely
due to my imagination. I had read in the books that I
was going to be depressed. Had the books said nothing
about it, I think I should have failed to notice it. Anyway, I have since spent nine winters in the North and
have never again felt any particular exhilaration at the
return of the sun. I have always been glad, however, to
see it rising higher and higher in the sky, for, although
the two or three months following its return are the
coldest of the arctic winter, they are on the whole much
the pleasantest part of the year, especially for one who
enjoys activity and wants to work outdoors all the time.

By the middle of January Mr. Harrison's fish pile
was getting noticeably smaller. He had a little flour,
just enough to make you wish you had more bread with
your fish. We could not eat more bread than we did or
it would not have lasted him till spring. He was anxious
to have it last, for he had the view (which I have since
found to be the opposite of practical) that it was best
to save such delicacies as you had so as to have a little

every day.  With men who are fonder of bread than they are of fish or meat, it is simplest to let them eat up the flour as fast as they like.  When it is gone they worry for two or three weeks and then forget all about it.  But if they have a little taste every day, they worry every day and every meal because they have less than enough.

To remove temporarily from his fish supply the burden of all the dogs, and also to deliver me back at Tuktuyaktok, Harrison and his party left for the coast on January 26, and three days later we were welcomed by Ovayuak at Tuktuyaktok.

# CHAPTER XII

It was only after my return to Tuktuyaktok that I began to live like a real Eskimo. Up to this time there had always been some difference between me and the natives. Sometimes I had salt when they had none, and generally my fish had been cooked in a special way. When they had been eating theirs boiled or raw frozen, mine had been roasted or baked; and when they ate heads, I seldom joined them although occasionally I allowed myself to be coaxed to taste this great delicacy of theirs. Ovayuak told me now that he would have things specially prepared for me if I wished it, but I decided to stop pampering myself, partly because it was a bother for the Eskimos to look after me specially and partly because I wanted to live exactly as they did so as to get their point of view.

The house we lived in had a framework of driftwood and the roof was supported by numerous wooden pillars. The earthen walls were five or six feet thick at the base and became thinner towards the top of the wall, which was only about five feet high. Then the roof sloped up from all sides in "cottage" fashion, and at the peak was a level square space about six feet each way. There was about a foot of earth on top of the roof planking. In the center of the roof was a window about three feet in diameter, made by sewing together translucent strips of polar bear intestines. On a clear day in midwinter this window gave enough light so that all the lamps could have been extinguished for about four hours.

The lamps never were extinguished, for we needed them for heat. Usually there were three or four of them burning, each in a corner of the house. They were huge, half-moon shaped bowls that had been adzed out of blocks of soapstone. The wick was a ridge of powder lying along the straight edge of the lamp. This powder was sometimes hard wood sawdust, sometimes powder made by scraping or sawing walrus ivory and sometimes it was dried moss that had been rubbed into powder between the hands. Occasionally if other materials gave out, they would take small pieces of manila rope that had been secured from the whalers, and hack the fibers into lengths of one-twentieth of an inch or less, thus practically converting the fibers into powder. Sometimes we tried to use ordinary commercial lamp wicks but they were much more difficult to keep burning properly, for the Eskimo women are very particular that the lamp shall never smoke the least bit. No duty of a housekeeper is more important than to keep the lamp well trimmed.

For ideal burning the bowl of the lamp must always be almost full of oil but never quite full. This is regulated in a simple automatic way. A slab of polar bear or seal fat is hung almost over the flame. If the oil in the lamp gets a little too low, there is more of the lamp wick exposed and the flame becomes bigger. The increased heat of the flame tries out the fat hanging over the lamp and makes the oil trickle down more rapidly. This gradually raises the level of the oil in the bowl until it floods part of the wick and decreases in that way the size of the flame. This cools off the vicinity of the lamp enough so that the slab of blubber stops dripping. Then the flame gradually increases in size as the oil lowers in the lamp until a second flaring up again brings streams of oil down from the slab of fat. A lamp once properly prepared in this way will burn with regular fluctuations six or eight hours at a time.

Ordinarily the lamps that are properly trimmed when people go to bed in the evening are still burning brightly the next morning. Occasionally, however, some woman forgets to put quite enough blubber on the hook above the lamp. In that case the lamp will begin to smoke during the night. I do not think the Eskimos have keener ears or keener eyes than Europeans, but they certainly have a much more delicate sense of smell. The least bit of smoke in the house will wake up somebody who shouts to the particular woman that her lamp is smoking and warning her to look after it.

Because the walls and roof of the house were so thick, scarcely any cold penetrated in to us that way and the only chill came by way of the fresh air that ventilated the house. The floor of the dwelling was level with the ground outside. The entrance was a kind of tunnel about thirty feet long and covered by a shed. The tunnel was about four feet deep where it came in under the house wall, so that you had to stoop low to enter. Once inside the wall, you could stand up in the end of the tunnel with your shoulders in the house. We spoke of this entrance as the door, but it was really only a square hole in the floor about four feet in diameter. There was a lid available with which to cover the door, but I never saw it used. The temperature in the alleyway was about as cold as outdoors but our house was so full of warm air that the cold air in the alleyway could not enter, for cold air is heavy and will not rise into any space occupied by warm air.

In the roof we had a ventilator about four inches in

diameter. The even flame of the lamps kept the temperature of the house day and night fluctuating somewhere between 75° and 85° Fahrenheit. We had a stove but this was never used except for cooking, and that commonly only for a period of two or three hours in the afternoon. At that time the temperature of the house rose to the vicinity of 100° and sometimes above. It was much like living in a Turkish bath. But with the house at such a temperature and the air outdoors perhaps 40° below zero, there was so much difference in weight between the outdoors atmosphere and the air in the house that the pressure through the door was strong enough to drive the warm air out through the ventilator with the force of a blast. I once went on top of the house, held my hand over the ventilator to test the draught, and got the effect of a strong wind blowing. This showed the house, although stifling hot, was well ventilated.

Before coming to live with the Eskimos I had heard much about the bad smell of their houses and at first it seemed to me that they did smell bad. I soon came to realize, however, that this was only the odor of the food they ate, corresponding to the odor of coffee or bacon in our houses, or perhaps to the odor of garlic in the homes of certain Italians. If you are fond of bacon or coffee or garlic you do not dislike the smell. Similarly, I found that as I gradually became used to the Eskimo food and finally fond of it, these odors changed from their original unpleasantness until I eventually grew to relish them as much when I came in hungry from out of doors as a hungry camper in the woods relishes the smell of frying bacon.

Our house had a square open floor space in the middle about twelve feet by twelve. In three directions from

this ran three alcoves, so that the ground plan of the
house was not very different from the club in playing
cards.  In each one of the three alcoves was a sleeping
platform about eight inches higher than the floor.  Out
of one alcove there led a door communicating with a
separate house occupied by an uncle of Ovayuak's, with
his wife and family.  In our big house and in this little
connected house we were twenty-three all together, not
counting visitors and there were visitors nearly every
night.  There was just room on the bed platforms for all
but me to sleep, and when every one else had gone to bed
I used to spread my blankets on the floor near the door
so as to be where it was as cool as possible.  Whenever
there were visitors there were others besides me sleeping
on the open floor space.

There is very little furniture in an Eskimo house.  They
have the sensible way of getting along with the least
possible, and much of what they do use they use only
temporarily and then take it out of doors.  Ordinarily
there is in the alleyway leading out from the Eskimo
house a side chamber where certain articles of furniture
are kept that are frequently used.  Whenever one is
needed somebody goes to bring it in.  Other things less
frequently used are kept on an elevated platform outside
the house.  Here are kept also the food and any property
the people may own, such as rifles that are not in use,
bolts of cloth purchased from the whalers, or the like.

But it is the custom to keep in the house the cooking
gear and the little movable tables upon which the food is
prepared and eaten.  These took up some floor space and
so did our sheet-iron stove that was used for cooking.
When visitors were numerous the tables were moved out
into the alleyway, and occasionally the stove also had to

be taken down and moved out so as to give sleeping room. If that did not suffice, then the visitors had to make a camp of their own outside, coming into our house to visit and join us at meals.

I found nothing so hard to get used to as the excessive heat at night.  The Eskimos take off all their clothing and sleep under some light cover.  Being lower down and nearer the door than the rest, I was a little cooler and soon got so I found it tolerable.  Eventually I became so reconciled to the excessive heat that I almost liked it.

There was no regular time of getting up in the morning. Most of these Eskimos were great smokers and I used to be wakened by the crackling of a match at perhaps four or five o'clock when somebody woke up to have a smoke. Commonly those earliest ones took a few puffs at their pipes and then went to sleep again.  But about five or six o'clock some smoker would not go to sleep but would instead open a conversation with another smoker.  The bed platforms were wider towards the center of the house than they were towards the walls, so that all the people slept with their heads towards the center of the house. This made it easy for a man to rise on his elbow and talk to somebody across the floor.

After half an hour or so of conversation in which more and more people joined, somebody would finally say that it was time to be having breakfast.  Then would arise a discussion among the women as to which of them should go out and fetch the fish.  This was all amiable and with a great deal of laughter.  When two or three women had been decided on, they would generally have a race to see which could dress the fastest.  Putting on Eskimo clothes is about as simple as it is for firemen to dress.  There are no buckles, everything slips on easily, and the only things to be fastened are belts and drawstrings. There are some slight differences in the clothes of men and women but they are about equally easy to put on.

I never actually timed these breakfast-getters but I do not think it took them more than from thirty to forty-five seconds to get completely dressed. Then they ran out and presently returned with armfuls of frozen fish, carried somewhat as a farmer carries an armful of firewood. The fish were thrown upon the floor with a clatter and more conversation went on for about half an hour, until it was considered that the fish were suitably thawed. Then the women would take their half-moon shaped knives and cut off the heads of the fish, to be saved till the afternoon's cooking. Then they would run a straight cut along the back of each fish from neck to tail, and another along the belly. They would then take one corner of the skin between their teeth and strip it off somewhat as one might a banana, if one did strip a banana with his teeth. If the fish were large, they were cut into segments but if they weighed no more than a pound or two they were left in one piece.

In a big family like ours the fish was put on several platters so that no one would have too far to reach. Before the platters were distributed Ovayuak's wife used to look them over and pick out the best pieces for the children, for it is the custom that in all things children are more favored than even the most influential member of the family or the most respected visitor. Next after the children the visitors would have their choice in a family where one fish tray served, but in a big family they take their chances more or less. If there are three sleeping platforms there would be a separate tray for each platform, and the visitors would share with those members of the family that slept on that platform.

We did not commence eating until the fish were nearly thawed, so that their flesh was not much harder than typical ice cream. We ate as much as we liked of any piece and then put the remainder back on the tray or into another tray. Eskimos are careful that no food goes to waste, but leaving half your piece means no waste, for the dogs have to be fed and the leavings go to them.

By seven o'clock every one is dressed and ready to go about the day's work. Ovayuak himself was always the first to go out to the fishing grounds. Certain members of his family always followed. It was optional with visitors whether they helped with the fishing but all of them did unless they had something else to do. Had some one refrained entirely from work of all sorts, I do not think our host would have done anything about it, nor would the rest of the community. But a lazy man is despised by everybody, and what keeps anybody at work is not the fear that he may be turned out of the house, but rather the dread of a public opinion which would eventually give him a low rating in the community. Such low rating would not be followed by any formal punishment, but no Eskimo seems to be able to bear the disapproval of his countrymen. This is one of the reasons why so few of the uncivilized Eskimos are lazy. I judge from my own experience that the stimulating climate is another important reason. I often feel lazy in southern countries, but I find activity a delight in the North.

I used to go with Ovayuak to his fishing. We were on one of the branches of the Mackenzie delta and the river ice was at that time about three feet thick. I did not understand very well how to use an ice chisel and at first it took me half an hour to make a fishing hole ten inches in diameter through three feet of ice, but Ovayuak could do it in a few minutes.  For a rod we each had a stick about two feet long and attached to it a slender line of braided caribou sinew about four or five feet long.  On the end of this was a little fish carved out of ivory about two inches in length.  A hole had been bored in the head of the fish, a shingle nail stuck through, bent and sharpened.  This sort of tackle is bait and hook in one.  When a fish bites you must not give him any slack; if you do he will get off the hook, for there is no barb to hold him.  There are only two tricks in this fishing: one is to keep jiggling the hook so that the ivory fish squirms around in the water much as a live minnow would; the other is to pull suddenly and keep pulling when you have a bite until your catch is on the ice.

We were getting several kinds of fish; the largest variety are called by the Eskimos *sit* and by the Hudson's Bay traders *connie*.  The Eskimo name is merely plain Eskimo but the white man's name is said to come from the French "l'inconnu," which means "the unknown" fish.  It is pretty hard to classify.  It used to be called "Mackenzie River salmon" but now I believe it has been decided that it is not a salmon at all.  It is a scaly fish with white flesh and may attain a huge size.  I have seen some more than three feet in length, weighing over forty pounds and have heard that they sometimes weigh sixty or seventy pounds.  At Tuktuyaktok we seldom got any weighing more than thirty pounds, and fifteen-pounders were perhaps above the average.

In six or seven hours of work we would catch on a good day four to eight fish of various sorts, or anything from ten to forty pounds per man.  There were seldom more than five or six of us fishing, and counting visitors we had on an average more than thirty people to feed and about fifty or sixty dogs. I imagine the people ate about five pounds each and the dogs two or three pounds each. This meant that, although we were catching fish pretty rapidly, our store of them was getting smaller each day. There were several tons that had been accumulated in the fall, but Ovayuák said he thought we would do well if we did not come to the end of it before the end of March. I applied my mathematical knowledge to the case and assured him that the fish would last longer than that, but he replied that so they would if our family did not increase in size; but he fully expected that shortage of food would come upon various neighboring communities presently and that people from these would gradually gather at Tuktuyaktok.

In this connection Ovayuak explained to me why he was a chief. He was two kinds of chief. The Hudson's Bay people called him chief because they had picked him out as the most influential man in the community with whom to deal on behalf of the rest of the Eskimos. This was purely a Hudson's Bay Company's idea and Ovayuak said it had at first been incomprehensible to himself and the other Eskimos. I knew from the traders that they were used to dealing with Indian chiefs all up the Mackenzie valley and, indeed, all over Canada. Most of these Indian chiefs have real legal power over their tribes, the power having either been inherited from the father who was also a chief or else having been given by a formal election to chieftainship. When the Hudson's Bay men penetrated north to the Eskimos they took it for granted the Eskimos would also have chiefs and inquired who the chief was. When the Eskimos were unable to point to any man who was chief, for such an idea did not exist among them, the traders watched and found out who were the most active and influential people. They then decided for themselves that these were the chiefs, and called them so.

Ovayuak's uncle had been a man of good judgment and great energy and had been influential in consequence, for that is the Eskimo way. Him the Hudson's Bay people had picked out to call chief and had made him their representative. This trust on the part of the Company in turn increased this uncle's influence, so that eventually he came to have more power than any Eskimo had had before him. This was not comparable to the authority an elected officer has among us, but rather comparable to the influence exercised by a public-spirited and successful man. When Ovayuak's uncle died, the Hudson's Bay Company had found that Ovayuak himself had the most influence and had concluded that he had become chief. It was for this reason that Firth had introduced him to me as such.

This was the white men's aspect of the chieftainship. So far as the Eskimos were concerned Ovayuak was a man of influence because of his good judgment in part but also because he had kept to the ways of his fathers better than most of the others. When the rest spent nearly the whole summer in long journeys to Fort Macpherson and Herschel Island for purposes of trading, he made only a quick journey to Fort Macpherson, returning immediately to the fishing grounds. As I have mentioned above, the best run of fish ordinarily comes while the main body of Eskimos are still engaged in selling their furs either to the Hudson's Bay Company or the whalers. But when these people returned to the fishing grounds with their silks, photographs, chewing gum and whatever else they had bought from the traders, Ovayuak would already have tons of fish laid up.

When the trading season was over, all the Eskimos would fish energetically each in the location which he had picked out that year (for they seldom keep the same location more than one season at a time). But with the best efforts few of them secured even half as much as they needed, for their late start had handicapped them too much. Ovayuak told me it was his great pride that in midwinter or towards spring when these people came to the end of their food supply, they would always say to each other, "Let us go to Ovayuak; he will have food if anybody has."

This was the main reason that gave him influence among his own people. It would never have occurred to him to refuse food to any one; in fact, it seemed to him that they had as much right to his fish as he had himself, for his people are communists and that is the way they look upon things. He never said to any one, "You must take orders from me if I am to give you food." Neither did he ever issue orders. The fact was, however, that if it was known he wanted anything done, everybody was eager to do it for him. Though he had no formal or legal power, he had the respect and good will of every one so fully that it amounted to the most absolute power.

Ovayuak's fishing hole and mine were only a few feet apart. The wind naturally changed from day to day and each morning he would build a semi-circular wall of snow about five feet high to shelter us against the wind. Dressed in our furs we sat very comfortably and talked. Really it was he who did most of the talking, for I in-

sisted that we must not speak anything but Eskimo. Of
this I knew almost none. He had the greatest patience in
first saying a thing to me in plain Eskimo and then explaining it in the jargon (of which I had secured complete
command at Herschel Island and Shingle Point). However, I now know that I misunderstood many things when
he first explained them, and doubtless there were many
things which I did not understand at all.

Adequately dressed and seated on blocks of snow in
the shelter of our wind-breaks, we talked as comfortably
as if the weather had been warm, though the mercury
in my thermometer frequently fell to $40°$ below zero.
That was no colder than what I was used to in Dakota
and, as my clothes were now much more satisfactory
than they had been in Dakota, I was more comfortable
than any one could conceive who has tried to protect
himself against winter cold merely by putting on a heavy
fur overcoat over a business suit.

We used to fish till about four in the afternoon. The
people who were at home would have about noon a lunch
of frozen fish similar to our breakfast. This we fishermen missed. About an hour before the rest of us were
ready to quit work, Ovayuak's wife, who usually fished
with us, would precede us home to start the cooking.
Nearly every one of my Eskimo friends had a watch,
but our return in the afternoon depended not on the time
as shown by their watches, but on the daylight, and that
depended on the cloudiness. Also Ovayuak liked to stay
at his work as long as he felt like it. When we got home
we usually found that the meal was not quite ready, but
by the time we had taken off our outer garments and
removed the hoar frost from them, we would have before

us huge platters of steaming boiled fish. This was my fifth month among the Eskimos and by now I enjoyed a meal of boiled fish as much as any Eskimo.

After dinner no formal work was done although everybody was always busy at something—carving ivory, cleaning rifles, or even taking a watch apart to repair it. Most Eskimos are clever with their hands and some have besides a mechanical turn of mind. Kakotok, for instance, who worked for Harrison, had some years before bought a watch from a whaler. When it stopped one day he took it to pieces and found the mainspring broken. He then dismembered a cheap alarm clock and with a file and what other tools he had, he made out of the clock mainspring a spring for his watch and put it in so the watch ran. This I did not see myself but I had the story from a reliable whaling captain and do not doubt it. By the time I came among the Eskimos there were many of them who repaired watches with parts taken from other watches. Doing this had become a pastime and I am afraid that they sometimes injured a delicate watch by taking it apart when it was not necessary.

While the men were making and repairing things and the women sewing and doing other work, some one would usually sing or tell a story. The singing might or might not be to the accompaniment of a tom-tom, which is their only musical instrument. Their stories were of two kinds. Some were well-known folklore tales. Everybody knew them so exactly that the chief interest was in watching the narrator and laughing at him if he made the slightest mistake. The other kind of stories were the personal adventures of the narrators. In that case every one listened carefully without making comments until the end, when there always was a fusillade of questions.

They frequently asked me to tell about how conditions were in the white man's country, but I soon found that they were really not much interested and that this was largely courtesy. At first I thought their lack of interest might be due to my inability to make myself understood, but I found in later years after I got command of fluent Eskimo that this was not the case. They have far less interest in the white man's world than we have in theirs. The whaling captains told me that they had found no Eskimo who was willing to go with them to San Francisco (which was their outfitting port) except for wages. The idea of any one wanting to go to a place for the sake of seeing it struck them as curious. They had no intention of living in San Francisco and if they did not want to live there, why should they go there? The only possible motive they could see was that the whaling captains wanted them to work for them, in which case they were perfectly willing to go if they were promised sufficient wages so that at the end of a year they would return to their people with a larger amount of goods than they could have purchased for the foxes they might have trapped during the same year. It is only when an Eskimo community becomes "civilized" that some of the Eskimos begin to want to go south to see the big cities.

I used to try to explain to Ovayuak that the climate of San Francisco was very good. (We always spoke of San Francisco because the name was well known to the Eskimos. In general the Mackenzie Eskimos at that time took the name to mean the whole world of white men). When I praised the southern climate he asked me whether it was not always summer there. On my replying yes, he said that undoubtedly white men might like that sort of climate, but that an Eskimo could not understand that a country could be pleasant where it was always summer. He said that they do look forward to winter changing into spring and spring into summer, but that they rejoice still more when summer changes into fall and winter. After all, you soon get tired of the heat. In winter, he said, a hot house is good, for you can always go out and cool off; but where can you flee to from the heat of summer?

Had I been idle and with no interest in the language and customs of the people, I might have found the life at Ovayuak's tedious. But everything that happened was of vivid interest and I continually had my diary out scribbling information about strange customs and making notes of new words.

Nothing was more interesting than the way they dealt with the extreme heat of the cooking time in the afternoon. As I have said, the temperature sometimes rose above 100°. On coming into the house, we took off all our clothes except knee breeches, so that every one was stripped from the waist up and from the knees down. The children up to the age of six or seven were entirely naked. One of the occupations of the men was to sit for hours with blocks of beautiful white spruce driftwood, whittling them into long shavings resembling excelsior. These shavings were put into great piles in the corners and into bags and boxes. Because of the extreme heat there were streams of perspiration running down the faces and bodies of most of the people, although, of course, the Eskimos differ among themselves, as we do, in the freedom with which they perspire.

Those who perspired most would take handful after handful of excelsior, rub themselves with it towel fashion, and then throw each handful away.

In some respects the Eskimos are less cleanly than we but in other respects more cleanly. Many of us wipe frequently with the same towel; in later years when our towels became fashionable among the Eskimos they learned from white men to use each towel several times and eventually became much worse than almost any of us in using filthy towels. But of their native excelsior they never used a handful more than once, throwing it into a waste pile to be burned eventually.

Not really to get relief from the heat, but rather for pleasant stimulation (as we take cold showers after a turkish bath) one or another of the perspiring people would run out and stand for a few minutes outdoors, naked but for the knee breeches. I never knew of any bad results from this practice—why should there be, if we escape injury who like to finish off a warm bath with a cold shower?

An hour or two after the afternoon meal was over the house would cool down to the normal temperature of 75° or 80°, at which those are comfortable who are used to it.

# CHAPTER XIII

## LEARNING TO BUILD A SNOWHOUSE AND TO BE COMFORTABLE IN ONE

I HAD expected to stay at Tuktuyaktok until March or April but now I began to think that it might be important to get into touch with my expedition which, according to Captain Leavitt's guess, should be wintering somewhere along the Alaska coast two or three hundred miles west of Herschel Island. Accordingly, when the time came for Ovayuak and his wife to make their trip to Herschel Island to see their new granddaughter, I asked to be allowed to go with them. At first Ovayuak refused, saying that the time immediately after the sun returns is the coldest of the year and that a white man cannot stand traveling in such weather. I pointed out that he intended to take with him his youngest child, a boy of three or four. But he replied that if I were also a small child he would not mind taking the two of us, for you can bundle a baby up in furs and strap him into a sled, but I was too big for that. I asked where he got the idea that a white man could not stand cold, and he said he had heard about it indirectly from the whalers. His own observation had been that those white men he had actually traveled with were rather good travelers but he supposed they must be exceptional, for his cousin Roxy and others who had worked with the whalers had been told by the white men themselves how greatly the Eskimos excel in their ability to stand cold.

In general I think Ovayuak believed most of the things I told him, but when I explained that the cold of Dakota, where I was brought up, was about as intense as that of the Mackenzie district, he could not reconcile it with what he had always heard from the other white men of how warm "San Francisco" was. I tried to explain that the white man's country is large, with all sorts of climate, and that if the whalers were not used to cold, this did not apply to me. Eventually I argued him into allowing me to go along, but I know he looked forward to a rather worrisome time.

He estimated the journey would take about ten or twelve days. When I pointed out that it would not have taken Roxy and me that long last fall but for our getting lost, Ovayuak answered that the weather was now much colder and that, while a sled slides over the snow easily at such temperatures as we had in the fall, the runners would now grate on the sharp snow crystals almost as if we were dragging them over sand, and that we could not expect in midwinter to make much more than half the speed one could in the fall or spring. He expected that both he and his wife would have to pull in harness with the dogs and, while he did not expect me to do that unless I felt like it, I must understand that he could not allow me to ride.

Although I was a little worried about the journey in advance, partly from Ovayuak's talk and partly from the dreadful stories I had read in books of arctic exploration about the hardships of winter travel, I was still amused at the idea that I might have to ride when we were traveling at a speed no more than half of what we had made in the fall. Ovayuak admitted having had a rather favorable account of me as a traveler from Roxy, but he thought that a white man who does well enough in the fall might do less well in winter.

We started from Tuktuyaktok February 1st with our sledge heavily loaded with fresh fish. The first night we slept at the settlement of Kangianik, about fifteen miles to the southwest. We were stormbound there for the two days following and on the third day we camped in a deserted house, some twelve or fifteen miles farther on our road. After that we would have to make our own camps all the way to Shingle Point.

This was my first introduction to the real Eskimo snowhouse. On the journey east with Roxy we had built vertical circular snow walls five or six feet up and had put a flat canvas roof over. Ovayuak said that that sort of camp was all right in the autumn but now the weather was cold and we would be more comfortable in a dwelling entirely of snow.

When it came nearly camp time both Ovayuak and his wife began to look for good snow along the way. Sometimes one or the other of them would run a few yards to one side to examine a drift but they were either too hard or not hard enough. Eventually we came to one that was just right.

A drift just right for an Eskimo snowhouse is four feet or more in depth and of uniform consistency. First you determine the surface hardness by glancing at your footprints as you walk. With the soft Eskimo footgear, you should leave just enough of an imprint so that your trail could be followed. If your foot makes no mark the snow is too hard, and if it sinks in so that the entire outline of the foot is visible in the snow then it is too soft. If the surface hardness is right, you next drive a rod of some sort down through the snow to judge the consistency of it.  Commonly the Eskimos use a four-foot long walking stick, about as big around as a broom handle.  You drive this down with a steady shove, and if uniform pressure makes it go smoothly the snow is right.  But if the stick goes down easily enough for a few inches, then requires a much harder shove to drive it down the next few inches and then slips along easily for a few inches more, your snow is unsuitable for it is stratified and the cakes you cut from it will tend to break into layers.

When the right snowdrift has been selected you dig a little pit with a shovel to get a good starting place for cutting the blocks.  Occasionally you are compelled to build on a drift that is only a few inches deep and then you have to cut your blocks horizontally, but if the snow is uniform and the drift deep enough you prefer to cut them vertically.  The implement is a knife having a blade from fourteen to eighteen inches long.  The building blocks should be about domino-shaped, say from twenty to thirty inches long, from twelve to eighteen inches wide.  When you first cut them they may be any thickness from four inches up, but if the block is too thick you trim it down so that when finished it is only four or five inches in thickness.

In the case of the first snowhouse we built we had to cut the snow in one place and build the house a few yards off because in addition to hard snow you want soft snow nearby to bank the house with after it is erected.  I watched the building of this first house so carefully that I think I should have been able to build one similar to it the next day.  The procedure is really very simple.

Ovayuak took the first block and put it on edge the

way a domino would stand on a table. With his hunting knife he then undercut the inner edge slightly so that the block leaned in just enough so you could notice it. The second block was similarly put on edge, domino fashion, and in a position such that the circle eventually made would be about ten feet in diameter. The inner edge of this block was similarly undercut so that it leaned in. This block also leaned against the end of the first block so that a pressure from the outside could not have pushed one over without pushing both over. In a similar manner the other blocks were erected until the first circle had been completed.

I had always wondered how an Eskimo would start the second tier of blocks but this proved very simple. Ovayuak looked carefully over the whole circle and selected a place where the blocks were especially uniform in shape and of obviously good material. This was because he was a particularly careful builder. I learned later that no such nicety is essential and that you can start the second tier any place. From a point three blocks away from where he intended to begin the second tier Ovayuak made a diagonal cut downward so that he removed the upper quarter of one block, the upper half of the next, and about three-quarters of the third block, bringing the cut almost down to ground level. He then took a snow block of ordinary size and put it in the niche so that its right-hand end rested against the end of the whole block that was next to the right. (Had Ovayuak been left-handed this process would have been exactly reversed; the left-hand end of the first block of the second tier would have been set against a block to the left of it.)

Once he had started the second tier, Ovayuak built it

to the left, leaning each block against the one previously set up, so that the wall rose in a gradual spiral. He was going to build a dome-shaped house and the blocks of the second tier were, therefore, leaning in more sharply than those of the first tier. There was no change in method as the house approached completion. The higher the blocks are in the wall the more they lean in; if you lean each carefully against the one set up before it no block can fall unless the end of the preceding block against which it leans breaks off. If the blocks are set up at all carefully this will never happen.

Before we started the house building, Ovayuak himself had cut fifteen or twenty blocks. While he was building I carried these to him while his wife continued cutting more blocks. I think it took altogether between forty and fifty blocks to finish the house. When she had cut what she thought was enough the house was already three tiers high. Everywhere between the blocks there were crevices, some narrow and some wide. She now started rubbing soft snow into these openings, filling each one. That had to be done gently, for the wall is fragile at first.

When the house was three tiers high it became difficult for me to lift the blocks high enough to pass them to Ovayuak over the wall. He then cut a hole in the wall at ground level for me to shove the blocks in to him, he taking them up and placing them in position along the wall. The complete house required five tiers of blocks.

I had imagined that building the roof would be harder than the rest. But when you watch a house actually being built, you soon see that roofing it is easier than anything. In the ground tiers you are building in a circle so large that the two adjoining blocks are almost in a straight line. If you take two dominoes and place them on a table end to end in such a position that they are nearly in a straight line, then you will find it difficult to make them stand by leaning one against the other. But if you have the same two dominoes meet at an angle of from thirty to forty-five degrees and lean them against each other, they will stand supporting each other. The like is true of snow blocks. When you get near the roof the circle you are working on is less than half the

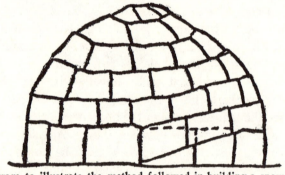

Diagram to illustrate the method followed in building a snow-house

diameter of the original ground circle. The blocks, therefore, meet at a much sharper angle and you can lean them together more squarely so they support each other better.

When the house is all but completed the builder finds in the center of the dome above his head a little irregular open space where the blocks do not quite meet. With experienced eye he decides how to enlarge this hole so as to make it big enough for an average sized block. With his sharp knife he snips off the projecting corners of the blocks, and now has above him an opening of regular shape. It may be square or triangular and occasionally it is domino-shaped, so as just to fit the block which he has ready. He next takes up a particular snow block, trims it so it is a little thinner than the average, puts it on end and lifts it vertically up through the hole, so that if you are outside you can see his two arms sticking up through holding the block. He now allows the block to take a horizontal position in his hands and lowers it gently down upon the opening so as to cover it like a lid. The block is somewhat larger than the opening, but with his long knife he trims it down to exact size gradually, and then allows it to slip into place.

By the time the snow frame of the house was finished Ovayuak's wife had all the crevices chinked up as high as the third tier. The cracks in the roof Ovayuak filled from the inside. When he announced that they had all been filled his wife began to shovel soft snow over the house. She threw shovelfuls up on the dome but none of it stuck there except what filled in the outer part of the crevices that had been chinked from the inside. Sliding down the sides of the house the soft snow formed an embankment all along the bottom of the wall. Eventually when the shoveling was discontinued, the house no longer looked like a hemisphere or a dome, but almost conical. With the snow piled at the bottom, the walls there were three feet thick. Two feet up, the walls were only eight or ten inches thick, and the roof was four inches—the thickness of the original blocks.

Ovayuak was now completely shut in, for he had filled up the little hole through which I had been passing the blocks to him. With a shovel his wife now dug a trench about three feet wide down to the river ice, four feet below. As if digging a cave she worked from the end of this trench in under the wall of the house to meet a hole that Ovayuak was digging down through the floor at that spot. Later we built of snow blocks a porch over this trench, making the regular Eskimo entrance.

As soon as the trench had been connected with the interior of the house, I crawled in and watched the rest of the process. Scattered all around him on the floor Ovayuak had fragments of blocks that had been unsound and had broken in handling, and there were other blocks which for one reason or another he had not used when I passed them in to him. Out of these he now made a platform a foot high, covering about two-thirds of the floor space. Over this platform his wife later spread a layer of long-haired caribou skins with the hair down. Over that she put a second layer of skins with the hair side up and on top of that our blankets—some of them reindeer and others cotton or wool.

A snowhouse is best suited to being heated with a lamp, either the Eskimo lamp or, even better, a blue flame kerosene stove or an alcohol lamp. We were, however, now traveling through a country well supplied with driftwood and for that reason we carried a sheet-iron stove instead of a heating lamp. We took two pieces of wood about four feet long each and placed them on the snow as far apart as the length of the stove. On top of these we put some sheet iron and on top of it the stove itself. A hole was made in the snow roof big enough for the stovepipe and over that part of the roof we spread a piece of canvas about four feet square that had a stove ring sewed to it through which the stovepipe projected.

I thoughtlessly imagined that when the fire was lighted it would soon thaw a huge hole in the wall back of the

BUILDING A SNOWHOUSE

All the men in this picture are young Americans, members of one of Stefansson's expeditions.

CAMPMAKING IN WINTER

stove and around the stovepipe. The stovepipe hole did
increase in size gradually as the flames shot up the pipe
making it red to where it disappeared through the roof.
There was a certain amount of melting of the snow wall
back of the stove and, indeed, the entire interior of the
house melted more or less. But as the snow was gradually turned into water, it was soaked blotter-fashion into
the dry snow outside of it. In the roof this process
continued until the four-inch blocks had been thawed
down to perhaps two inches. By that time the roof was
damp and had become a good conductor of heat, as
compared with the porous snow. This gave the intense
cold outside a chance to penetrate in and meet the heat
from the interior, stopping the thawing and turning the
damp snow blocks into ice. Thus the thickness of the
roof is automatically regulated. It thaws thinner and
thinner until a balance is reached between the outer cold
and the inner heat. It is only in warm weather that a
snow roof could be completely melted away even by
maintaining inside the house a temperature of 70°.

While we were cooking supper the snowhouse was
almost as hot as our earth and wood house at Tuktuyaktok. Ovayuak told me, and I later verified it, that had
there been no stovepipe hole the snow house would have
remained at an agreeable temperature all night. As it
was, however, when the fire went out a certain amount of
warm air continued to go up through the stovepipe. This
allowed a corresponding quantity of colder air to enter
through the open door. The result was that by morning
it was freezing fairly hard inside the house. Our bedding
was warm, however, and I did not mind it. In the
morning when we lighted the fire the house became fairly
warm in a few minutes and, of course, remained so until

we let the fire go out preparatory to packing up the stove
and the rest of our gear to continue the journey.

During the evening I had asked Ovayuak whether
there was no danger of the house caving in on us during
the night and he had laughed at me. When we were
about to start, this conversation apparently recurred to
him, so he asked me if I would like to try how fragile
the house was by climbing on top of it. I hesitated a
moment, and he ran up on the roof himself and stood
on the peak. I then clambered up after him. Had there
been ten of us our combined weight would not have
broken the house down. The structure had been very
fragile in the evening just while we were putting it up,
but after it had once been dampened by the overheating
of the interior and had then been turned partially to ice,
nothing but a sharp blow could have broken it. To begin
with, the half-solidified blocks of snow were now much
stronger than they had been; for another thing, the shape
of the house was just right to sustain a heavy weight.
The case of an egg is analogous. You can easily break
an egg with a sharp blow, but it is not so easy to crush
a raw egg by squeezing it in the hand if the pressure
is applied uniformly.

As we traveled west, the skies were clear every day
and the cold gradually increased. I did not have a
thermometer with me but I should judge it was frequently 35° and even 40° below zero: possibly it may
have been 45° below. This was no colder than what I
had been used to in Dakota. It surprised Ovayuak to
see how naturally I took to the conditions and he began
to believe me when I told him that certain parts of the
white man's country were as cold in winter as his.

On the twelfth day of our journey we arrived at

Shingle Point and found everything well there, both in Sten's house and in Roxy's. They had had during the winter numerous visitors with dogs and, for one reason and another, their store of fish had almost given out. As there is no winter fishing at Shingle Point and no sealing nearer than twenty miles from there, Roxy's household had decided on breaking up. When Ovayuak returned from Herschel Island Roxy and his family would accompany him back to Tuktuyaktok, while Oblutok's family would go up into the forest region of the Mackenzie delta where the spring fishing is tolerable and where there are rabbits and ptarmigan.

I had now been living for the last six weeks on fish (without salt) and water—no sugar, no flour, no vegetables, nothing whatever but fish and water—and before that for three months on about 95% either fish and water or meat and water. I had just passed through the supposedly depressing midwinter period called "The Long Arctic Night" and had just finished my first journey under the rigors of a polar winter. Apropos of all of it, Sten remarked I must have been putting on weight. I weighed myself—176 pounds. That was ten pounds more than I ever had weighed up to that time, and is twenty pounds more than I normally weigh when living in a city.

# CHAPTER XIV

ALTHOUGH Sten had been whaling in the Arctic for something like fifteen years, he had always lived on ships in winter or in their vicinity and had never been short of groceries. The supplies I had secured for him in the fall by the boat trip to Herschel Island had nearly given out, so he asked me to take his dog team and fetch a load of groceries which he thought Captain Leavitt would sell him. The reason why he could not go himself was that he had been troubled the last year with epilepsy and did not dare to take chances on traveling. I was willing to make the trip but preferred to do so two or three weeks later. Accordingly, I remained behind at Shingle Point while Ovayuak's party continued west.

There was now staying with Roxy's family an Eskimo named Kanirk, a name that may be translated into English as "Hilltop." The whalers, who had no idea of the meaning of the word, had apparently found in the sound of it a suggestion of a well-known English word and had called him "Cockney." When first I heard it I took it to be a nickname but Captain Leavitt told me later that it was merely a careless pronunciation of what the whalers believed to be his real name.

Apart from men who are students of languages, it is the general habit of those whites who come in contact with Eskimos or Indians to pronounce any words they hear, and especially the names of people and places, so as to resemble more or less closely some word of the white man's language. For this reason it is certain that were three traveling parties to pass through any given aboriginal region, one party English, another French, and the third Swedish, the three parties would bring back very different versions of the names of persons and places. This shows how unlikely it is that the Indian names that we use in America to designate our rivers, mountains and cities are even approximately similar to the real Indian pronunciation of those names.

When I first dealt with the Eskimos their names sounded very different to me from what they now do. The man whom I call Ovayuak was introduced to me by the Hudson's Bay people as "Levayuk," which some of the white men had shortened into "Levi." At first the name sounded to me a little like "Levayuk" and I used it until he himself took me in hand to instruct me. It was only after continuous listening to his slow repetitions that I began to hear it clearly as O-va-yu-ak. Another good example was an Eskimo woman Ikkayuak (Ik-ka-yu-ak), whom the white men called "Kashia" saying it was her native name. The next sandspit east of Shingle Point is called by the natives Akpaviatsiak (Ak-pa-vi-at-si-ak) which means "the little race course." The white men have turned this into "Appawuchi," which resembles the real name only faintly and which means nothing.

It was agreed that when I went to Herschel Island to do the trading for Sten, Kanirk and Roxy's boy would go with me, taking his team with the idea of possibly buying certain things for him. We started west along the coast February 15th. Nothing special happened the first day. The ice offshore had been crushed up into huge ridges by the wind and we could not travel over it but had to follow the narrow beach between cliffs two or three hundred feet high on one side and the impassable ice on the other.  There was soft snow under the cliff in places where there was a lee, and here and there the rough ice had been shoved actually up against the cliff in such a way that we had great difficulty in scrambling over.  Occasionally we had to use axes to hack away snags of ice to make a road for the sleds.

We spent the first night in Amundsen's abandoned house at King Point.  The next morning there was a howling blizzard and it continued for three days.  By that time we had eaten up all the food we had with us, for we had expected to reach Herschel Island in three traveling days.  It was still blowing rather hard on the fourth morning but we had to do one of two things—turn and travel before the wind back to Shingle Point and get a fresh start, or face the wind and travel some twenty miles against it to Stokes Point where we knew a family of Eskimos were living about ten or twelve miles our side of Herschel Island.  My companions were inclined to turn back, but I had a little pride in such things and urged that we should go on.  Accordingly, we set out and I had my first arctic experience with a blizzard in the open.

In Dakota I had seen many blizzards (and some of them are as bad as any in the polar regions) but there had been no occasion to travel against them any length of time, for houses or other shelters had always been available.  Dressed as we were in Dakota, we should have frozen to death anyway trying to walk twenty miles into a storm.  Dressed in Eskimo clothes it is another matter.  But although our lives were in no danger, we had difficulties of two kinds.

One difficulty was with the dogs. Their eyes kept getting filled with the drifting snow and caking with the freezing slush that resulted when the snow melted in their eyes. When a dog can see no longer he refuses to travel and commonly wants to curl up and sleep. We had to clean their eyes every few minutes to keep them going.

The other trouble was with my beard. One of my southern ideas was that a beard would be some protection against freezing the face. The Eskimos had told me that this was the opposite of the truth, and it was partly thoughtlessness that I did not take their advice and shave clean for this journey. As it was, I had a full beard. Had the weather been a little colder the condition might not have been quite so bad. I think the temperature was about 10° below zero and the wind perhaps forty miles an hour directly against us. The snow that struck my face melted in part and the water ran down my cheeks, freezing in the beard. This helped to cake the snow into the beard. I tried at first to keep my face clear by taking off my mittens and melting some of the ice off with my hands but I soon concluded that if I continued this my hands would freeze. Hands are worth a great deal more than faces, especially in the North, and so I kept them warm in my mittens, allowing my face to freeze. At first I kept both eyes open by clearing them occasionally with one of my hands but even this seemed a little risky, so I closed one eye and allowed the ice to form over it.

After some seven or eight hours of travel we got to Stokes Point. Instead of being cold I was too warm, if anything. But on my face there was a mask of ice which I suppose must have weighed more than ten pounds. When I went into the overheated Eskimo house, the warmth of my face combined with the warmth of the room soon brought the mask off in one piece. Under it my face had been slightly frozen all the way from the roots of my hair down to my neck, even including the eyelid of the eye that had been kept closed. The freezing was only skin-deep and no worse than a sunburn, except on the chin where it had gone almost to the bone. I had a sore there for two or three weeks and the scar did not disappear for a few months. The lesson was well worth it, however, for I have never since worn a beard in cold weather, nor have I since had my face seriously frozen.

The whole matter of keeping your face from freezing is to keep your hands warm so that you can use them for thawing purposes if your face begins to freeze. If you are traveling against a head wind with a temperature anything like 30° or 40° below zero, more or less freezing of the face is sure to take place. You keep making grimaces, for freezing is painless and you can detect it only by a stiffening of your chin or cheek. Occasionally you take one hand furtively out of the mitten and feel over the face to see if any part is getting stiff. If you find a little stiffening in the skin of the cheek or the chin you hold the warm hand on it for a moment until it is gone.

If the weather is exceedingly bad—say 50° below zero with a moderately strong wind—a different method is used. The cut of both your outer and inner caribou skin coats is such that if you want to you can withdraw your arm from the sleeve and hold it on your bare breast inside of the clothing, tucking the empty sleeve into your belt to prevent the cold getting in that way. The neck of both coats is made loose and you can shove your warm hand up through. If any part is getting stiff you hold your hand over it as long as may be necessary to thaw it out. Then you pull it in and hold it against your breast where it gets warm in a moment.

By being careful you can see to it that the freezing is never more than skin-deep. A little peeling of the skin takes place a few days later and there may be a moderate burning sensation for a few hours in the evening after a day when you have frozen frequently. These are minor discomforts and, as I have said, are no more serious than sunburn when you become equally used to them.

When we crossed over to the Herschel Island harbor the day after my freezing experience, we found not only a welcome at the police barracks and at Captain Leavitt's ship but also news of our expedition. Leffingwell and the Mate of the *Duchess*, Storkerson, had been to Herschel Island in the fall and had reported that the *Duchess* was wintering safe behind Flaxman Island just as Captain Leavitt had guessed. Leffingwell had left word for me that I might stay in the delta if I wanted to or come to Flaxman Island if I preferred. I decided to spend some more time to the east and proceed to Flaxman Island in April.

My return journey to Shingle Point was an interesting experience. The weather was good the first day and we made Stokes Point. The next day we were going to make the Amundsen cabin at King Point. We had scarcely more than started out when it began to breeze up from the east and to snow. The wind gradually increased until when we rounded Kay Point it was blowing a gale in our faces. We now had the usual trouble with the dogs in keeping their eyes free of snow. Finally the storm got so bad that their eyes filled as fast as we could clear them, and they kept curling up with their noses in their tails in spite of anything we could do. We had one whip with us, for the dog-whipping habit had come in from the Indians to the south enough so that some Eskimos now owned whips although few used them. Kanirk and the boy were ahead with Roxy's team and I followed with Sten's. Finally the dogs became so nearly unmanageable that Kanirk took hold of their leading dog, dragging the team ahead and bothering no more with their eyes. The going along the beach was so rough that the sleds were upsetting continually. The boy tended the forward sled in this respect and I managed the rear one.

We struggled along this way until my sled got a bad upset, or rather fell off a ledge into a low, soft place. I shouted to the men ahead but, of course, they could not hear me against the wind and they disappeared in a moment into the swirling snow. Eventually I got my sled righted but long before that my dogs had all been curled up snugly and now the drifting snow had nearly covered them from sight. I got hold of the leading dog and jerked on the harness until I had the team on their feet. While the other sled had been just in front of us they had struggled ahead bravely, but now when nothing was in sight the story was different. I got them started but neither they nor I could see the trail of the other sled which had been completely covered up by the drift, and I could not see ahead enough to guide them. I now tried to walk ahead, dragging the leading dog, but then the sled upset right away. At first I felt sure the Eskimos would come back to help me and I struggled on for perhaps an hour during which time I do not think I made more than one or two hundred yards between the up-settings of the sled and the refusal of the dogs to work because of being blinded by the snow.

When I realized the Eskimos were not coming back I

realized also that the situation was of a sort which according to all the books I had read should lead to tragedy. The Eskimo sled had been light, for they had bought very few things from the ship. But mine was heavy, for Captain Leavitt had sold me all the flour and other things that Sten wanted. My sled being heavy with groceries, the Eskimos had put on theirs all the camp gear and bed clothing and all the equipment. During the early part of the day a frying pan had fallen off their sled. I had picked it up and stuck it on mine, and this was the only implement I now had.

I remembered that somewhere in this vicinity on the way west we had seen a deserted Eskimo snowhouse. When I could not get the dogs to move ahead farther, I left them and taking the frying pan with me I plodded into the wind searching for the snowhouse. It turned out to be only a few hundred yards away.

It was an old house built in the early fall and repeated blizzards had cut away at the roof until a hole had been made by the wind. Through this hole the house had been packed full of snow. I did not have even a hunting knife big enough to use for a snow knife, so there was no use trying to make a new house. Furthermore, I had never tried to build one although I had seen Ovayuak build several. The only thing to do, then, was to try to dig out the soft snow from the interior of the house with my frying pan shovel. About two hours of work enabled me to do this sufficiently. I then went back to the sled and took a small piece of canvas that was on it, unhitched the dogs and led them to my proposed camp. While I was doing this a good deal of fresh snow had drifted in so that I had to do some more shoveling with the frying pan. I then dropped two of the dogs into the house with the idea of their furnishing me with some warmth, followed them in and tried to cover the hole over with the piece of canvas. I succeeded in this only partially and during the following night a good deal of snow kept sifting in.

I was pretty tired by the struggle of the day and it was not long from the time the dogs and I got into the house until I went to sleep with one of them for a pillow. I slept well until morning when I began to notice that I was getting wet. My clothes had been pretty well filled with snow and then the house was overheated by myself and the dogs, so that I was everywhere damp and on parts of my body soaking wet. I feared this might be serious, for the clothes would become stiff as soon as I went into the outdoors cold. But there was nothing to do but to try it as soon as it was daylight.

Shortly after the first glimmering began to show through the translucent snow roof I went out, hitched the dogs to the sled as quickly as possible, and started off. There was no trouble now for the weather was beautiful—clear skies and hard frost. About four miles of driving brought me in view of the Amundsen camp at King Point and I saw the other sled hitched up and the men ready to start. When they saw me coming they waited and started a fire to cook my breakfast.

I learned later from the boy that they had gone ahead probably half a mile or so the previous evening before noticing that I was not following. The boy had then wanted to stop and go back for me but Kanirk had said I would doubtless come along. When they got to the cabin and cooked supper without my coming, the boy had again proposed that they go to look for me but this Kanirk had simply refused to do. The next morning the boy had wanted to go back and look for me but Kanirk

SEA ICE PILED AGAINST THE COAST IN WINTER

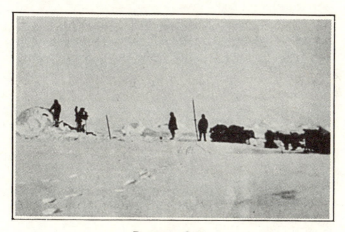

BREAKING CAMP

had wanted to keep on for Shingle Point and they were standing arguing about this when I came in sight.

I have never rightly understood Kanirk's position in this. He already had a bad reputation (as I learned later) by reason of having abandoned on a journey a sick Eskimo companion who would have frozen to death had he not been picked up by others who followed. His own statement was that he had considered it no use looking for me in the morning for I would undoubtedly have frozen to death during the night. White men usually did freeze to death when they were lost over night.

The idea which the Mackenzie River Eskimos had at the time about the ease with which white men freeze to death had no doubt grown up from the frequent tragedies that occurred to sailors who tried to run away from the whaling ships. Captain Leavitt told me many such stories. Men brought up in cities and sailors who knew nothing about land travel had frequently tried to run away from Herschel Island to the interior of Alaska, especially during the time of the Yukon gold excitement (between 1899 and 1902). Commonly these men had little idea of which way to travel or of the distance they would have to go and no idea of how to take care of themselves. It seems unbelievable but some froze to death under clear skies at distances of no more than six or eight miles from the ship. They had sneaked away from the vessels perhaps about nine or ten o'clock in the evening, had stumbled along through half-darkness over rough ice on the way towards the mainland for six or eight miles, had become tired and with clothing wet with perspiration had lain down to sleep, never to waken.

Among white men in the North, such as Hudson's Bay Company's men and whalers, there is prevalent a superstitious fear of going to sleep outdoors in cold weather. It is not the sleeping, however, that is dangerous to a tired man but rather that he does not go to sleep soon enough. If you exert yourself only moderately you will not perspire, and so long as you do not perspire your clothes will keep reasonably dry, at least for the first day or two after you start on a journey. The Eskimos know how to keep their clothes dry indefinitely but the runaway whalers did not know how to do that. This was not the trouble, however, but rather that they worked themselves into a sweat, struggled along until they were soaking wet and dead tired, and then finally went into a sleep that ended in death.

My own practice through many years has been to lie down in the open and go to sleep whenever I feel like it. I have frequently done this on winter nights under the stars, with a temperature in the vicinity of 50° and 55° below zero, or as cold as it ever gets in the arctic regions. I find that in fifteen or twenty minutes the cold wakes me up. That is not much of a nap, but when I get up from it I feel a good deal refreshed and go on until I get too sleepy again, when I take a second nap. The fear of going to sleep in extreme cold is not only unfounded but is actually the cause of many deaths in the polar regions. Men struggle ahead and keep awake as long as they can. Finally exhaustion compels them to sleep. It is then they are in danger of freezing and never waking.

The Eskimo sled had contained besides our food and camping gear a bag of my clothing. In the warmth of the Amundsen cabin I changed after breakfast into dry clothes. We reached Shingle Point easily by mid-afternoon.

# CHAPTER XV

WE GO IN SEARCH OF OUR OWN EXPEDITION

ALTHOUGH it still looked like winter, I considered spring to begin April 7th when I started to follow the coast westward in search of Flaxman Island which I had never seen and my own expedition which so far had been mine in name only.

My companion on this trip was an Eskimo from Cape York on Bering Straits who had been with the whalers so long that everybody seemed to have forgotten his rightful name. Even the Eskimos called him "Cape York" and he introduced himself to me by that name.

Cape York had never been farther west in winter than about halfway to Flaxman Island, but he had often seen the place from shipboard as he passed by in summertime aboard one or another of the whaling vessels and he thought he would be able to recognize the vicinity when we came to it. One might think that finding a ship anchored behind an island would not be particularly difficult, and neither would it be in good weather. But in the Arctic the weather gets more disagreeable and more difficult to deal with when spring approaches.

In mid-winter it is cold in the Arctic but when you are dressed Eskimo-style you don't mind it. Fifty or fifty-five below zero is a little too cold, for if you run or exert yourself violently and take the air rapidly into your lungs in consequence, it has a sort of burning and half-stifling effect. Forty below is about right and on the north coast of Canada it is not likely to be colder than that more than ten or twenty days in any one winter.

It is only in the interior of a continent or large island a hundred miles or more from the coast that you may occasionally get a temperature of sixty below zero. Your first morning of that kind of weather is a marvelous experience. The air is so clear that you can see three or four times as far as you can in any lowland in the South (mountain air is clear in all parts of the world). You can see with the bare eyes almost as well at 50° below as you can with opera glasses at 50° above. But if your eyesight is improved two or three times over, your hearing becomes ten times keener. I have heard distinctly at a mile the footfall of caribou walking quietly through slightly crusted snow. Firth told me that in the mountains west of Fort Macpherson he had frequently heard Indians chopping their firewood in camps that were ten miles away.

From Christmas until April the arctic skies are clear most of the time and you have such experiences as I have just described. But when the temperature begins to rise towards zero Fahrenheit, the skies begin to cloud over, fogs are frequent, the snow storms are twice as numerous and the snowfall heavier than in the next worst period, which is the late fall.

When Cape York and I started west we still had clear weather, but Captain Leavitt warned me that it was unlikely to continue that way and that we might miss Flaxman Island and the ship unless we were careful. Fearing this difficulty, he gave me as good a description of the topography as he could, but unfortunately he had seen it only from shipboard in summer. The land then has an appearance quite different from that of winter, and the point of view of a traveler by sled is necessarily different from that of a whaling captain, for the sled traveler's eyes are less than six feet above sea level as he follows the beach, but the captain gets almost a bird's-eye view from his masthead, more than a hundred feet above water.

However, Captain Leavitt thought we could not miss Barter Island, for that is the first land west of Herschel Island higher than fifteen or twenty feet above sea level. Herschel Island is about five hundred feet high and Barter Island, Captain Leavitt thought, would be about a third as high, consisting of rolling hills where the rest of the coast is flat. On a clear day we could judge roughly also by the distance of the mountains from the seacoast. Just east of the boundary between Canada and Alaska at a point some twenty miles west of Herschel Island, they come nearer to the coast than at any point between the Mackenzie River and Cape Lisburne near Bering Straits. There are only six or eight miles of level prairie separating the coast from the first foothills, and the mountains proper are not over fifteen miles from the sea. At the Alaska boundary they are twenty or more miles inland and as you go west they become farther and farther away until in the vicinity of Barter Island Captain Leavitt estimated them to be about thirty or thirty-five miles inland. They would be at least forty miles inland from Flaxman Island, which is about fifty miles west of Barter Island.

But the mountains would be unlikely to guide us for the spring fogs and snowstorms would prevent that. Our hope was to recognize Barter Island when we came to it. We would then estimate carefully our daily traveling distances beyond that and when we got fifty miles west of Barter Island we would search carefully or wait for clear weather.  In case of clear weather Captain Leavitt thought there would be no difficulty in finding the *Duchess of Bedford*.  He described Flaxman Island as being five or six miles long, a mile or two wide and in few places more than fifteen or twenty feet high.  The masts of a ship anchored behind the island would, therefore, be visible above it.

Those unfamiliar with the north coast of Alaska might think that distinguishing at a distance between the mainland and the islands would be easy.  It is difficult, however, for the islands, although some of them grasscovered, are little moré than overgrown sandpits.  Flaxman Island, for instance, is only about three miles from the mainland and a sledge traveler viewing it from seaward is likely to mistake it for a low promontory rather than a separate body of land.

Our dog team was the poorest I have ever seen in the Arctic, either before or since.  Captain Leavitt had seen nothing like it.  There were only two passably good dogs in it, one belonging to me and one to Cape York.

As related before, I had purchased two dogs from Sten in the fall but one of them had died under peculiar circumstances.  There had been a woman and her adopted son staying at Sten's house.  They decided one day they wanted to make a trip and, as they had only one dog to pull a small sled with their bedding, I lent them the better one of mine.  He was a powerful and in every way a good dog and had had an interesting history.

Two years before when Captain Amundsen had been wintering at King William Island to the north of Hudson Bay there had been in Hudson Bay the ship *Arctic,* under command of Inspector Moody, of the Royal Northwest Mounted Police.  Hearing that Amundsen was wintering in the North, Inspector Moody wanted to offer him some courtesy and purchased a team of the best dogs obtainable in that region to send to Amundsen as a present. But Amundsen already had all the good dogs he could use and was having the difficulty all northern travelers know of finding sufficient food for them. To show his appreciation of Inspector Moody's gift he kept one dog from the team but returned the others with an explanation of the cause. The next year Captain Amundsen had tried to sail west to the Pacific but had been frozen in (as we have explained) at King Point and had spent the winter there as a neighbor to Sten, for Amundsen's winter camp was but a few hundred yards away from the wreck of Sten's schooner *Bonanza*. The next summer when he sailed away Amundsen made Sten a present of a whole dog team which he had brought from Greenland and of this one dog from Hudson Bay. The Hudson Bay dog was so much bigger and stronger than the Greenland dogs and was so likely to injure them if they got into a fight, that Sten was glad to sell him to me although he was the best of all his dogs.

So when the widow and her son wanted to make their trip, I loaned them The Owl—that being our name for the Hudson Bay dog. This was some months after my trip across the Mackenzie delta with Roxy and I had forgotten the peculiar Eskimo point of view when it comes to feeding dogs. On the trip the woman and boy were stormbound several days at King Point and during that time they ran out of food. I happened to be making a short trip at that time. When I met them I was astounded to see that although their own dog was fat, mine that I had lent them looked like a skeleton. When I asked how this happened, I was told they had run out of food and that, as I had provided none for my dog, naturally they had stopped feeding him before they stopped feeding their own.

This meeting took place at an Eskimo camp. I unhitched The Owl from the widow's sled and took off his harness, which was made of braided hemp. I then went into the Eskimo house to ask for a fish to give to the dog. I was handed the fish at once, but when I got out with it I saw the last of the hempen harness disappearing down the dog's throat. He had been ravenously hungry, and some grease at some time or other had been spilled on the harness. This made it smell to him like food and he had eaten it. I knew his death was bound to follow unless I could make him throw it up. We poured a pint or more of seal oil down his throat, hoping to induce him to vomit. He threw up the oil sure enough, but the harness stuck in his stomach. Two days later he was suffering such agony that he had to be shot.

This was to me a tragic experience both because I had been fond of the dog and because I was getting fond of the Eskimos as a people and did not like to find such disagreeable characteristics cropping out. I must say before leaving this subject that, although both the woman and Roxy were justified by a theory which the Eskimos well understood, in starving my dogs when they fed their own, the rest of the people disapproved of them for doing such things and both of them were thought less of by their countrymen after than before.

After The Owl's death I had one fairly good dog left and Cape York owned a willing enough dog, but tiny. It was the intention that Cape York should return to Herschel Island after delivering me at Flaxman, and so we tried to borrow several other dogs for the trip. I succeeded in borrowing four but it turned out that none of them was worth his feed. They were small and also poor in flesh. One was larger than the others and looked better but he turned out to have fits resembling epilepsy with which he was seized two or three times a day. He used to foam at the mouth, lying in a fit for a few minutes, after which he got up but was dizzy and apparently out of his head for an hour or so. After two or three hours of normal pulling he would have another fit.

This spring journey gave me several new experiences. One of these was with "diffused light," which is among the chief annoyances of arctic travel. This trouble comes when the sky is uniformly clouded over and the clouds just thick enough so that they let through most of the sun's light without revealing just where the sun is. If the position of the sun in the sky is even faintly visible, then the case is not so bad, for discernible shadows will then appear in the lee of snowdrifts, ice snags, etc. But when you cannot see the sun there are no shadows. The snowdrifts are white and the ice snags white and there is nothing to enable you to distinguish between them.

The storms of winter sculpture the snow into ridges which we call drifts. If you have not seen snowdrifts, just imagine that the surface of an ocean or a big lake is first ruffled by a moderate storm and then suddenly frozen solid so that every wave and billow retains its position as they do on a painted canvas. Traveling over such a snow surface is disagreeable enough when the sun is shining and gives you shadows enough in the low places so that you can distinguish a ridge from a trough. But under the conditions of "diffused light" the snow before you, no matter how rough in reality, looks perfectly smooth. And still that is hardly the word. It rather looks as if there were nothing there and as if you were stepping into space each time you lift your foot. You never know when you are going to step into a hole or stub your foot against a ridge and, consequently, you must walk with the caution of a blind man who cannot see the things he may stumble over.

All this would not be so bad if you really had the strength of mind to realize that your eyes are useless. But you are continually trying your best to see, and the strain brings on the condition known as snowblindness. You may become "snowblind" on shipboard from the glare of a smooth sea or lake, and you may become snowblind on a snow field when the sun is bright in the sky and the light is so intense that it is difficult to keep the eyes open. But neither of these conditions is half as bad as the subdued glare of diffused arctic spring light.

One thing about snowblindness is that each time you have it your eyes are weakened a little and you are predisposed to a second attack. For this reason white men who are new in the Arctic are at first some of them comparatively immune. An Eskimo who has been exposed to this light condition from childhood is likely to become snowblind before a white man or negro feels the least twinge in his eyes.

This happened to Cape York when we had traveled something over a hundred miles west of Herschel Island and thought we must be approaching Barter Island. Captain Leavitt had given us some flour and I had secured seal oil from an Eskimo. This made the necessary ingredients and in the evening after camping I was frying doughnuts when Cape York asked me whether the grease was not getting too hot. I assured him it was not and asked what made him think so. He said it seemed to him that there was smoke in the tent—for it was now too warm for snowhouses and we were using a tent instead. After he had looked carefully at the pan in which the doughnuts were simmering and had assured himself there was no smoke, he announced that he must be getting snowblind and said we should probably not be able to travel the next day. He hoped it would not be a bad attack; perhaps one day's delay would be all.

But it turned out to be a bad attack. Before we had supper eaten the tears were beginning to run down Cape York's cheeks and his eyes, instead of feeling as if there were smoke in them, felt as if there were grains of sand under the eyelids. As usual, I made a long entry in my diary. This took me about half an hour and by that time my companion had begun to moan with a pain in the eyeballs which resembles the shooting pains of toothache. This was the first time I had seen snowblindness and the severity of it was a revelation to me. I had imagined that it was a kind of temporary blindness and had not realized that it was painful.

That night I was awakened now and then by Cape York's moaning. I offered to do whatever I could but he said there was nothing to do but what he was doing, which was to crouch on all fours with his head covered by a blanket. The cover was necessary to keep out the light for it was spring now and the nights were no longer dark except for two or three hours around midnight.

All the next day the pain in Cape York's eyes was unabated. The first sign of improvement was that towards midnight he fell asleep. Next morning when I woke up he was cooking breakfast with his eyes protected by colored goggles which we had secured from Captain Leavitt. The pain was no longer intense, he said, but tears were still running from his eyes and the eyelids were swollen—perhaps partly because he had been rubbing them so much. By evening of the second day he could keep his eyes open within the tent, but he told me that everything looked double. He said that when he looked at me it sometimes seemed as if I had three eyes and sometimes as if I had four.

The morning of the third day Cape York had gone outside the tent door and came in with great excitement, saying there were caribou on a nearby hillside. I went out and sure enough there they were about a mile away. These were the first caribou I had seen, for the Mackenzie district is a fish and rabbit country with a few moose in the willows but ordinarily nowadays no caribou. We had seen caribou tracks when I was on the way with Roxy to Tuktuyaktok. These had been animals crossing from the mainland to Richard Island. On the Eskimo Lakes with Harrison we heard of Eskimos living two or three days' journey away from him who had killed a few, but in general that is not a caribou country either, at least nowadays.

The Eskimos say that before the whalers came and induced the Eskimos to kill so many caribou to feed the ships, there used to be considerable numbers just east of the Mackenzie. Captain Leavitt told me that on the mainland just south of Herschel Island they often had caribou in the spring, and thirty or forty miles south of Herschel Island in and beyond the mountains there were supposed to be a good many. None had been seen north of the mountains this winter in that locality but Captain Leavitt had told me that as we traveled west the chances of seeing them would become greater and that he believed that south of Barter Island we might find some. This forecast was now coming true. Not only were the caribou there but they were on a hillside and, therefore, probably on Barter Island, for Captain Leavitt had said it was the first hilly country we would come to.

I know now that I should have gone after those caribou myself. The Eskimos of northwestern Alaska are excellent seal hunters but they do not see any caribou unless they leave their own country to go southeast into the Kuvuk or Noatak valleys or unless they join a whaler and later become caribou hunters in the service of the ships in the Herschel Island district. I did not realize this fully at the time and took it for granted that Cape York was a good caribou hunter. I thought only of the condition of his eyes, but he said that they were not bad now and he would try it. We could not both go because one of us had to watch the dogs to keep them from making a noise. So long as one man was around the tent they would remain quiet, but if both of us left they would probably set up a howl because they were tied and could not follow. If they were not tied they would follow us. Either would have been fatal to any chance of getting caribou.

I did not see how Cape York hunted the caribou, for before he got started from the tent they had wandered over the hill to the far side. In half an hour I heard shooting and in about an hour he came back with a long explanation of just why he had failed to kill anything. One thing was that he had miscalculated the wind and they had heard and perhaps winded him while he was still behind the cover of a hill. When he got to the top of the hill they were running some distance off. According to his account, he should have been able to kill them, nevertheless, had it not been that when he aimed the rifle he saw two rifle sights where one should have been, for he was still suffering the last effects of the snowblindness. The comfortable part of the story he brought back was that he felt sure this was Barter Island. He said we could soon verify that for he had heard there was a sandspit running west from the island on which there were ruins of an ancient Eskimo village.

When we started traveling this was verified, for we came to the sandspit and to the ruins of several Eskimo houses made of earth and wood. To the south on the mainland we saw a house that looked as if it were inhabited. This turned out correct, but the people were off on a journey. We went into the house, for that is the custom of the country. As Cape York's eyes were not fully recovered and as I found several books and magazines to read, we decided to spend the night. There was also the possibility of the occupants coming home.

Evidently the owner of this house was a white man, for there were books on mining, assaying and the like. Some of the books had on them the names of Leffingwell and Mikkelsen and had evidently come from our ship.

The second day after leaving this cabin the weather was thick and we walked out of a snow squall almost into an Eskimo camp. This was a tiny house occupied by a couple with an infant child. Now we learned exactly where we were and got information of various sorts. To begin with, the man whose house we had occupied two days before was Ned Arey. I had heard much of him from Captain Leavitt. Arey is of Pilgrim descent, born and brought up in Massachusetts. He first came to the Arctic as a whaler but soon became interested in mining and has traveled over a large part of northern Alaska, prospecting for gold. At first he had a good income which came to him annually from his parents in Massachusetts. Later this failed and he made his living from the foxes he trapped, for he was never very lucky with the gold. All this I knew from Captain Leavitt, and also that Arey was one of the most amiable and entertaining of men. We learned from these Eskimos that he was now on a visit to our ship at Flaxman Island.

About the expedition we received two pieces of serious news. The lesser of the evils was that the ship had sprung a leak. As she was for the present frozen into six or seven feet of ice, she could not sink. Her hold was full of water, however, and she was expected to sink in the spring when the ice thawed which now held her up. Accordingly all her cargo had been removed to the land, she had been partly broken up, and from the lumber a house had been built ashore.

The more serious piece of news was that Leffingwell, Mikkelsen and the first mate, Storker Storkerson, were dead. Against the advice of all the Eskimos they had gone away from land north over the moving sea ice. A week or two later one of their dogs had come back. Evidently this was the only survivor of the party. The Eskimos thought that the two sleds and all the men and dogs had probably sunk through thin ice in trying to make a crossing from one solid floe to another, and that this one dog had wriggled free from the harness and had eventually made his way to land. For some days after the dog came ashore the Eskimos had hoped that perhaps one of the men would also get ashore. This hope had now been given up. An Eskimo might make a living for a long time by hunting but white men would surely die unless they got back to people within a few days.

We were told that the camp at Flaxman Island was now

under the command of Dr. Howe and that Ned Arey had gone over there to give Dr. Howe the benefit of his long experience in the country and to make himself generally helpful.

The bad news inclined us all the more to hurry on to Flaxman Island. It was late in the day, however, so we slept over night. The next morning we started early and made the remaining twenty miles to Flaxman Island by midafternoon. On arrival at the camp we found the physical conditions as described by the Eskimos. The ship had been dismantled and a house had been built on shore where the party were now living under command of Dr. George P. Howe, of Boston, Massachusetts, a Harvard man whom I had known in Cambridge. He had three white men and there were some Eskimos helping about the camp. As a visitor we found Ned Arey with his Eskimo wife and family.

But we got a new story as to the death of the three officers. Dr. Howe did not think they were dead. The Eskimos had from the first believed that any journey out over the sea ice would be suicidal. The start had been made under ordinary ice exploring conditions, but the party had not been gone more than a few days when the Eskimos already knew they were dead. Later when a dog came ashore this confirmed them in the belief. Dr. Howe thought everything was all right. The intention of the ice party had been to stay away about two months. The time was not quite up and they might come back any day.

Ned Arey's opinion was intermediate between that of the Eskimos and of Dr. Howe. He thought that the party might have survived a certain length of time out on the ice but that they had now been gone too long and the chance of their safety was small. Furthermore, he considered that the arrival of the dog was a fairly conclusive evidence of tragedy.

On the whole my own opinion was a little more optimistic than even that of Dr. Howe, for I had gathered from the polar books I had read that ice travel was possible, although dangerous, and could not see why it should be much worse to the north of Alaska than in other parts of the world. I have since learned that it is somewhat more dangerous than the average in this locality, for the currents are specially violent and the ice, in consequence, particularly treacherous. Even had I known this, I should still have expected the party to come back, for they had been outfitted with provisions ample for a time somewhat longer than their absence had as yet amounted to.

Dr. Howe's opinion was that our expedition would be over that summer. The *Duchess* would probably sink in the spring and we would have to take passage with whaling ships to the outside world. This was a great disappointment to him, but even more disappointing to me, for my heart had been set upon visiting the Victoria Island Eskimos.

When Leffingwell had first proposed to me in Chicago that I go with him to Victoria Island the prospect had seemed attractive. It is an island much bigger than England. More than half a century before our time some British explorers had examined a considerable part of the coast and had met some Eskimos in two or three places. It seemed probable that these explorers had not seen more than a small fraction of the native population. Furthermore, most of the Eskimos actually seen by the explorers had probably died since then. It would be a fascinating thing to visit these people, the ancestors of most of whom had never seen a white man and who themselves certainly never had. If there were a few living who remembered from their childhood the days of the early explorers this would make the case still more interesting. Most thrilling of all was the possibility that we might find some old man who could give us from memory a solution of what to the world of Europeans is still the mystery of the fate of Sir John Franklin's men, whose two ships had been set fast in the ice just to the east of Victoria Island. All of his men were supposed to have died there or to the southeast but it was possible that some of them came ashore in Victoria Island. They might even have lived there for a few years, if not indefinitely.

When I had met Captain Klinkenberg at Herschel Island the past summer my interest had been increased. He had actually seen the Victoria Island people, but presumably only a small fraction of them. He had described them as having copper weapons where other primitive Eskimos usually have stone. But mysterious above everything, was his information that a certain small percentage of them differed from the rest and differed from the Alaska Eskimos Klinkenberg knew so well, in having a complexion which made them resemble Europeans. He had said that some of them had blue eyes and light hair.

Dr. Howe and I talked much about this fascinating problem and both said we would give anything to be able to go there. We agreed, however, that the best way of getting there would probably be to leave the country for now and to organize a new expedition later. All our plans had hinged on the *Duchess of Bedford* and when she was sunk we would have to make a new start.

This problem of the strange Eskimos occupied my mind continually more and more as time passed. We knew that no whalers had been there, for the first whalers in the western Arctic had come in to Herschel Island only in 1889 and the captains of most of those early ships were still captains in the present fleet. I had learned from them that no whaler had ever gone ashore in Victoria Island, except that Captain Cottle had once landed a small party of Alaska Eskimos to pursue some caribou they saw from shipboard. The caribou had been killed and the Eskimos had come aboard with the meat without reporting having seen even signs of people. It had been the common whaler belief that Victoria Island, although formerly inhabited by Eskimos, was now uninhabited, and Klinkenberg's discovery had, therefore, seemed even more remarkable to them than it had to me. Whalers have never reached Victoria Island from the east side, as I knew in advance and as I verified later by inquiries from Captain George Comer, a veteran of the eastern whaling fleet, who still lives in Connecticut.

I gradually made up my mind to solve sometime and somehow the mystery of the white Eskimos of Victoria Island. The opportunity did not come for three years.

## CHAPTER XVI

### A SPRING JOURNEY IN AN ESKIMO SKIN BOAT

AT Flaxman Island I found a well-stocked library and the leisure to write and to think. After an active winter under strange circumstances, the change was welcome. The shelves were full of scientific books. I read Osler's "Practice of Medicine," fascinating as a novel, and Chamberlain and Salisbury's three-volume geology, which has for its theme the greatest romance of all the romances— the ancestry, birth and development of our world. Then there were books labeled romances, such as the marvel stories of H. G. Wells. There were whole shelves of Tolstoi and of the English classics. Between reading these I wrote long dissertations on what I had seen and heard during the winter and on what I thought about it all.

But under the stimulation of an arctic climate inactivity soon palls upon one who has tasted the wine of action. I had not been at Flaxman Island more than a week when I proposed to Dr. Howe, who was in command for the time being, that he outfit me for a trip back to Herschel Island. He did this and I made the journey, but as it was uneventful I shall tell nothing about it.

During my absence at Herschel Island the men whom the Eskimos had reported dead came home all safe from the ice. They had made a fine exploration a hundred miles north from Alaska. The theory upon which they started was that the ocean would be shallow and islands would, therefore, probably be found rising here and there

from the sea bottom, or else a large land. So sure did
they feel about the shallowness of the ocean that, although they intended to take soundings wherever they
went, they carried a line of only 2,000 feet, expecting it
to reach bottom whenever desired. This was so far from
being true that they had gone only about thirty miles
from land when they came to where the sea floor settled
rapidly down to abysmal depths. This was taken to
mean that the probability of land beyond was small.
They, nevertheless, kept on for some distance. But the
ice was in rapid motion and everything was more difficult
than they had expected, so they presently turned back
to survey some more of the "continental shelf," as we
call the beginning of the steep slope where the shoal
waters of the coastline meet the deeps of the ocean proper.
The location of this slope is considered a matter of great
scientific importance.

While engaged in determining the continental shelf the
party were struck by an easterly gale which carried the
ice they were on so swiftly to the westward that they
were in danger of being taken into the open sea beyond
Point Barrow. A calm came just in time and they were
able to get across from the moving floes to the landfast
ice to the south of them, and thence ashore.

When I got back to Flaxman Island Leffingwell and
Mikkelsen confirmed what Dr. Howe had conjectured—
that the expedition was practically over. Leffingwell
would spend another year in the vicinity, for he was a
geologist by training and wanted to study the mountains
to the south. Mikkelsen had first thought of making a
journey eastward in a small boat with only Storkerson
as a companion but he later gave that up.

At Flaxman Island I now awaited eagerly the coming

of my first arctic summer. The winter I had liked very well. It had resembled in general the twenty winters I have lived in Dakota. The cold had been no more intense than the Dakota cold although somewhat more uniform and lasting about two months longer. The storms had been rather milder than the worst Dakota blizzards. The long periods of clear and cold weather had been more exhilarating than any climate I had known before.

But although the winter had been pleasant, I looked with the keenest interest toward the coming of spring. The beginnings of spring were disappointing. The latter part of April resembled January in Scotland or Nebraska, and was rather disagreeable. May was worse. It resembled the worst kind of January you get in the south of England or in Missouri. The first rain came on the 6th of May.

One of the pleasant things about the North is that the winter snow is perfectly dry. But in May the northern snow has the sogginess familiar in southern countries and makes your feet wet unless you wear water boots. We did commence wearing the Eskimo style seal skin water boots, which are lighter and in every way better than any other water boots known to me. But although they are good water boots for summer, they are cold footgear for spring, for the chill of the damp snow outside of them penetrates through and produces the same sort of condensation on the inside that you get from wearing rubber boots wading in cold water. Although perfectly waterproof, neither rubber boots nor seal skin boots can keep your feet dry, for they become wet inside with the condensation of the body moisture. You can travel through six months of winter with feet dry every day inside deer skin boots that are not waterproof, but you become wet in six hours of May travel though your boots be water-tight.

At Herschel Island the mountains are only twenty or thirty miles to the south but at Flaxman Island they are ten or fifteen miles farther away. The spring heat takes effect sooner on the mountain slopes than on the level prairie and, accordingly, the more easterly rivers opened earlier. On my last trip east I found the Firth River open the 10th of May and the water from it spreading in a wide fan over many square miles of sea ice just west of Herschel Island. The Kugruak River at Flaxman Island did not open till the middle of May. The water from such a river flows several miles out on the ice, perhaps six or eight, and finally meets a tide crack through which it can join the sea beneath. These tide cracks are formed where the shore ice that lies solidly on the bottom meets the ice farther out that lies over deeper water and rises and falls with the tides. These cracks are kept open all winter by the ice movement and are ready to receive the river water when the spring freshets bring it to the ocean.

Most travelers of the polar regions have remarked how suddenly spring comes. It does come more rapidly than in more southerly countries, but gradually nevertheless.

There are many signs of coming spring besides the increasing warmth that we dislike because it is accompanied by increasing cloudiness and a heavier and heavier snowfall. The birds are one of these signs. A few kinds have been there all winter—ptarmigan by the thousand, hawks, owls and ravens by the dozen. The first snow buntings appear on the coast early in April. If you were far out on the sea ice where it is in rapid movement with much open water between the cakes, you would have the seagulls as early as the snow buntings come to the coast. But near land the gulls do not appear until about the same time as the geese, and that would be about the same time as the first rivers break up, or anywhere between the first and middle of May. There are half a dozen different kinds of geese and a little later there are dozens of kinds of ducks, including four kinds of eider ducks. A very few cranes and a somewhat larger number of swans come about the same time as the ducks, and so do the loons. About a hundred varieties of smaller birds come, too, some of them early and others later—plovers, snipes, sandpipers, etc.

In the fall at Shingle Point I had seen great rejoicing among the children when the first snow fell and when the first ice came. Now at Flaxman Island there was also rejoicing among the people. They like to see summer change to fall but they also like to see winter change to spring, although the joy seemed to me more exuberant in the fall than in the spring. One reason why nobody in the North can wholly like the summer is that it makes travel so difficult. In winter all the rivers and lakes are frozen over and you can walk or travel by dog sled without interruption in any direction. In the summer time you cannot use sledges at all; nor could wagons be used for there are no roads, the ground is rough, and there is sticky mud in many places. In summer the dogs can be used for carrying packs only and, as their legs are short, they cannot be trusted to carry anything that must be kept dry, for they will accidentally drag their packs through water in crossing streams. In hot weather they intentionally lie down in streams and in ponds to cool off, thus making their loads wet. The people themselves are, accordingly, the chief beasts of burden in summer.

This makes travel much less pleasant and much slower than in winter.

Of course, the same summer heat that makes overland travel difficult makes boat travel possible, and the Eskimos take advantage of that. The spring is, therefore, the time for making boats and putting boats in order. In 1906-07 a good many of the Eskimos owned whaleboats purchased from the ships. These boats are about 28 feet or 30 feet long, will carry a ton of freight and sail beautifully, but they are fragile, difficult to keep in repair and not very seaworthy when heavily loaded. The big Eskimo skin-boat called *umiak* is for most purposes far better.

When the white whalers first came to the north coast of Alaska they had great contempt for the driftwood on the beaches and brought with them lumber which they thought would be preferable for use in making the frames of the Eskimo umiaks. At first the Eskimos were talked into this, but they soon gave it up for they found that a frame made of spruce was lighter and stronger for any given dimension than a frame made of the commercial lumber. Thus the Eskimos found out for themselves what many white men never knew until the World War came with its demand for spruce as framework for airplanes. The same quality that makes spruce suitable for airplane frames makes it suitable for the frames of the umiaks.

The standard size umiak is designed to be covered with the skins of seven bearded seals and is from thirty to thirty-five feet long. The boat is flat-bottomed, or roughly dory shaped.

The bearded seals (*Erignathus barbatus*) that furnish skins for the covers weigh from six to eight hundred pounds. They have been killed sometime during the winter or previous summer. A month or two before it is time to make the skin-boats, the hides are put into tubs or bags and kept in some warm place until all the hair rots off. At the same time that the hair is scraped off one side the fat is scraped off the other side of the skin. The women then sew the hides together with a double seam. The thread is braided caribou sinew and has the property of swelling when it gets wet. The careful sewing by the women and the swelling of the sinew together produce the only waterproof seam that is known to be made by any people, European or other. This is the same seam they sew in making their seal skin water boots.

The seams of the commercial leather hunting boots sold in our sportsmen's outfitting stores are generally made waterproof by rubbing grease into them. A boot seam made by an Eskimo woman does not need any waterproofing with grease and she will consider it an insult if she sees any one rubbing grease on the seams of boots she has made, the implication being that you do not trust her sewing. In the case of the umiaks, however, it is the custom to rub grease on the seams just before launching if the boats are dry at the time. When once water-soaked they never leak.

The seal skin is sewed in the beginning so as to fit the boat frame, but only roughly. It is then stretched and lashed on the frame in such a way as to make it fit tightly. When it dries it is as tight as a drum.

An umiak big enough to carry twenty men will weigh only four or five hundred pounds. Two stout men, one at each end, can carry it, and four men can carry it easily. In the spring the Eskimos often put their umiaks on low sledges, then put their household gear inside the

AN UMIAK AND CREW—NORTH COAST OF ALASKA

THE BREAK-UP OF THE SEA ICE IN SPRING

umiak and commence their spring journey (if it is going to be a long one) several weeks before the ice on the rivers or ocean breaks up. They travel along until the water from the coastal rivers floods the ice. At first this water makes travel impossible, for it soaks into the snow that is on the ice and converts it into a foot or two of slush. Two or three weeks later holes will have opened all over the ice, the water will have drained off and then you can travel by sled for two or three more weeks until the ice finally breaks up completely under the heat of the sun and the influence of the winds and currents. Then begins the boat travel proper. This may be by any of three methods.

In traveling up river, "tracking" is ordinarily employed. A long rope is fastened to the mast of the boat three or four feet up and a dog team is hitched to the other end of the rope. One man walks along the river bank ahead of the dogs and the rest of the party ride in the boat, one of them acting as steersman. By this method you can travel upstream, even against a strong current, with a speed of from two to four miles an hour. When you are going down stream or traveling on a lake or on the ocean in calm weather, you can use either paddles or oars. As a matter of fact, both are frequently in use at the same time. In Greenland the men are said to have a prejudice against oars, only women using them. But in Alaska either men or women may use oars and either may use paddles.

The most serious defect of the umiak is that it has no keel and will not sail into the wind. But if you have a side wind or a fair wind it sails very well with a leg-of-mutton or any other type of ordinary boat sail.

In addition to its lightness and the ease with which

it can be carried on the shoulders of men over a portage or freighted by dogs on a sled, the umiak has many other peculiar advantages. For one thing, the hides it is made of are so exceedingly tough that you can sail with a speed of four or five miles an hour into a piece of ice as solid as a rock with little danger of serious injury. You may break one of the ribs of the boat but that will merely make a little dent in the side of your craft and can be fixed whenever you like. If you tear a hole in the boat it can be readily patched up by the Eskimo women with their needles. Another great advantage is the ease of landing. You can land on any beach except among actual rocks even in fairly bad weather. This is partly because the boat is so light that it draws very little water and partly because the bottom is flat. The light draft is an especial advantage in river travel. A whaleboat carrying a ton of freight will draw about eighteen inches where an umiak carrying the same amount of freight would not draw more than eight or ten inches.

In some ways an even better boat than the umiak is the kayak. This has the outlines of a racing shell. The frame is made of light wood and whalebone. The entire craft is closed in so that the waves can dash over it without entering. In the old days the Eskimos used to go in waterproof shirts that were fastened tight around the neck of the wearer, around his wrists and around the mouth of the kayak in such a way that even if it capsized no water could get into the boat. A good boatman would be able to right himself even in fairly heavy weather. For this reason the seal hunting Eskimos go out on the ocean in summer weather where no other craft of the same size could possibly live. A special use of the kayak is in spearing caribou when they are swimming rivers or lakes.

The season of spring, while the birds are becoming more numerous day by day and while the snow is slowly disappearing, is one of great activity among the Eskimos in getting their boats ready for summer travel. Either before the ice breaks or else just after it does they move from their winter camps to some good fishing locality. These are places where the water is muddy so that the fish cannot see the nets in the perpetual summer daylight.

On the north coast of Alaska there are about two months when the sun does not set at night. The midnight sun comes before the snow is entirely gone from the prairie and the snow does not come back until long after the sun has begun to set at night. At Flaxman Island where we had the ice-filled ocean outside of us and about three miles of cold water between us and the mainland, the weather never became very hot, but some parties who went inland reported that up towards the mountains it was on an average more than twenty degrees warmer than we had it on the island. This meant that when we were just comfortable at Flaxman Island at a temperature of $55°$ or $65°$, people in towards the mountains were sweltering at from $75°$ to $85°$, which is very hot indeed up there, for the air is about as humid as air can be, and there is little relief from the heat at night for the sun does not set.

With the increasing heat came swarms of mosquitoes. We have already described how bad they are on the Mackenzie. They were not very bad on Flaxman Island because we had cool breezes from the sea continually, but ten or fifteen miles inland they were just as bad as they are anywhere on the Mackenzie River or as they are anywhere in the world.

Besides mosquitoes, there are many other kinds of flying insects—bumblebees, butterflies, dragonflies, horse-flies, blue-bottles, and the like. There are also many kinds of beetles, worms and other crawling things. This rich insect life corresponds to the rich vegetation of the prairie. It seems to me that in most places, prairie is the best general name for the arctic grasslands, but in many places you would speak of them rather as meadow. There are also patches here and there where mosses and lichens prevail, so that the name of neither prairie nor meadow fits exactly. I never speak of "tundra," for that word is misleading because it conveys a sense of barren-ness to the average reader. In many places there are acres and acres where flowers of one kind or another form a veritable carpet. There are not likely to be in any given locality more than a hundred or so different kinds of flowering plants, but the individual flowering plants are numerous and the flowers are brilliant in color.

It was not till June that it began to rain to any con-siderable extent. That summer we had only one heavy thunder shower.

Our plans had been made to leave the country this year and Captain Mikkelsen decided we would go out by way of Point Barrow. On the 14th of July we started west along the coast in two boats, a wooden sailing boat be-longing to the *Duchess* and an umiak belonging to a local Eskimo.

I found it a delightful adventure sailing along an un-known coast with a fair wind, by the light of the mid-night sun. Occasionally we came to Eskimo encamp-ments and frequently we went ashore to hunt geese, eider ducks or other birds. We saw no caribou and the Eski-mos told us they were not likely to be found near the coast at this time of year. It is a belief common among those who write about caribou that in the spring and early summer they come down to the sea to avoid the mosquitoes. This is a complete misunderstanding, so far as my observation goes. If they do come down to the coast, it is usually in the early spring, a month or two before the mosquitoes arrive. During the height of the mosquito season, as the Eskimos told us, it is only rarely that bands come to the coast and you usually have to go thirty or forty miles inland before you find caribou in any numbers. In September after the mosquitoes are gone you are far more likely to find them near the sea. It appears, then, that the caribou do not come to the ocean because of the mosquitoes and that their movements are determined by entirely other causes—probably the lack of preferred foods, the change in the palatability of certain grasses as they become ripe in autumn, or by the direction of the wind. Caribou usually travel against the wind.

We had proceeded without incident as far west as the eastern edge of the Colville delta when an accident happened that changed all our plans. Storkerson was playing with a rifle and shot himself through the foot. After preliminary attention to the wound, Dr. Howe gave it as his opinion that Storkerson should be taken back to Flaxman Island immediately, for he thought that trouble with the wound might develop and that an operation might be necessary. He had taken with him an emergency kit but had left behind at Flaxman Island his anesthetics and many of his instruments, and did not feel that he could attend to Storkerson properly elsewhere. To make this decision was no great hardship for most of us, for it meant only that we would go by whaler from Flaxman Island to Point Barrow to reach the revenue cutter instead of getting there a few weeks earlier by means of small boats.

I don't think any of the men worried much about the accident except insofar as they were sorry for Storkerson. As for me, I was delighted with one aspect of the situation, for the Eskimos had told me that in prehistoric times (before the memory of the fathers of the old men living) there had been a big Eskimo settlement on one of the Jones Islands which lay in a row parallel to the coast a few miles offshore from where the accident occurred. This island was a little bigger than Flaxman. I say *was*, designedly; for it and all the other islands are growing smaller year by year. It seems the north coast of Alaska is sinking gradually. So long as the sea ice remains in winter and spring, nothing happens to the injury of the islands. But when the ice goes away, as it does nearly every summer, and when a gale comes from the open sea, the waves will undermine the cliffs of the islands at a great rate, so that the coastline sometimes recedes as much as a hundred yards in a single summer. When the early whalers came to the north coast of Alaska, Flaxman Island was probably some eight or ten miles long. It is now no more than half that long and less than half as wide as it used to be. The Eskimos said that similarly the ocean was rapidly cutting away the sites of the villages on the Jones Islands and that all sorts of ancient implements and other relics were being washed away by the sea.

It was, accordingly, decided that while Storkerson and the rest of the party returned as fast as they could to Flaxman Island, I should remain on the Jones Islands with an Eskimo companion and a sailor, investigating these ancient ruins until a whaling ship came along to pick us up.

The island containing the house ruins was a low, rolling prairie similar to Flaxman Island. There was a great abundance of driftwood on the north coast and we erected a comfortable camp near the ruins. As I had been told, the sea was cutting this island and it appeared as if half the village site was already gone. I found awash on the beach a number of carvings of bone and ivory and a number of weapons and implements of bone and wood. These differed in some respects but not fundamentally from those that were in use by the Eskimos when the whites first came to the country. The houses had all fallen and looked superficially merely like so many mounds. I found on investigation that the ground plan had been similar to that of the houses now in use along the coast. In my opinion this village was inhabited no more than two or three centuries ago.

I was enjoying myself thoroughly, both because I was discovering things of scientific interest and because I was having a good time hunting and merely living in this delightful place. It was rather a disappointment for me than otherwise when on the 25th of July the first of the whaling ships came in sight from the west. We struck camp hurriedly, loaded our gear and our trophies into the boat and paddled out to meet the ship. It turned out to be the steam whaler *Belvedere*, owned at San Francisco but under command of Captain Stephen F. Cottle of Massachusetts (Martha's Vineyard, I think). Mrs. Cottle was with him. They received me hospitably and gave me fruits and vegetables and various civilized foods for which I had been hankering greatly.

My experience since has shown that when you have been without potatoes and apples for a year you are so hungry for them that a boiled potato makes a banquet and an apple is delicious beyond your vocabulary to ex-

press. But when you have been without these things for
five or six years, as happened to me later, you not only
cease to long for them but actually find them much less
pleasant when you first come back to them than you
would if you had been eating them every day. If you
went without fruits and vegetables for ten years at a time,
you might imagine for the whole ten years that you were
longing for them. But if, like me, you first go without
them for a year and later for two years and eventually
for five years, you find that a total of ten years is ample
to cure you of all your hankering. It goes even farther
than that. I used to be almost a vegetarian by taste. At
the end of ten years in the polar regions I much preferred
a meal where both fruits and vegetables were completely
absent and meat the only food.

We sailed pleasantly with the *Belvedere* to Flaxman
Island where we took aboard Captain Mikkelsen. We
then continued to Herschel Island where we arrived July
27th, which was up to that time the earliest date that a
ship had ever arrived there from the "outside world."

# CHAPTER XVII

WHEN we got to Herschel Island we heard news that worried both Captain Mikkelsen and me, although for different reasons. I have mentioned in the preceding chapter that after first getting to Flaxman Island I made a hurried trip back to Herschel Island for a conference with Captain Leavitt. At that time I had said to the captain and to some of his officers that the Eskimos around Flaxman Island believed the ice exploratory party —Leffingwell, Mikkelsen and Storkerson—to have lost their lives. We had discussed this a good deal. Captain Leavitt had inclined to the view that the ice party were safe but most of his officers and all the Herschel Island Eskimos had agreed with the Flaxman Island Eskimos that they were undoubtedly dead. During the spring several boats had gone from Herschel up to Macpherson to meet the Mackenzie River steamer, *Wrigley*. These people had paid no attention to Captain Leavitt's minority view that the ice party were safe and had reported the death of Leffingwell, Mikkelsen and Storkerson. The *Wrigley* had left Macpherson about the middle of July, carrying the news of the supposed tragedy. The bearers of this report would arrive at the telegraph station at Athabasca Landing probably between the 5th and 10th of September, and the news of another polar tragedy would be flashed to the world. When sent out this news would have the weight of the authority of Mr. Harrison, who was one of the outbound passengers and who was said to have been as convinced as the rest at Macpherson that the ice party had lost their lives.

What concerned me particularly in this situation was that the story would be published on my authority, it having been said at Macpherson that I had brought to Herschel Island the news of the death of the three men. What worried Captain Mikkelsen especially was that he had an invalid mother who he feared might possibly die of the shock of reading in the morning paper the definite announcement of the death of her son. Captain Mikkelsen felt almost equal concern about the parents of Mr. Leffingwell and about several other near relatives of the three reported dead.

Captain Mikkelsen took counsel with the whaling captains in the harbor and with the police at the barracks but was told that there was little chance of overtaking this bad news. A pursuit up the Mackenzie under a month's handicap was unthinkable. The alternative was a journey over the mountains to the United States Government wireless station at Eagle City. If this were tried failure was considered probable by some and certain by others.

Previous to this Captain Mikkelsen and I had talked a good deal about the possibility of my remaining with him another year to continue the exploration north of Alaska. I had considered still more definitely the possibility of staying with Leffingwell and helping him with his geological survey of the Endicott Mountains to the south of Flaxman Island. Had Leffingwell and Mikkelsen been able to agree on coöperating at either of these enterprises, I should doubtless have stayed with them. But as one had his heart set on the mountains and the other on the sea ice I could not please one without displeasing the other, so I thought it better on the whole to sever my connections with their expedition and to try to organize one of my own the following year. My heart was neither in the mountains nor on the sea ice but rather in the mystery of the strange people with blond faces and copper weapons whom Klinkenberg had reported from Victoria Island.

Captain Mikkelsen may have realized already that I would probably not accept his offer to stay and help him another year with exploring, or it may have been that in his anxiety for his mother and for the relatives and friends of Leffingwell and Storkerson he had forgotten temporarily the plans he had been discussing with me. At any rate, he came to me and with no reference to what might be done in the North if I stayed another year, he asked if I would undertake the forlorn hope of outspeeding the bad news now on its way up the Mackenzie by journeying south across the mountains to the Yukon with the hope of getting to the wireless station at Eagle City before Harrison got to the regular telegraph at Athabasca Landing. He said this would have to be done by me or no one, for I had greater experience in overland travel than any one else at Herschel Island. Furthermore, all of the others were in such circumstances that they could not very well consider going. Mikkelsen could not try it himself, for he would have to return to Flaxman Island to close up the affairs of the expedition. It was now the plan that all of the expedition except Leffingwell would take passage west with an outgoing whaler in September, connecting with the United States revenue cutter at Point Barrow, or possibly in Nome or Unalaska. Leffingwell alone would remain at Flaxman Island for the purpose of his geological studies.

It took me but a few minutes to decide to try it. The decision once made there was no time to be lost. A whaleboat belonging to the Mounted Police and manned by a crew of three Macpherson Indians was now in the Herschel Island harbor. The police had intended to send the boat to Macpherson in a few days anyway, and now they said it might as well start in a few hours. It did not take us even a few hours to get ready; we were under sail inside of two hours, speeding eastward with a fair wind.

A whaleboat sails beautifully when well handled and one of the Indians was a fair boatman. The breeze slackened gradually, however, and it took us eighteen hours to reach King Point, a distance of thirty-five miles. I was for taking turns sleeping on the boat and keeping on but the Indians pretended to know that by mid-forenoon there would be a fair breeze. Accordingly, we camped beside the wreck of the *Bonanza* shortly after midnight and slept till nine o'clock.

I had felt sure when we went into camp that the Indian forecast of a breeze was based on nothing more substantial than the desire to sleep soundly on shore. But a breeze did come and with it we made the mouth of the Mackenzie and got some distance up stream. After this the Indians worked as hard as any one could desire. We were lucky in having a sailing wind fully half the time. When it dropped calm or when there was a head wind we got out our tracking line. One man remained in the boat to steer it and the other three of us walked along the river bank, pulling on the tracking line. Thus alternately sailing and tracking we reached Macpherson August 12th, breaking the record in summer travel from Herschel Island to Fort Macpherson. We had made the

WE SAILED UP THE MACKENZIE DELTA TO MACPHERSON

PORCUPINE RIVER IN EARLY SPRING

two hundred and fifty miles in a few hours over three days, which was about two days better time than any one else was known to have made.

At Herschel Island I had considered the possibility of walking straight south over the mountains and I should have tried this had there been any natives available to go with me. I am writing this story, from memory and notes, fifteen years later and with ten years of arctic experience to my advantage. It now seems silly to me that I did not go straight south from Herschel Island over the mountains alone. With nothing heavier to carry than a message, a man needs no companion for a journey of one or two hundred miles through uninhabited country. Those are my ideas now, but I did not have them then nor did it seem to occur to any one who was then at Herschel Island that a man unaccompanied could safely make such a journey.

I had decided to go by way of Macpherson because the police had assured me that I would have no trouble in getting Indians to help me across the mountains from there. I now took the case to Firth and he said there should not be any great difficulty about it, although the arrangements could have been more easily made had I been there two weeks earlier while large numbers of Indians were at the Fort for their summer trading. There were no good men available now and I would have to take what I could get. He thought it could be managed somehow.

It took only a few hours to negotiate with the Indians and to make all arrangements. During that time Firth gave me valuable information and advice. He had himself been in that country for more than thirty years, stationed not always at Macpherson but sometimes at La

Pierre's House on the Bell River to the west, or at Rampart House on the Porcupine to the southwest. He knew the mountains between thoroughly. There were two ways open: One was to get a canoe, go a few miles down the Peel River to the mouth of the Rat River and then up the Rat about three days' journey, paddling, poling and tracking the canoe. We would eventually come to a portage over which the canoe could be carried to the Bell River. The men who accompanied me would then return on foot and I would paddle the canoe down the Bell and Porcupine to the Yukon. But this canoe route was hardly open to me because there were no good canoes for sale just now at Macpherson. That practically limited us to the "portage route."

The portage route was a footpath leading about eighty miles west over the mountains to the Bell River. In the early days when the Hudson's Bay Company had posts on the Bell and Porcupine Rivers, the freight to supply these used to come down the Mackenzie to Macpherson and was then carried by porters over the mountains to La Pierre's House. It was the feet of these porters that had made the trail which we were now to follow.

Firth told me many interesting stories about the old portaging days. The goods of the Company used to be made into ninety-pound packages each of which was known as a "piece." They would employ no man in the portaging who could not make eighty miles in four days carrying in addition to the ninety-pound piece whatever he needed in the way of food and bedding. Many of the men could carry two pieces or 180 pounds, and Firth had known three or four who would carry three pieces each and their food for four days, a rifle, and some ammunition, a frying pan, teapot, and even sometimes something in addition.  He told me I would have to manage with boys whom he could not recommend in any way and that they would probably fail to make the distance in four days unless their loads were lighter than eighty pounds.

The Indians eventually engaged were Joseph, who was over twenty years old, and William, who was about seventeen.  William was, however, the bigger of the two.  When it came to outfitting, it was they rather than Firth or I that insisted on heavy loads.  They wanted to take along so much corned beef and so much bacon and so much of various other things for provisions.

I found out from Firth that the regular wages were four dollars a day for the journey to the Bell, the Indians receiving no pay on their way back home.  Thinking that I would get better service by offering a lump sum, I told the Indians (through Firth as interpreter) that instead of paying them four dollars a day, which would give them only twenty dollars for the trip if it took five days, I would pay them thirty-five dollars each, no matter in how few days we made it.  I also offered a prize in case we made it in less than the regular time.  The bargain seemed to please not only the men themselves but all their relatives who had gathered to help in the negotiations.

August 13th we got away from the Fort and were ferried across the Peel River by a boat belonging to Mr. Harvey, a Free Trader who had set up at Macpherson a rival establishment to that of the Hudson's Bay Company.  Harvey had been no less kind to me than Firth.  As the general arrangements for my trip were in Firth's hands, Harvey had made up for his lack of opportunity in helping with the general outfitting by insisting on

making me several presents.   He said I would be sure
to find along the road Indians who would have to be paid
for their services.   There is a certain type of silk handkerchief which at that time passed practically for money,
and of these Harvey gave me several.   He also gave me
certain delicacies of food.

The police at the barracks insisted that I must not
go unarmed, and gave me one of their service revolvers.
I had left my rifle behind at Herschel with the idea that
the journey would be almost entirely by boat or raft,
first on the ocean and the Mackenzie River and later on
the Bell River and Porcupine, and that I would not have
time to stop along the road to hunt.   I did not, therefore, really want the revolver, but because I valued the
kind intentions of the police in this matter I took it.   I
was to return the revolver to the head office of the police
at Regina when I got out.

Once across the river our journey with pack loads
began.   The two Indians were carrying about eighty
pounds each and I was carrying about forty pounds.
This division of the packs had been made to conform
with Firth's ideas of practicability and propriety.   I
understood it was not considered good form for an
employer to carry as much as his Indians did.

We had no trouble following the path for about five
miles when we came to the place where I had said
good-bye to Elihu Stewart the year before.   Stewart had
started out from Macpherson in the evening and his
camping five miles from the post had, accordingly,
seemed to me logical.   When my Indians now insisted
on camping at the same place I saw no logic in it for it
was not yet evening, but they said that all people who
went across the mountains camped there and that,

while this counted regularly for one day so far as wages
were concerned, it was not counted when people were
saying they could do the eighty-mile portage in four
days. They also explained that on the fourth of the
counted days we would camp a few miles away from
Bell River and make that distance the next morning
without counting that as a day either except in the payment of wages. There would, accordingly, be six wage
days although we would say that the journey had been
made in four days. All this might have been amusing
had I been on an ordinary journey but when I was
racing with Harrison and his bad news the idea did not
suit so well. There was nothing to do about it, however, for the Indians reminded me that they were still
near home and if their ways did not suit me they could
easily go back and I could hire some other Indians.

I have learned it better since but I understood even
then that there is nothing to do except to make the best
of this sort of situation. I showed no hard feeling and
presently we were all laughing and chatting together. It
was then that the Indians explained that there was a
reason for their camping here, for to-morrow we would
find no suitable camping place until evening. They said
that if we proceeded now we would be tired out before
we could get to a tolerable camp site. All this I believed
that evening and it was a good thing I did, for it made
me sleep better. Next day I discovered there was no
truth in it, for there were good camp sites along the road
the whole day. Thereupon the Indians owned up that
they had not been over this road before. They said
they had always understood there were no good camping
places and professed to regret having misinformed me
the day before.

Looking back to it, this journey is one of the most interesting I ever made. At the time it was one of the most disagreeable. I noticed the first evening that William did a good deal of coughing. He spoke no English, but Joseph explained to me that some weeks before William had had a hemorrhage from the lungs and that people expected him to die the next year from tuberculosis. I could tell that William knew what Joseph was explaining to me. As he seemed in no way depressed, I wondered whether that was a sign he did not worry about dying or whether it indicated that the story was a fabrication. But the more I saw of William the more I believed that he was seriously sick and that the story was true.

William's illness showed itself not only in coughing but also in weakness and in shortness of breath. The next morning Joseph took twenty pounds of William's pack, so that now he had a hundred and William only about fifty pounds. We had not been many miles on the road when it became evident that a hundred pounds was too much for Joseph to carry and I took some of it. We agreed that William's share of the load should be the heaviest food, such as the corned beef, and we ate four times a day hugely. This lightened his load so rapidly that by the third day he had scarcely anything in his pack although Joseph and I were still carrying moderate loads.

When we left Macpherson the mosquitoes had been bad in the lowland but as we got higher into the mountains they ceased to bother us much. Had the journey been made a month earlier the reverse would have been true, for in no place are mosquitoes less tolerable than above the treeline in arctic mountains. The season had advanced enough so that we now had severe frosts at night which had a quieting effect on the insect world, although the temperature in the daytime still rose to about 80°.

The first day and a part of the second the road led mainly through a spruce forest; then we began to cross ridges covered with grass. This was my first real experience with the "nigger heads" that are described by so many travelers who have dealt with the northern part of the American mainland. Essentially the ground is covered with hummocks, varying between the size of an orange and that of a man's head, or sometimes larger. These hummocks are really shaped like mushrooms. There is a wobbly head to them, covered with vegetation, and between are deep crevices. You try to step from the middle of one hummock to the middle of another and about once in three times your foot slips off and you go halfway to the knee in mud. I know no experience more heartbreaking than the struggle towards the evening of a long day if you are carrying sixty or eighty pounds.

Were it not for my great respect for Firth's general veracity I should doubt whether any Indians or other human beings could carry loads of three hundred pounds across such country at the rate of twenty miles a day. It was all I could do to carry eighty pounds twenty miles. I judge from my later experience, however, that part of my trouble was due to inexperience in handling a back load.

The third day from Macpherson we crossed the ridge of the mountains. I do not know how high above sea level this took us—probably not over two or three thousand feet. Still, we were above the treeline. There was even some snow from last year in small banks in the lee of steep cliffs. The Indians said, however, that this snow would all be gone in two or three weeks and that there would be a month or so between its disappearance and the coming of the next winter. I judge that a mountain in this vicinity would have to be six or seven thousand feet high to be cold enough for any snow to remain permanently.

The evening after crossing the divide we had a delightful camp site in a grove of tall spruces by a small river that flowed west towards the Bell. We were high enough up so that it was cold towards morning and when we awoke there was hoar frost on the grass. Before leaving our camp we had a discussion as to where we should strike for the Bell. The Indians said the nearest way would be to go directly towards the site of La Pierre's House but that the trees in that locality would be too small for building the raft on which I wanted to travel down the river. I should have liked to see the ruins of this mountain outpost of the Hudson's Bay Company, but the main consideration was to try to reach a telegraph station ahead of Harrison's bad news and I could not afford time for sightseeing. I told the Indians, therefore, to head as nearly as they could for the nearest point on the Bell where there were trees large enough for a raft. I think that had we gone to La Pierre's House we might have followed the little branch river at which we had been camped, but now we had to climb out of its valley and march all day at an angle to the streams, so that we had to cross several small rivers and climb a good many hills. We did not quite make the Bell that day, but the Indians said it was not far.

The next morning we got to the Bell after a march of

two or three hours. I was eager to start at once building a raft but the Indians were slow about it. I had noticed the previous evening that they had been less cheerful than usual and this morning they had been sulky. On arrival at the Bell River they sat down and acted as if they did not know if they would ever stand up again. When I asked them what the trouble was they said they were feeling injured about not getting the same wages as all other packers. Ever since the gold rush (1897-99) there had been a standard wage for this sort of work. Their fathers and uncles and all their friends always used to get four dollars a day, and why could they not get four dollars a day? I reminded them that the wages I offered them had been satisfactory when we talked it over with Firth and pointed out in addition that they were getting thirty-five dollars for the trip which would be more than four dollars a day. They expressed themselves as very doubtful as to whether thirty-five dollars was more than four dollars a day and said that, as they had worked hard for me and faithfully, they did not see why they should not get the same wages as everybody else.

We haggled about this for an hour but I was unable to make it clear to them that thirty-five dollars is more than four dollars a day for six days. Accordingly, I agreed that I would pay them four dollars a day. The arrangement had been that I would give the Indians a letter to take back to Firth, certifying that they had performed their task properly, whereupon he was to give each of them thirty-five dollars. I now wrote Firth, explaining that they were dissatisfied with thirty-five dollars and wanted instead four dollars a day. I said he was to use his judgment whether to take them at their word or whether to give them the larger amount.

As soon as I had written this letter and translated it to Joseph, both Indians became cheerful and commenced at once chopping down trees to make the raft.

[When I was on my way north on my second expedition (1908) I saw Firth again and asked him what had happened to the wages of the Indians. He said that when they had come back he had received news of it right away and had expected them to come that same day to get their wages. They did not come, however, until the next day and were then accompanied by a large number of their relatives and friends. When they handed him my letter and he read it over, he asked whether it was correct that they preferred four dollars a day, whereupon not only they but also their relatives spoke up and said that it was only fair. Everybody else had been getting four dollars a day for years and they did not see why these young men should not get the same wage. Thereupon Firth paid each of them twenty-four dollars and they went home well satisfied. This left him twenty-two dollars to refund to me.]

Although the Indians and I worked hard at the making of the raft, it took all the rest of the day. For making the raft we had brought along a sharp new ax and several hundred feet of strong but slender rope. The logs we used were about twenty feet long, about a foot in diameter at the big end and four inches at the small end. To make a good buoyant raft we should have had dry logs, but others had built their rafts in this locality ahead of us and, although we went as much as half a mile afield, we got only enough dry wood to make half of the raft. The rest, then, had to be green.

When all was done I had a raft twenty feet long, about ten feet wide at the big end and six feet wide at the small end. On the middle of this raft we made a fireplace of stones so that I could cook meals without losing any time in landing. Firth had told me that there were few rapids in the river and none dangerous. It was my intention, accordingly, to sleep on the raft and travel both day and night.

# CHAPTER XVIII

THE morning of August 19th my Indians turned towards Macpherson and I began my long drift alone down the Bell and Porcupine Rivers. I did not then realize how long it was to be, for this was my first journey at the mercy of a river current. By the map and as the crow flies the distance did not seem so formidable. But the Bell is one of the slowest of rivers, flowing through the most crooked of valleys, so that my estimate of the distance was multiplied by two and my hope of speed cut down by at least half. Under ordinary circumstances I think I might have enjoyed the lackadaisical Bell but now I was in a race. I estimated that by this time the bad news would be somewhere on the Slave River between Great Slave Lake and Athabasca Lake. To be sure of winning I had to get to a telegraph office by the first of September. If I were much later than that, nothing but some bad luck to Harrison could give me the good luck of winning.

The current varied a great deal. Once or twice a day it cheered me up for a while by speeding along at three miles an hour. But much of the time it was only half a mile an hour and I think the average was somewhere between a mile and a mile and a half. Traveling twenty-four hours a day I would be making at the most thirty-six miles, and thirty-six miles by the river would be no more than twenty miles in a straight line. By what Firth had told me it was less than three hundred miles to Rampart House, but he was referring to the sledge trails which do not follow the river and are much shorter. I had been told that at Rampart House I would be sure to find Indians whom I could hire with their canoes to paddle me rapidly the remaining two hundred miles to the Yukon.

My Indians had said there was a possibility that I might fall in with some fishing Indians or some moose hunters almost any time. If fishing, they would be camping beside the river, but if hunting moose they might be some distance back. They told me to watch carefully for smoke inland, for if Indians have the luck to kill a big moose, and more especially if they kill two or three, they will camp by the kill to smoke-dry the meat. They had also told me that at this season of year I might find some bad rapids in the river and had warned me to be careful.

With these two ideas of moose-hunting Indians and possible rapids in my head I found excitement in rounding each curve in the river, for the next stretch held the promise of an Indian smoke and the threat of a rapid. These uncertainties helped wonderfully to pass the time, but occasionally I would get into a placid stretch where I could see the river below me for a mile or two ahead and where the current was only half a mile an hour. These were undeniably tedious spells, even if they gave me the best possible chance to study the scenery.

Although I was still a hundred miles north of the arctic circle, I found the scenery here not very different from that of the Athabasca River, a thousand miles farther south. I suppose the trees along the Athabasca must be stouter and taller but as you travel along the river you do not notice that, and here as there are the forest-clad hills rolling away into the distance. On the Athabasca there are no mountains in sight and on the Bell when I looked at right angles to the river's course I saw no mountains, but whenever a long vista opened either ahead or behind I was likely to see mountains in the distance. None of them was snow-covered but their tops were bare of trees, for the forest went only a third of the way or half the way up their slopes. The highest of the peaks would be under ten thousand feet.

The down-river journey was monotonous but every day something happened to vary the monotony a little. One day a moose was standing on the river bank as I drifted around a bend. I sat motionless on my raft wondering how near I would pass, for the raft was at the mercy of the current and was carried sometimes along one bank and sometimes along the other. The river here was about two or three hundred yards wide. When I was still several hundred yards above the moose he noticed my raft and began to watch it carefully. It is the nature of animals that they do not recognize a man as long as he makes no movement, and apparently the moose took my craft and me for half a dozen tangled spruce trees drifting together. Still, it must have seemed to him that there was something peculiar, for when we got abreast he suddenly plunged into the river and came swimming towards me. He came within eight or ten feet and then started to swim around me on the downstream side. There was no noticeable wind but I suppose the air must have been moving downstream, for when he got in front of the raft he was scared by something, turned around suddenly and swam back to shore. He was not badly frightened for he stopped on landing to look back. Then he walked into the forest and disappeared.

But for this meeting with the moose I should have had no chance to kill game with my revolver so long as I was on the river. This chance I did not take for I considered I had enough bacon and groceries to take me all the way. But I suppose I could have killed some fish for they were jumping out of the water all around me nearly all the time. I have at other times shot fish both with rifles and shotguns and had no doubt of my ability to get some with the revolver. If you are in a position to seize a fish you do not actually have to hit him, for the impact of the bullet on the water right near him will stun him temporarily.

When the mind is strongly preoccupied with any idea your eyes will play curious tricks on you. There was scarcely a long stretch of the river when I did not discover in the blue distance an Indian smoke curling up. But as I drifted nearer and nearer the smoke became less and less certain until it generally disappeared. Some persisted, however, until I came abreast of them, whereupon I used to land and walk half a mile or so inland to the top of a hill. As these hilltops were frequently covered with trees I used to have to climb a tree to get a view, whereupon I failed to see smoke and returned to the river.

But in one case the smoke was indubitable. I saw three or four wisps of it curling up among the trees about half a mile inland. I think this was on the third or fourth day. Sure now of having found people, I fired three shots from my revolver to attract their attention, but got no reply. This was strange, for a number of shots in rapid succession are recognized by the northern

Indians everywhere as a signal and are always replied to. There was no doubt about the smoke, however, so I went inland and found its origin in some burning peat. There had been an Indian campfire there a month or two before and since then the fire had spread to cover several acres of ground. It had not blazed up but was smoldering its way through the peat.

The reason why the peat fire had not developed into a real forest fire was undoubtedly in the frequent rains. I have never seen such regularity of weather. There used to be clear skies until somewhere between eleven and one o'clock, whereupon clouds gathered and by three there would be at least one light shower followed sometimes by several others. By six or seven o'clock the skies were clear again and remained so during the night. This rain had soaked me every day not at all to my advantage but had been a blessing thus far in saving the forest. There was a much heavier rain three or four days after this which probably killed the peat fire. Had there been a dry spell instead, and especially dry weather accompanied by a high wind, there would have developed one of the fires which so frequently destroy hundreds and even thousands of square miles of the vast forests of the North.

It was a curious chance which guided me inland at this particular place, for on my way back I discovered evidence of what was probably one of the many untold tragedies of the North. The story, as I have deduced it from the evidence, needs the historical background of the gold rush.

In the history of the northern gold fields the year 1898 takes the place of 1849 in the gold days of California. In 1897 stories had come to the world of newspapers,

telling of fabulous riches in the Klondike section of the
Canadian part of the Yukon valley. The idea presently
crystallized that there were four routes by which this
El Dorado could be reached. One lay by Seattle and
Skagway and the mountain passes that lead to the upper
Yukon near White Horse and then down the Yukon to
the gold country. Another trail was from Edmonton
through the Peace River Valley. A third went from
Edmonton down the Athabasca and Slave Rivers and
through Great Slave Lake to the mouth of the Liard and
then up the Liard and thus across the mountains. With
none of these are we concerned here but only with the
fourth route which came on down the Mackenzie past
the Liard to Macpherson and then over the mountains
either by the route I had just traversed or else by the
Rat River portage which we had considered taking. I
had not taken the Rat River route because I had not
had a boat, and exactly so had it been with the miners
in 1898. Those who had boats went up the Rat and
then down the Bell. Those who had no boats carried
pack loads over the mountains as I had done, and then
built rafts or boats on the Bell to continue the journey.
Some took a third way, going up the Peel River and then
crossing from the upper Peel to the Klondike.

The men who came down the Mackenzie in hundreds
were of all sorts. Only a few were fitted for their adventure through previous experience such as might be
gained in the winter woods of Michigan or Ontario.
Others, although miners of long experience, came from
Australia or South Africa and were as little trained for
the northern journey as if they had come from farms
in Illinois. Some did come from farms in Illinois or
from shops in England or New England. A few of these

had such natural gifts that they adapted themselves to northern conditions, but in the main the Klondikers were hopeless incompetents. It seems difficult now to believe how many of them found a way of dying by drowning or some other accident or by starving or committing suicide. Many died of scurvy.

For the scurvy they were not individually to blame, for their ignorance of how easily it can be prevented was merely the ignorance of the medical profession of that day who supposed that scurvy could be prevented only by the drinking of lime juice or the eating of vegetables and fruits. We know now that scurvy can be cured by an underdone steak no less than by a raw potato or an orange. We know also that while uncooked foods, whether fruits, vegetables or meat, are good antidotes for scurvy, they lose their power on being cooked. But in their ignorance the prospectors used to eat mainly the beans and bacon and other things they had brought with them. A few of them only had the luck or skill to kill game, in which case they ordinarily overcooked the meat until it no longer had any value as a preventive or cure for scurvy. When they actually became ill with the disease some of them took the boughs of the spruce trees, considering them a vegetable and a possible cure for scurvy. They probably would have been a cure had they been eaten raw in the manner of a salad, but the miners ordinarily put them in pots and boiled them for hours, making a decoction which they called spruce tea. This was drunk without any beneficial effect so far as the scurvy was concerned, and many who had escaped drowning in the rivers or hunger on the portages died of this loathsome disease.

On my way back from the fire that had led me half

a mile into the woods I came upon what I supposed to be the evidence of one of these tragedies. It was a partly-built log cabin, but beautifully built so far as it went. The logs were of uniform size, hewn smooth and well fitted together. The walls were of the ordinary full height for a log cabin but there the building had stopped. No openings had been cut in the walls for windows or for a door, and there was only a partial roof composed of poles with some brush on top. I climbed up on the wall and dropped inside. Here I found a Bible decayed to pieces, a rusted teapot, a heavily silver-plated Winchester rifle, a fur robe so decayed that it resembled wet brown paper, a china saucer that had been used for a grease lamp, and some other odds and ends.

It seemed to me that these were articles which under ordinary circumstances would not have been left behind. And had they been left, they would have been piled up in a corner or arranged in some orderly way. I imagine at the time the tragedy occurred the men who were building the house were still living in a tent camp down by the river where they had most of their belongings. After some misfortune had happened to them, some Indians or other miners had probably found the tent camp and taken it away but the house had escaped notice, for it was so hidden by trees that there was no sign of it from the river. The logs out of which the house had been built had all been chopped nearby and the trees close to the river left intact.

I should probably have taken with me at least the silver-plated rifle but for the plan which I had already formed of some day soon leaving my raft behind and walking along the river till I found Indians. I was beginning to lose patience with the raft; and if I undertook to walk the added weight of the rifle would be a burden.

The night after my discovery of this deserted cabin I was as usual sleeping on my raft as it drifted. Midsummer was now long past; furthermore, I was traveling south so that it was dark for two or three hours around midnight. Because of the uncertainty of everything I never slept soundly. Now I was awakened by what I took at first for the rustle of leaves. I was lying quietly looking up at the stars and listening to what sounded like wind among trees, when it suddenly occurred to me that this could not be the sound of any wind for there were no leaves to rustle—an evergreen forest makes no such sound as that made by aspen leaves or those of other deciduous trees.

If it was not the noise of leaves it must be the only logical noise of the same sort that one may hear in this locality—the murmur of a rapid or a waterfall. It was so dark that I could not see the land clearly on either bank of the river and apparently the stream at this particular point was especially wide. I had no idea on which side the rapids would be worse, but knew that the most favorable place to run them would be where the current was strongest. The chances were that my raft would keep to the strongest current and would find a safe place (if there was one) if I left it to its own course.

It was a tense half hour as I sat motionless in the middle of my raft with the noise of the rapids gradually increasing. I don't think it ever became loud enough to deserve the name of a roar but it sounded quite loud enough to make me feel uncomfortable.

When I got almost to the rapids the current had taken

the raft near enough to one river bank so that I could see the trees plainly. They were flitting by rapidly which showed my speed was increasing. Then the raft began to bump on an occasional boulder. The bumps became more and more frequent and I was wondering whether the rope would hold by which the logs were tied together, when all of a sudden the downstream end of the raft stuck fast. Then the raft swung broadside to the current and bumped along over two or three more boulders, stopped, and the upstream edge began to rise as if the raft were about to flop over. I grabbed all my belongings, including the stones which made the fireplace, and shifted them and myself to the rising edge. This was enough to bring it down and lift the downstream edge so that the raft commenced moving again. There were half a dozen more serious bumps and then we drifted into quiet water below.

It was not particularly likely that there would be a second rapid just below this one. But drifting through an unknown rapid in the dark is no fun, and it had taken so much of my nerve that after a little debate with myself I started poling ashore. I landed about half a mile below the rapids, and decided to sleep there and wait for daylight. After this I traveled each day only while there was light enough to see some distance ahead, which was about eighteen hours of the twenty-four.

The next day I wrote in my diary: "Home has never seemed as far away as it does moping down this infernal river on a headstrong and lazy raft." The feeling of impatience indicated by this entry kept growing. The next day I came to the end of my patience, poled the raft ashore, packed on my back the twenty or thirty pounds of food and other things I had with me (little beyond my diary and some mail I was carrying out for the police), and started to walk along the river.

But if rafting had its disadvantages, walking had them no less. To begin with, the river bank was made up of angular blocks of rock which began to hurt my feet right away and promised to hurt them more as I walked further. Then my clothing and especially my footgear was not in the best of condition. On the rest of my body I was wearing woolen clothes but on my feet I had Eskimo style water boots. The uppers of these are made of seal skin as thin and soft as a kid glove but perfectly waterproof. The soles are of the thick leather of the bearded seal. This is almost perfect footgear for the summer if it is kept in condition. But that can be accomplished only with extreme care. You must never wear the same pair of boots more than at the most two days in succession, when you take them off and dry them thoroughly. Well taken care of, two pairs of boots regularly alternated may last four or five months, but if you wear one pair continuously it will rot to pieces in a few days. On the march over the mountains from Macpherson I had taken the boots off in the evening and managed to dry them fairly well every night so that, although I did not have another pair to change into, I still kept them in fair condition. But it was chilly sleeping on the raft and I had kept my boots on. Similarly when I went ashore I had kept all my clothes on, for I had no bedding and shivered as it was, especially as I got soaking wet every day in the afternoon showers.

After I had been walking a few hundred yards along the river bank I stopped to adjust the laces that are bound around the ankle of the water boot. When I pulled on these one of them came off. A little later

when I was fixing the other boot and gave a pull on the
upper I tore a great opening in it along the edge of the
sole. I now realized that my boots were rotten and that
I should not be able to walk in them many days.

I might have turned back in an hour or so because
of the boots but what actually turned me back was that
I came to a tributary river so deep that it could not be
waded and so turbulent that trying to swim it would
have been dangerous. I was carrying the same ax and
could perhaps have gone half a mile upstream and found
a place where I could make a raft for crossing out of
two or three trees, but rather than do this I went back
for my old raft.

The walk from the place where I had left the raft
behind to the uncrossable stream and back was only four
or five miles but my feet were so badly bruised by the
rocks in that short distance that I was thoroughly reconciled to the raft. Although at the time I regarded this
as a useless delay, I think now it was really worth while
through the peace of mind it gave me. Before that I
had been thinking and planning continually and worrying about whether I should not leave the raft behind.
Now I had no doubts about the advisability of sticking
to it to the end.

The interest of the down river journey was heightened
by my absolute ignorance of the country. The decision
to start south had been made so hurriedly at Herschel
Island that we had not thought of asking the whalers
for a possible map. At Macpherson none was obtainable. Firth had told me a good deal about the river but
much of what he told me I had forgotten. I knew so
little that when a river the same size as the Bell joined
it on my left-hand side, I was surprised, for I thought

the Porcupine ought to come in on the right-hand bank. Indubitably this was the Porcupine, however, for I knew it to be a stream somewhat larger in reality than the Bell and that these two are the only rivers of comparable size. I remembered Firth had told me that although the Old Crow was large, it was a good deal smaller than the Bell.

Not far from the Porcupine mouth I saw the second moose. It was walking along the river bank, headed downstream, and a quarter of a mile away from the raft. Just to see what it would do, I fired my revolver into the hillside above it. Either the actual noise of the bullet striking the hillside or the echo of the shot deceived the animal into thinking the danger was up the hill, for after trotting along the bank a few steps it plunged into the river to swim across. When it got abreast of my raft and about a hundred yards downstream from it, it suddenly turned and swam back again. I think this was because I was trying to row (for the river just here was too deep for poling) and it probably heard the splashing.

Rafts are ordinarily handled with poles and I had one about fourteen feet long. I seldom used it except for sounding purposes. I found by that means that the water is more than fourteen feet deep in a good many places. Apart from the rapid through which I went in the night, I think the river could have been navigated at that season by a boat drawing three or four feet of water. But this seemed to be about the season of high water. Now that I was sleeping ashore nights, I used to put a mark in the water's edge in the evening and take it up the next morning. I would find by this means that the river had risen some nights as much as an inch per hour. By the water marks along the beach I could tell that the water seldom got higher than it now was except in spring freshets.

At various points I had seen signs of old Indian campings. In some places there were merely the sites of camp fires and the pegs driven in the mud to which the Indians had fastened their nets when they were fishing. In other places were the conical teepee frames over which they had spread their tents. Occasionally there was a platform cache.

Shortly after passing the juncture of the Bell and Porcupine I came to a village site which in addition to the teepee frames had a platform cache with something on it. I went ashore to investigate and found some bundles of Indian property and a good deal of dried moose meat covered up by a large piece of moose skin. My provisions were beginning to run low and I am fond of dried moose meat, so I took several pounds of it and left in payment a silk handkerchief. Had I had nothing to pay with I should have been entitled by the custom of the country to take what food I thought I needed to carry me to the next settlement. But I had been provided by Harvey with silk handkerchiefs for just such payments.

Day by day my raft was getting lower in the water. Some of the logs had been partly decayed and were rapidly getting watersoaked. I had to throw away my stone fireplace to lighten the raft. A day later the water was washing over whenever I came into a slight ripple, so I went ashore and got an armful of dry willows out of which I made a kind of nest on the middle of the raft and sat or slept on that. The day after I built this the water-logging process had gone so much farther that there did not show above the water anything but my nest and some humps of two or three crooked logs in the raft.

After throwing away my fireplace I had to do whatever cooking there was on shore. The first morning of this cooking I left beside the fireplace on shore my package of tea. This was two or three pounds and far more than I could possibly have needed. I had been carrying it for trade with any Indians I might happen to meet.

The evening of August 26th I came to a deserted village just as it was getting dark. The houses appeared as if they might have been inhabited the previous winter and as if the people intended returning to them. Still, the half-dozen cabins were empty of furniture and the doors of some of them open. It had been raining particularly heavily that day and I was soaking wet, so I was glad of the shelter of a roof. The reason I knew the houses were entirely empty was that I went into every one of them in search of a possible blanket or robe that an Indian might have left for me to sleep under. Although it was dark, my exploration of each cabin was thorough, but I found no beds or bedding.

I have said that after my midnight adventure with the rapids I was in the habit of sleeping ashore six hours. Sleeping is merely a courtesy description, for when the wetness due to the afternoon showers was combined with the chill of the night, it kept me from any real sleep. I did get good naps on my craft, however, in the forenoons while the sun was shining.

After my night in the deserted village I was up at dawn and made a huge bonfire. It is much easier cooking over a small fire but this one was primarily for warmth. As I was finishing breakfast I was startled to hear a voice behind me. On looking around I saw an Indian a few yards away coming up from the river where

he had beached his canoe. I should have been glad to
see anybody, but I was particularly glad to recognize this
old fellow for I had met him at Macpherson the year
before. He had been there in his capacity of deacon of
the Church of England to confer with the missionary and
had later been the man who undertook to help Stewart
across the mountains. The Deacon spoke passable
English and I soon knew how everything stood.

The house I had slept in was the Deacon's. He and
his family would occupy it after the freeze-up some two
months from now. They and the other Indians that
belonged in this village were now camped about half a
mile away beyond the next bend, and if I had not gone
ashore just here because of seeing the houses I should
a few minutes later have drifted into sight of their camp-
fires and should have had a far more pleasant night. We
proceeded to their camp now. The Deacon's canoe was
so small that two of us could not ride in it and I had
to pole my way to the village with my raft. Once there
my regrets for an uncomfortable night were soon forgotten in the warm welcome of the Indians.

At the village there were small canoes, all made of
birch bark. It is one of the signs of intimate connection
between these Indians and the Eskimos to the north that
their canoes are much the shape and size of the Eskimo
kayaks, although differing, of course, in not being covered
over. They are one-man boats. One of them was almost
big enough for two men, however, and I asked the Deacon
whether he would not undertake to carry me in that down
to Rampart House. At first he said it could not be done.
We considered the possibility of my paddling my own
canoe, but this type of craft is so exceedingly cranky and
there would be some rapids to run, so the Indians were

all against my trying it. At first they thought of building a large raft for me, for they said my small and water-logged one would never do for running the rapids. Later, however, we made an actual trial of the biggest canoe and it turned out that we had about two inches of free-board with the two of us in it. We decided that this would be all right in quiet water. The Deacon knew where all the rapids were and said he would land me above each series of rapids and run them alone, picking me up again below the dangerous water.

Up to now I had thought it probable that the Indians would know about the cabin I had found and about which I had woven the story of a gold seeker tragedy. Careful inquiry showed that they had no knowledge of the place, although they had been up and down that river every summer by canoe and every winter by dog team their whole lives long. I tried my best to describe the location, and they said they would look for it whenever they went up that way. I have never heard if they found it.

But a story that interested them more than the deserted cabin was my account of how I had cooked breakfast ashore and had forgotten several pounds of tea tied up in a silk handkerchief. I had not been at the village an hour when one of the men got into his canoe and started upstream in search of the tea and handkerchief. I estimate he had forty miles to go. However, he said that he might get a moose on the journey, thus killing two birds with one stone.

Compared to my sluggish drift, the canoe journey from the mouth of the·Old Crow seemed like flying. Between paddle and current we made from six to eight miles an hour. There were no rapids that could not be easily run in a good canoe or even in one of these bark canoes with a reasonable load, but overloaded as we were I had to go ashore a few times to walk around a rapid. Occasionally we took a chance and ran through a ripple, but it never really paid, for the canoe always sprung a leak and each time we only barely got ashore before sinking. Then it took two or three hours to make a fire, melt some spruce gum and patch up the cracks in the bark.

It took two days from Old Crow River to Rampart House. A few miles above that trading post we came to an encampment of a white man, Archie Linklater, who was living there with his Indian wife and family. We had a pleasant visit with them, after which Linklater took me on his raft to Rampart House, for the river between was swift and would not have been safe to run in a bark canoe carrying two men.

At Rampart House I had the warmest sort of welcome from Daniel Cadzow, the local trader and only resident white man (there were several other white men who made up a sort of floating population). It would have been pleasant to linger there as he urged me to do but it was now the 30th of August and in two or three days Mr. Harrison might reach Athabasca Landing and send out over the world the report that I had told at Herschel Island of the death of Leffingwell, Mikkelson and Storkerson. As soon as Mr. Cadzow understood how pressing the case was he ceased his urging that I should stay and devoted himself instead to helping with preparations for my continuing the journey. I had thought of hiring Indians, but Cadzow said that Linklater would take me to Fort Yukon much more rapidly than any Indian. Linklater undertook the job, and in a few hours he and his family were on their way with me in a flat-bottomed rowboat.

I have never seen a man who could work as Linklater did.  He was over six feet in height, powerfully built and used to the roughest kind of work.  For years he had been a member of the Royal Northwest Mounted Police at Dawson, at which time he had gained a reputation as a traveler.  He had never been a sailor, but he must have done a good deal of rowing in his time, for he kept steadily at the oars something like sixteen hours a day.  The current was sluggish and we had little help from it, so that with all our hard work we did not get to Fort Yukon until the evening of September 3rd.  It turned out, however, that somewhat greater speed would not have helped particularly, for there was only one logical way of proceeding upstream from Fort Yukon to the telegraph station at Eagle and that was by the river streamer *Hanna,* which was due about noon of the 4th.  She came some ten hours earlier than that and I was awakened from a sound sleep to scramble aboard in the early morning.  Then everything went well for a while.

The *Hanna* was carrying a huge cargo, a part of which consisted of several hundred tons of oats in bags.  She was loaded deeper than usual and the river had been dropping rapidly, so that I found soon after getting aboard that there was great concern as to whether we should be able to get through the Yukon flats.  This is a long stretch where the river, normally about a mile or two in width, spreads out to six or eight miles and winds its way through a maze of low islands.  We soon began to have trouble with shoal water and eventually came to a channel not deep enough for passage.  There was nothing to do but pull up to the bank and unload some of our freight so as to lighten the draught of the steamer.

There were on board the boat about a hundred laborers

who were returning to Seattle after a season in the Alaska gold mines. The captain offered these men a dollar an hour if they would turn to and help the crew unload the bags of oats, but it appeared that the miners had had their fare paid by their employers all the way out to Seattle and that this fare included board. They said, accordingly, that they did not care how long they were stuck; in fact, the longer we were stuck the better it suited them, for they would get that much more free board. Furthermore, they said they were through working for the season, and that they were miners anyhow and not stevedores.

There happened to be on the ship a number of passengers who were eager to get to Dawson and Seattle. I was in no particular hurry to reach Seattle but I was in a hurry to get to Eagle. Accordingly, I was one of the passengers who volunteered and six or eight of us worked hard with the crew for about twelve hours carrying ashore bags of oats. I think we unloaded six hundred tons before the *Hanna* was light enough to pass the shallows above.

We kept running aground again and again in spite of our unloading, and all together we lost about fifty hours' time. We should have reached Eagle September 5th but actually got there September 7th. When I sent my despatch out it got to the newspapers thirty-six hours too late. In a sense I had won the race, for my reaching the Yukon would have been in time if the steamer had only kept to its schedule. As it was, my news did not prevent the shock caused all over the world by the announcement of one more polar tragedy, nor did it prevent the writing of many editorials, some praising the heroism of the dead and others declaiming against the futility of such hare-

brained adventures. A few of the relatives of the supposedly dead had had the good sense not to believe the
announcement but were, nevertheless, in suspense, and
the rest who had believed were in grief. But whether
suspense or grief, it was better for all concerned that it
lasted only thirty-six hours. Had I not made the journey
over the mountains the good news would not have reached
the telegraphs until about two months later when the
whaling ships carrying the other members of our expedition got to Nome or Unalaska.


To a person who comes to the Yukon from the South it
has many thrills. Some call it the frontier and some call
it the wilderness, and to most such travelers the story
of a journey along the Yukon River and across the
Alaska mountains would seem worth writing. But I
came from the North and to me this was "civilization."
I ceased to make entries in my diary after boarding the
river steamer, and began instead to plan my next arctic
expedition.

Those plans were soon carried out. With the fever of
the North in my veins I remained in New York only
seven months and then started on my second expedition,
to spend in the Arctic the years 1908-12.

# SHORT STORIES OF ADVENTURE

# CHAPTER I

## HOW I LEARNED TO HUNT CARIBOU

FROM childhood I have been a hunter of animals from rabbits to wolves and antelope, from partridges to swans and cranes. When I went to the Arctic I had a good opinion of myself as a hunter, but most of that was soon talked out of me. The theory was in the air everywhere that a white man could not be a good hunter. On my trip down the Mackenzie River, two or three of the Hudson's Bay traders had told me that the best white hunters were better than the best Indian hunters, but the great majority of the traders were of the opinion that ability to hunt was an inborn gift with Indians and Eskimos and that no white man could be really good at it. When I came to the arctic coast I found this opinion universal. The whalers had much to tell of the uncanny prowess of the Eskimos and of the misadventures of such white men as had thought they were able to hunt and had tried it. According to the stories, the white men not only failed to kill game, but they used to get bewildered whenever they got beyond sight of ships and habitations. Sometimes they wandered back to their own camp or hit upon some other camp by accident; sometimes they had to be rescued by Eskimos who went out in search of them; in many cases they starved or froze to death.

This was the view of white men as hunters which I got almost unanimously from the whalers. There were only two or three who disagreed. But what impressed me even more than this nearly unanimous opinion of the whites was the entirely unanimous opinion of the Eskimos. According to their account, the white men who had gone hunting with them were uniformly incompetent. Most of them could not hit anything they tried to shoot. A few white men were wonderful marksmen when they were shooting at a still target, but were so badly afflicted with "buck fever" that they could not hit caribou or other big game. No white man was supposed to be able to find his way about. According to the Eskimo view, a white man was an amiable, overgrown baby and had to be watched and protected and helped in every way. At first these opinions did not impress me very strongly, but I heard them from all sides and gradually they began to soak in.

I spent my first arctic winter and summer with Eskimos who lived mainly by fishing. If I applied myself, I found I could fish as well as they, nor did that surprise them for they were all of the opinion that white men are good at catching any kind of water game with hook or net. To see a white man do well at any such work, from herring fishing to whaling, did not surprise them. They knew also that white men can catch seals in nets. But white men were unable to get seals that had crawled out on top of the ice, for then the tactics of getting them had to be those of the hunter and not the fisherman.

During my first summer I found I could kill ducks and geese as well as the Eskimos. This did not surprise them either, for it was in accordance with their general view. White men were good with fowling pieces and could even kill rabbits.

By the fall of 1908 (my second year in the Arctic) I had, in spite of myself, become obsessed with the idea that

Autumn Camp of Caribou Hunters a Hundred Miles North of the Arctic Circle—
Sun-drying Meat and Skins

a white man cannot be a good hunter, and that it is not safe for him to be out alone away from the wise Eskimos. Had any one put it to me in just those words I might have argued against it, for my reason was unconvinced. But subconsciously I had absorbed a profound mistrust of my own ability to take care of myself.

Later in September, 1908, a party of us were on our way by sledge east along the north coast of Alaska. I had one white companion, Storker Storkerson, with whom I was destined to be continuously associated through most of the following nine years of polar work. He was a sailor and full of confidence in himself in every way, except that like me he had been talked into the belief that he would not be able to make a living hunting and that he was in danger of losing his way if he got separated from his Eskimo guides.

The Eskimos of my party were a middle-aged man, by name Kunaluak, and my old friend, Ilavinirk, with his wife Mamayauk and their young daughter. Ilavinirk differed from the general run in several ways. For one thing, he had a greater admiration for white men than was common among his countrymen at that time. The general Eskimo view was that the white men are rich and fortunate, but unskilled and incompetent in the things that really matter. They felt about the whaling captains and about travelers like me somewhat as farmers or sailors might feel about grand opera singers or men who have inherited riches. But Ilavinirk used to maintain that the white men really had considerable native ability and that some of them were capable of becoming good winter travelers and even good hunters. I had heard him argue along those lines several times and now he had frequent talks with Kunaluak on this subject. Kunaluak maintained that white men had gifts of a certain kind entirely above the comprehension of an Eskimo, but that in such every-·day matters as getting back safely to camp when it is dark and when you are ten miles away from home they are hopelessly incompetent. To illustrate their incompetence in caribou hunting, he told stories of the adventures of sailors he had hunted with. We all had to join in the laughter. Ilavinirk was forced to admit the truth of the particular stories told by Kunaluak but he stoutly maintained that a few white men were exceptions to the rule.

Privately Ilavinirk told me that I must not be too much impressed with what Kunaluak and all the rest were saying. He gave me careful instructions in all the laws of caribou hunting and encouraged me as best he could to think that I would be able to make a good showing when the time came.

The time came just east of the Colville River. Kunaluak was walking ahead of our caravan of sleds when suddenly he brought us to a halt. I had been watching the land no less carefully than he and I found later that my eyes were just as good, but I then lacked the experience needed for identifying what I saw. I had seen a group of little specks on the hillside, but there were so many other specks elsewhere that I had given these no attention. Kunaluak's practiced eye recognized them as caribou, and when we stopped our field glasses confirmed him. There were nine animals, one a bull with spreading antlers, and the others of all sizes from yearlings up.

It was important for us to get these caribou. We were not short of food for we had been killing seals, but we were inadequately dressed for the coming winter. Storkerson's woolens and mine did very well for September, but against November we needed the warm caribou clothes which the Eskimo women would make for us if we only could get skins out of which they could make them.

We held a council. Kunaluak suggested that Storkerson and I should go with the Eskimo woman, child and dog teams the shortest distance towards the land and make camp while he and Ilavinirk went after the caribou, but Ilavinirk said that he wanted me to learn caribou hunting and that Storkerson and Mamayauk could easily make camp. Kunaluak demurred at first, saying that it was very important that no mistake should be made and that we get all the caribou. Like most Eskimos, he was kindness itself and was obviously of a divided mind between the courtesy which prompted him to invite me to come along and the caution which urged him to get me to stay behind. But Ilavinirk and I had our way.

Just as we were separating from the sledges, Mamayauk pointed out that while we needed especially the skins of the younger caribou for our inner clothing we should also secure the bull if possible, for his thick hide was needed for the soles of our winter boots. As we walked along Kunaluak and Ilavinirk discussed this point. They decided to leave the killing of the bull until the last for at this season bulls are very thin and their meat is considered nearly unfit for use (except for dog food) and they are valued chiefly for the hide. So they agreed they would shoot the other eight animals and the bull last.

We were still a mile away from the caribou, Kunaluak was walking rapidly and Ilavinirk and I dropped a little behind. He now told me that he had laid a trap for Kunaluak. Both of them had agreed not to shoot the bull until the last. Ilavinirk now told me to be sure to kill the bull while they were firing at the others. To his mind this would be a great joke on Kunaluak, for he had only that day been saying that he had known white men to fire many hundred shots at caribou and the only time he had known them to hit was when there were several caribou in a band and when a bullet intended for one had struck some other animal.

It is sometimes difficult to approach caribou, but in this case it was easy for there was a little ridge about three hundred yards away from them. We crawled to the top of this ridge and found conditions ideal, except that twilight was stealing on and we could no longer see the sights of our rifles plainly. The eight caribou were strung out almost in a straight line at right angles to us, and the big bull was at some distance from the others. It was agreed that Kunaluak should begin shooting at the right hand end of the line and Ilavinirk at the left hand end. In this conversation the two Eskimos agreed that I was to shoot at the middle of the line, but Ilavinirk gave me a wink to remind me that I was not to shoot at the line at all but at the old bull.

I think it took the Eskimos about twenty shots all together to kill six out of the eight animals, for two escaped. In the excitement of the shooting they had not been watching the bull. The other animals had been dashing round in various directions and in the half dark it would not have been strange if the bull which originally had been some distance away from them had got mixed up in the band without being noticed for in that light his antlers would not be conspicuous. When we went up to the dead caribou and found the bull to be one of them, Kunaluak said that Ilavinirk must have killed it for he felt sure that he had never aimed at any animal excepting a young one. Ilavinirk denied having shot the bull and said he thought I had done so. This Kunaluak evidently took for an amiable fib on the part of Ilavinirk and so as not to hurt my feelings he did not argue against it. But when it came to the skinning, it turned out that the bull had a peculiar wound that could not have been caused by their black powder rifles and must have been caused by my more powerful soft-nosed bullet. This evidence compelled Kunaluak to admit that I had killed the bull. But he seemed to consider it only a lucky stray shot.

A week later I had a chance about forty miles east of there to kill a caribou when I was off hunting alone. In that case there was no arguing as to who had been responsible.

We were camped on the coast and had gone hunting in different directions. The Eskimos had invited me to go along with them but I had preferred to hunt alone. The weather was so beautiful that it was impossible to conceive of any one getting lost. The topography, too, was simple. The mountains were in sight inland and from any small hill the coastline could plainly be made out even when you were three or four miles inland. Our camp was perched conspicuously on a high cutbank and both the tent and the smoke could be seen from afar. Even a sailor ashore could not get lost in such country and such weather. It seemed to me a good chance to try myself out and see if I could really stand on my own feet.

I had hunted inland seven or eight miles and had seen some caribou which I could not approach. The weather was very still, they heard my footfalls half a mile off and were gone. On my way back to the coast I noticed at a distance of two or three miles a small speck moving over the snow. My glasses showed this to be a big bull caribou. He was traveling in a straight line. I watched him carefully for about a mile and found that he was going to pass about half a mile from me.  I then ran as hard as I could to a place I judged to be directly in his road and there I lay down.  I was so badly out of breath that had he come along directly I should probably have missed him, but something induced him to stop for ten or fifteen minutes and when he finally came over the ridge about two hundred yards away from me I was over the worst effects of my running, although I am not sure that my hand was really steady.  The magnificent animal crumpled up with the first bullet.  That evening Kunaluak did not argue that it had been a chance shot, but I am not sure but it was.

From this time on I did my own hunting.  I have usually been in command of the traveling parties and it has been optional with me what to do.  Because hunting is pleasanter than taking care of the dog teams or building the camps, I have generally assigned the hunting to myself while my Eskimo or white companions have had to do the harder and more difficult work.  Still this has been not wholly because I was in command, but partly because many years of hunting have made me an expert in that line of work, just as any ordinary person can become an expert in anything through long practice.

When you consider that an experienced hunter is an expert in a very simple task, you will not think it remarkable that we count on being able to secure at least three out of every four caribou we try to get.  The same proportion applies to seals and polar bears.  This is why we feel no hesitancy in making journeys of hundreds and even thousands of miles in the arctic regions, depending on hunting entirely for our food.  If you read of travelers starving to death up there it will be through some special misfortune, or else because they either did not try to hunt or else did not know well the technique of finding and securing game.

A common mistake about caribou is to suppose that they are more difficult to hunt in districts where they are frequently hunted by people than in countries where they are never hunted at all. I find there is no such difference. The reason is simple. They have one great enemy, the wolf. On the prairies in the northern half of Canada and on the islands to the north of Canada there are many millions of caribou. Some say there are ten million all together and some say there are thirty million. In these great herds there must be born every year anything from two million to six million calves. The number of caribou killed by human beings in all of northern Canada is far less than one million per year. Accordingly, the caribou would increase very rapidly were it not for the wolves which kill several times as many as do the human hunters —Indian, Eskimo and white. Wolves are found wherever caribou are found and the caribou are in continual dread of them. They are, therefore, almost equally harried in countries that are uninhabited by men as in countries that are inhabited. I have, accordingly, found that even in the remote new islands which we discovered in 1915 caribou are about as difficult to approach as in northern Alaska or on the Canadian mainland where they are continually hunted by Eskimos.

Apart from the islands actually discovered by my expedition, there is no known country in the northern hemisphere that has been so little visited as Isachsen Land in north latitude 79°, west longitude 103°. We feel sure that no Eskimos ever saw that island. From the beginning of the world to our time it had been visited only once—by Captain Isachsen in 1901. Isachsen made a hurried sledge trip around the island. The journey took him about a week. In one place he saw some caribou tracks and I think he may have seen some caribou at a distance, but he did not try to hunt them. The next visitors were my sledge party in 1916 and on that occasion we saw no caribou and had to feed ourselves and our dogs entirely on seals.

My second visit, and the third visit of human beings to the island, was in 1917. We were then on the most dangerous adventure that has ever fallen to our lot. By the road we had to travel we were some five hundred miles away from the nearest Eskimos and six hundred miles away from our own base camp. Four of us had been on a long journey out on the moving sea ice to the northwest. When we were more than a hundred miles northwest from Isachsen Land, two of my three companions were taken seriously ill. We turned towards shore immediately and it was a hard fight to make land. When we got there after a struggle of two weeks we found ourselves with one man so sick that he could not walk, another who could barely walk but was of no use otherwise, and with two teams of dogs that were exhausted with hard work and so thin from short rations during the forced march towards shore that they were little more than skeletons. It had been my pride through many years never to lose a dog. Furthermore, I was exceedingly fond of every one of these dogs for they had worked for me faithfully for years. I was concerned for their safety, and still more concerned for the safety of the sick men. By that time, however, my confidence in our ability to make a living in the Arctic had become so strong through eight years of experience that I felt more worry for the lives of the men on the score of illness than for fear they might actually die of hunger.

But the first day on Isachsen Land was a depressing contradiction to my hopes and expectations. The one man in good health and the two men who were sick had to make their way as best they could along the coast while I hunted inland parallel to their course. I walked that day twenty miles across one of the very few stretches of entirely barren land that I have seen in the Arctic. Under foot was gravel without a blade of grass. Much of the land was lightly covered with snow as in other typical arctic lands in winter, and I looked in vain in the snow for track or other sign of any living thing.

That evening my men were depressed partly because of their illness and also because it looked as if we had at last come into a region as barren as many people think the polar countries generally are. It was clear that if we saw game the next day we would simply have to have it. Where game is plentiful, you may lose one chance and soon get another; but where it is scarce, you must not allow any opportunity to slip through your fingers.

I am telling this particular hunting story rather than any other to illustrate the principle of how you must hunt caribou in the polar regions if it is essential that you shall get every animal you see. It certainly was essential in this case, for I wanted not only to stave off immediate hunger but to secure meat enough so we could camp in one place for several weeks to give the sick men a chance to become well.

Our second day on Isachsen Land the men again followed the coast line with the sledges, cutting across the shortest distance from point to point while I walked a much longer course inland. I had gone but a few miles when I came upon the tracks of a band of caribou. You can seldom be sure of the minimum number in a band from the tracks if there are more than ten animals, for caribou have a way of stepping in each other's foot-prints. There are always likely to be more animals in a band than you have been able to make out from the tracks.

The trail showed that these caribou were traveling into the wind as they usually do. There were only light airs and the snow had on it a crust that broke underfoot with a crunching noise. Under such conditions the band were likely to hear me four or five hundred yards away. The country now was a rolling prairie—not barren gravel as yesterday. It was impossible to tell which ridge might hide the caribou from me, so instead of following the trail ahead I went back along it for about half a mile studying the tracks to see just how fast they had been moving. They had been traveling in a leisurely way and feeding here and there. I estimated their average rate of pro-gress would not be more than three or four miles per day. I could not rely on this, however, for a wolf may turn up any time and begin a pursuit which takes a band twenty-five or fifty miles away. Should a wolf pass to windward of them so that they got his smell without his knowing about them, they would be likely to run from five to ten miles.

When I had made up my mind that these caribou were moving slowly, I went to the top of a nearby hill and through my glasses studied the landscape carefully. With good luck I might have seen some of them on top of some hill and the problem would have become definite. But I watched for half an hour and saw nothing. Clearly they were either feeding in some low place or else they were lying down, for caribou are like cattle in their habit of lying down for long periods. I now commenced a cautious advance, not along the actual trail but crisscrossing it from high hilltop to high hilltop, hoping to get a view of the animals while they were at least half a mile from me and while I was beyond the range of their eyesight, for they cannot see a man under even the most favorable conditions farther off than half a mile. Under ordinary conditions they would not see you much beyond a quarter of a mile.

Finally I saw the band lying quietly on some flat land. There was no cover to enable me to approach safely within five hundred yards and that is too far for good shooting. I thought these might be the only caribou in the whole country. We had thirteen hungry dogs and two sick men, and now that I had a large band before me it was my business to get enough food at one time to enable us to spend at that place two or three weeks while the men had a chance to regain their health and the dogs to regain their flesh and strength.

On a calm day when caribou can hear you farther than you can shoot, there is only one method of hunting. You must study their movements from afar until you make up your mind which direction they are going. Then you must walk in a wide curve around them until you are in the locality towards which they are moving and well beyond earshot. This takes judgment, for they usually travel nearly or quite into the wind and you must not allow them to scent you. You, therefore, have to choose a place which you think is near enough to their course so that they will pass within shooting distance, and still not directly enough in front so that they can smell you.

On this occasion the glaring light on the snow had been so hard on my eyes that I did not feel they were in perfect condition, and no one can shoot well if his eyes are not right. Unless there is a change of wind caribou are not likely to turn their course back along the trail by which they have come. I accordingly selected a hill across which they had walked that morning and half a mile away from where they now were. On the top of this hill where I could see them, although they could not see me (because my eyes were better than theirs) I lay down, covered my head with a canvas hunting bag to keep the sun away, and went to sleep. Sleeping is the best possible way of passing time, but my object now was not only to pass the time until the caribou began moving but also to get my eyes into perfect condition.

When you go to sleep at twenty below zero you have in the temperature an automatic alarm clock. My clothes were amply warm enough to keep me comfortable while I was awake, but I knew that when I went to sleep my circulation would slow down. This reduces the body temperature and the same weather that will not chill you when you are awake will chill you enough to wake you from a sleep.

In this case the chill woke me in about half an hour to an unpleasant situation. A fog had set in and I could not see the caribou, nor had I any means of knowing whether they were still lying down or whether they had started to move. If this had been a good game country, I might have taken chances on advancing through the fog a little, but I was so impressed with the possibility that these were the only animals within a hundred miles that carelessness was not to be considered. At this time of year we had twenty-four hours of daylight. The fog was bound to lift sooner or later and whenever it did I would commence the hunt over again.

The fog did lift in about two hours and I did have to commence the hunt all over again, for the caribou were gone. I was to the north of them and I felt sure that they had not gone by near me; so they must have gone east, west or south. I was probably so near them that I could not with safety go on top of any of the adjoining hills, so I went back north half a mile and climbed a high hill there. From that hill I saw nothing and went half a mile to one side to another hill. Then I saw the caribou. They were now feeding half a mile south of where they had been when the fog covered them up. In the meantime the breeze had stiffened enough so that now there was no longer danger of my being heard. I did not, therefore, have to circle them and lie in wait in front but could follow up directly behind.

Eventually I got within about three hundred yards. But I wanted to get within two hundred, so I lay still and waited for them to move into a more favorable locality. During my wait an exceedingly thick fog bank rolled up, but with it the wind did not slacken. Under cover of this fog I felt safe in crawling ahead a hundred yards, for I knew that I could see through the fog quite as well as the animals and that they could not hear me because of the wind. The reason I had not approached them in the previous fog was that the weather then had been nearly calm and they would have heard me.

At two hundred yards I was just able to make out the outline of the nearest caribou. I did not dare to go closer and, of course, I could not begin shooting with only one or two animals in sight where I wanted to get them all. I had before now counted them carefully. There were twenty-one, which I estimated would be enough to feed our men and dogs between two or three weeks, giving them a chance to recuperate.

After about half an hour the fog began gradually to clear and in another half hour I could see all the animals. I was near the top of a hill and they were in a hollow, the nearest of them about a hundred and fifty yards away and the farthest about three hundred.

In winter the ground in any cold country will split in what we call frost cracks. These are cracks in the frozen surface of what in summer is mud. They are ordinarily only half an inch or so wide but I have seen cracks four or five inches wide. These cracks form when the mercury is dropping and with a noise that resembles a rifle shot. Under the same conditions the ice on the small lakes cracks similarly. These loud noises are so familiar to the caribou and the report of a rifle is so similar that the mere sound of a rifle does not scare them. Of course, we have smokeless powder so they cannot see where the shots come from. What does scare them is the whistle of the bullet and the thud as it strikes the ground. It is instinctive with all animals to run directly away from the source of any noise that frightens them. It is another instinct of caribou when they are alarmed to run towards the center of the herd. A band that has been scattered feeding will bunch up when they take fright. When you know these two principles, it is obvious that the first caribou to kill is the one farthest away from you. On some occasions when I have been unable to get within good shooting distance of a band, I have commenced by firing a few shots into a hill on the other side of them, hoping that the noise of the striking bullets would scare them towards me. Frequently it works. On this occasion, however, I merely took careful aim at an animal about three hundred yards away. It dropped so instantaneously that although the sound of the bullet striking it induced the other caribou to look up, they recognized no sign of real danger. They were, however, alert and when they saw the second caribou fall they ran together into a group and moved somewhat towards me. I now shot animals on the outer margin of the group and as each fell, the others would run a little away from that one. Their retreat in any direction was stopped by killing the foremost animal in the retreat, whereupon the band would turn in the opposite direction.

It would not have been difficult for me to kill the whole band alone, but I was not shooting alone. From a point somewhat above and behind me I could hear other shots, and some animals I was not aiming at were dropping. Without looking around I knew what this meant. My companions traveling along shore on the ice had seen the caribou and had waited for some time until they began to fear that I might have missed the band. The two sick men had then been left behind in camp while their Eskimo companion had come inland to try to get the caribou. When he got near he saw that I was approaching them and very wisely did not interfere. There is nothing so likely to spoil a caribou hunt as two hunters whose plans conflict. Even when they have a chance to consult at the beginning of the hunt, two men are less likely to be successful than one. For one thing, caribou may see a black dot on the landscape and take no warning from it, but if they see two black dots and later notice that they are either closer together or farther apart than they were a moment before, this makes a danger signal which they understand. That is the main reason why I always hunt alone. If there are two hunters to go out from the same camp on any given day, they should go in opposite directions. That way they double the chance of finding game and each has a fair chance of getting the animals he does find.

On our journeys we never kill more animals than we need, but in this case we needed the whole twenty-one. The Eskimo and I went down to the ice with my hunting bag filled with the tongues of the caribou. This gave the sick men a more appetizing meat than they had had for a long time. The dogs had to wait for their food until we were able to move camp right to where the caribou had been shot. Although they were thin and tired, they became so excited with the smell of the fresh killed caribou which they got from our clothes that they pulled towards shore as if they had been well fed and of full strength.

On the hill from which I had shot the caribou we pitched camp. During the next two weeks the invalids rapidly gained in health. We called the place Camp Hospital. Few hospitals have ever been more successful. When we left it three weeks later, the dogs were fat and the men well.

# CHAPTER II

## HOW I LEARNED TO HUNT SEALS

SOME Eskimos make a living almost entirely by hunting seals, and I have had to do the same occasionally. The seal is the most useful of animals because it furnishes all you really need for living in comfort.

The lean and fat of the seal make together a diet upon which whole groups of Eskimos live in good health to a reasonably old age. On some of my later expeditions my white companions and I have lived exclusively on seals for months at a time. Some people do not like the meat at first just because it differs considerably from any meat with which they are familiar; but you gradually get to like it, and the longer you live on it the better you like it. You may be dreadfully tired of seal after three weeks, or even three months, but I never saw any one who was tired of it after three years. It is in living with the Eskimos on seals as it is in living with the Chinese on rice that no matter how much you dislike it at first, you are likely eventually to become as fond of it as they are themselves.

In addition to giving meat and fat for food the seal furnishes fat for fuel. Many thousands of Eskimos have no other fuel in winter, and it does them very well. They burn the fat in stone lamps made for the purpose. These are carefully trimmed and should not smoke. A woman is considered a very bad housekeeper if you can notice the smell of lamp smoke in her house or see stains of lamp soot on her hands, or on anything in the house. The first real Eskimo house in which I lived (at Tuktuyaktok) usually had four seal oil lamps burning, maintaining the temperature of the interior, day and night, steadily between 70° and 80°. We had a wood stove which we used for cooking only, but many Eskimos cook entirely over their lamps. This serves well, but takes a little longer.

Besides food and fuel, the seal furnishes clothing. The Eskimos use water boots in summer that are made entirely of seal skin, and in winter they use caribou skin boots which in some cases have seal skin soles. Rain coats are made of seal skin and so are mittens intended to be used in handling fishnets or anything that is wet. Coats and trousers for winter may be made of seal skin, but this is seldom done except when caribou are scarce.

Whalers, traders and explorers have for a century been in contact with the Eskimos in Greenland, even as far north as Smith Sound where the most remote of them live. These people buy canvas and other tents from traders and so do all the Eskimos of Alaska—and, indeed, all the Eskimos in the world except some small groups that are especially inaccessible because they are in the middle of the north coast of North America halfway between the Atlantic and Pacific oceans. These small groups still use skin tents and they are of seal skin in districts where seals are more abundant than caribou.

Lastly, seal skins furnish material for boats. The small seals are used for the kayaks and the big seals for the umiaks.

I like to travel with Eskimo companions, but I never liked to feel that I was wholly dependent upon them. Being helpless is never pleasant. To become self-sup-

A Woman Fishing Through the Ice

Bringing Home a Seal

porting, nothing was so important as to learn seal hunting, for then I could supply myself with food, fuel,
clothing and, if need be, material for a tent or a boat.

It is said that experience is the best teacher; but she
is a slow and painful teacher.  Any one at all intelligent
or thoughtful can learn without experience, or rather
from the experience of others.  That is why we have so
many schools and that is why they are so useful.  I am
a great believer in schools and like to learn things by
being taught.  I therefore asked the Eskimos to explain
to me just how they hunted seals.  They told me clearly
and fully.  If I were to repeat what they said, I should
give a description of seal hunting from which any one
could learn the principles so well that he could hunt seals
successfully the first time he found himself in the polar
regions.  But I found later that while the Eskimos had
told me the whole truth they had told me a great deal
more than the truth.  They are a kind and charming
people; but they are very superstitious, and about half
the things they told me I would have to do in order to
hunt seals successfully I have since found were pure
superstition.  Seal hunting is very much simpler than any
Eskimo will ever tell you; for he tells you how he hunts
seals, and half the things he does while hunting are done
merely because his father and grandfather before him
always did them that way.

So instead of telling how Eskimos hunt seals, I shall
tell how I do it and how the other white men do it who
(on my various expeditions) have accompanied me when
we were living on seals.

On my first expedition (1906-07) I was in a fishing
country and never saw a caribou or a seal.  On my
second expedition (1908-12) I was nearly the whole time

in a caribou country and lived mainly on caribou. Furthermore, my Eskimo companions at that time had been brought up as caribou hunters, and if they knew how to hunt seals they did not care much about it. One of them, Natkusiak, came from Cape Prince of Wales in Alaska and had learned sealing as a boy. He had explained to me how it was done and I felt sure I could do it whenever the need arose. But the need never came until in May, 1912, when he and I were making a 1000-mile sledge journey from Langton Bay to Point Barrow. We were on the last lap—the 400-mile stretch between Herschel and Barrow.

We could have carried almost enough groceries to last us the trip from Herschel to Barrow but we did not like to because such a heavy load would have lessened our speed. So we took only about one-quarter of what we needed, expecting to live mainly by hunting. This was the best time of the year for sealing on top of the ice, and Natkusiak assured me he would be able to get all the seals necessary to feed ourselves and our dogs.

But soon after we started west from Herschel Island he began to complain about a pain in one of his fingers. This developed into a felon and the pain became so intense that he could not sleep at night. He could not even ride on the sled daytimes for the jarring hurt too much. Delay was out of the question for we had to reach Point Barrow before the summer heat turned into water the sea ice we were traveling over, so he used to walk along slowly and as carefully as he could, carrying his afflicted left hand in front of him supported by his right. Crippled as he was he could not hunt seals, so I had to do it.

I felt I understood the theory and that I should be

able to kill my first seal. The principle was simple. You had to go on the assumption that the seal would see you when you were far away. Your task was to approach him slowly, crawling along the ice like a seal and making him think all the while that you were another seal. Natkusiak had explained to me both by words and mimicry how this should be done. But I did not want to make any mistake with my first seal, and thinking that possibly the seals themselves might know even better than Natkusiak how a seal acts, I decided to find out from them just how they do act.

That was a simple matter. The eyesight of seals is not very good, and when they are lying sunning themselves on the level ice they cannot see you much beyond four hundred yards. With this in mind I watched for seals as we traveled, climbing on top of ice hummocks now and then and examining the ocean with my field glasses. Finally we saw a seal lying on the ice ahead of us. We made camp about half a mile from him. I then went to the top of an ice hummock and studied him carefully through my glasses. Previous to this I had often watched seals and had checked them with my watch to find out how long at a time they sleep. I found that they take short naps, but that their waking spells between the naps are even shorter. I learned that while on top of the ice the average Alaskan seal sleeps about seven times as much as he stays awake. The average length of his naps was about thirty-five seconds and the average length of the waking periods between was about five seconds.

It may seem strange to those unfamiliar with the lives of the arctic seals that they should sleep so fitfully. Nothing else would do, however. If they slept thirty

minutes at a time instead of thirty seconds, there soon
would be no seals left. They would all get killed and
eaten by the polar bears.

The polar bear is the great enemy of the seal. He
is white in color and difficult for the seal to see at a
distance. He is also a very skillful hunter. Eternal
watchfulness is, therefore, the price of a seal's being able
to live at all. Accordingly, he usually goes to sleep on
large expanses of level ice so as to give the bear no
opportunity to creep up behind the cover of a hummock.
Then after the briefest nap, during which the seal sleeps
like a small boy on a lawn, he lifts his head as high as
he can above the ice (about eighteen inches) and surveys
the whole horizon carefully. Having satisfied himself
that nothing dangerous is in sight, he takes another nap.
While the average nap is thirty seconds, the seal may lift
his head suddenly after five seconds of pretended sleep,
or possibly after a real nap of fifteen seconds. They
seldom sleep more than a minute at a time, but north of
Prince Patrick Island, where we never saw polar bear
tracks, I have known them to sleep five or even ten
minutes at a time.

All these things I had heard already, but I wanted
further confirmation of them and I wanted to learn
certain finer details of how to act. Watching the seal
through my glasses, I noticed that he was seldom still for
a moment. He was continually squirming and rubbing
himself against the ice as if he were itching. Occasionally he would scratch his side with one of his front flippers. The front flippers are short and inconvenient for
that purpose, but the hind flippers are long and flexible
and he can curl himself up in such a way that he can
scratch with them as far up as his waist. I concluded,

therefore, (and long experience has verified it) that when I came to play seal it would be advisable for me to squirm and scratch myself as I had seen him doing.

When my hour of study was over, I began the hunt with every rule in mind which Natkusiak had given me and not forgetful of the things I had just learned by watching. Knowing that he could not see more than at most five hundred yards, I walked to a spot directly to the leeward of him five hundred yards away. I now saw that the ice between him and me was not quite level. This would be bad, for if he once saw me I must keep in sight all the time. If I had any hollows in the ice to crawl over, I should disappear from his sight occasionally and this might scare him. I therefore stepped a few yards to one side and examined the ice between him and me with the glasses. This was still hummocky, so I kept going a little more to one side until I found that all the ice in a direct line to the seal was level. Then I commenced the approach.

It may seem that it would be advisable to dress in white clothing for this sort of hunt. That would be the worst thing you could do. The seal is continually watching for polar bears. If he sees something that is suspicious and white, he takes it to be a polar bear and dives into his water hole at once. The seals themselves are grey and when they have just come out of the water their sleek sides look black at a distance. The hunter may, therefore, wear any color between grey and black. I have used blue and it seems the seal cannot distinguish between this and black. Green I have never tried because I never had green clothes, nor have I heard of it being tried. Eskimos have told me that red will not do, and that seems reasonable. I have tried to get at seals when dressed in white, but have never succeeded except when I have been able to shield myself behind some cover.

So long as you are more than three hundred yards away from the seal you need not be careful. He might see you at four hundred yards if you were upright, but you should begin crawling somewhat before the four hundred-yard mark is reached. I crawl ahead on all fours while he is asleep, and when he wakes up I drop flat instantly and remain motionless until he goes to sleep again. This sort of approach will do until you are about three hundred yards away, but after that you must be more careful for he now may see you at any time.

When I felt myself well within the seal's range of vision, I began to crawl ahead seal-fashion, which practically means snake-fashion. I moved as rapidly as I could while he slept and I stopped motionless while he was awake until finally, at a distance of 175 yards, he saw me.

It was easy to tell when the seal first saw me. He stiffened up suddenly, lifted his head a little higher than ordinary and crawled a foot or two nearer his water hole so as to be able to dive instantly if necessary. Being now in what he thought a safe position himself and considering me so far away that there was no immediate danger, he watched me carefully. Had I remained motionless for two or three minutes, he would have become restive, and in a few minutes more he would have dived into his hole, for he knew very well that no real seal would remain motionless for long. Accordingly, I waited until he had been watching me about half a minute, which is the average sleeping spell of a seal. I then did my best to act like a seal waking up. I lifted my head about eighteen inches above the ice, looked around in all directions, and moved as if I were squirming seal-fashion on the ice. After spending about five seconds looking around, I allowed my head to drop on the ice. I then counted ten of my breaths and raised my head a second time, dropping it after a suitable interval. Occasionally I would flex my legs at the knee so as to imitate a seal scratching with his hind flippers.

In about ten or fifteen minutes of this sort of acting I had the seal convinced that I was another seal. After that the whole thing was easy. I have since found by long experience that most of the seals you lose are lost at this critical time. It may be that they are of a specially nervous temperament, perhaps they have had a narrow escape from a bear just recently, or possibly they may have been lying up on the ice so long that they are hungry and ready to dive into the sea in search of the next meal. I should say that one seal out of four will dive at this stage, no matter how good a seal hunter you are. To lose a seal that way is nobody's fault. If you lose him thereafter, it is your fault or because some accident happens. It may be that a sudden gust of wind flaps your clothing so that he notices it. There is nothing about a real seal that flaps in the wind, so he will recognize this as a danger sign. Possibly you may make some loud noise by carelessly breaking a snag of thin ice. Still, that should do no more than make him suspicious over again for seals do break ice snags sometimes, and a few minutes of playing seal should put him at his ease.

I do not know how to explain it, but a seal certainly cannot tell a man from a seal by merely looking at him even at so short a distance as five yards. But if he is stupid as to a man's appearance, he is very keen as to his actions. When within ten or fifteen yards of a seal you must mind your P's and Q's very strictly or he will detect the fraud.

I am inclined to think that the seal's inability to detect the trick that is being played on him is not due to simple stupidity, but is rather self-deception—auto-suggestion. He has made up his mind that you are a seal; and once made up, a seal's mind stays made up. There is nothing fickle about a seal.

In the case of my first seal I was 175 yards from him when I got him convinced that I was a seal. When eventually he began to take his regular alternate naps and waking spells, I began a systematic advance, moving ahead while he slept and stopping motionless while he was awake. If at any time he watched me as much as half a minute at a time I played seal some more by lifting my head to show I was awake or by bending my legs at the knees to pretend that I was scratching.

Eskimos sometimes crawl within five yards of a seal before throwing a harpoon and I have known of them crawling so close that they could seize him by a flipper with one hand and stab him with a knife with the other. This is done only to show off their skill as hunters or else in an emergency when the rifle or sealing harpoon has been lost or forgotten at home. I ordinarily crawl within about fifty yards and did so in this case. Then I waited until the seal raised his head, took a careful aim and shot him through the brain. Next I dropped my rifle on the ice and ran at top speed to catch him, for although he was dead there was still a chance of my not getting him. He was lying on a slippery incline of ice so near his hole that the mere shock when the bullet struck might start him sliding. It had started him, and I got there just in time to seize a hind flipper as he was gliding into the water. On other occasions I have had to slide for a dead seal as a runner in baseball slides for a base. Sometimes I have just caught the seal and sometimes I have just missed him. In a few cases he has slid so rapidly that I was no more than halfway from the shooting place to his hole when he disappeared.

Three seals out of four have buoyancy enough to float, but if they slide into the water the momentum gathered by slipping off the ledge of ice is enough to send them diagonally down into the water fifteen or twenty feet. They come up diagonally under the ice. The ice may be as much as seven feet thick and you do not know exactly where they are. We, therefore, consider that a seal is lost if he once slips into his hole, and we do not even try to search.

In about one case in a hundred the dead seal may rise in the hole. It is, therefore, worth while to stand by for two or three minutes on a chance that he has sunk vertically and that he will come back up vertically.

It would be easy to shoot a seal at a distance greater than fifty yards, but experience shows that this is wasteful. If you have a hundred yards to run the seal's dead body has at least an even chance of sliding in before you get there. It takes so much cautious effort to get within a hundred yards of a seal that you had better not spoil it all by shooting until you are nearer. Furthermore, nothing will do but a brain shot or one through the spine at the base of the brain. If there is the least life in the animal, a wiggle will send him into his hole.

I have spoken of the seal's hole without describing it for that is more easily done in connection with an account of our second method of hunting. The way already

described the Alaskan Eskimos call the *auktok* or crawling method.  We occasionally kill seals by the more
ingenious *mauttok* or waiting method.

In most of Alaska the mauttok method is now only a
tradition.  The older men in the Mackenzie district know
the theory but I have never seen them use it.  My first
experience with mauttok hunting came in 1910 when I
was with the Copper Eskimos in Coronation Gulf.

Through the eyes of a southerner nothing can be a
more desolate or more hopeless desert so far as food is
concerned than the level expanse of winter ice along the
polar coast.  If the coast is open as in northern Alaska,
you can go five or ten miles to seaward and find a place
where the wind has broken the ice and where the cakes
are in motion.  Here you will find seals swimming about
in the water like bathers in a pond, and the tracks of
polar bears that live on the seals may meet you anywhere.
But in places like Coronation Gulf there is land on every
side and the ice does not move from November, when
it forms, until the following June or July, when it
eventually breaks up some two months after summer and
green grass have come upon all the surrounding lands.
There are no polar bear tracks on this ice except in rare
years, and no obvious sign indicates the presence of game.

We were in a village on the level ice some ten miles
from shore.  There were twelve or fifteen snowhouses
with two families in some and one in others.  The
population of the village was around fifty, among whom
there were about fifteen able-bodied hunters.  A few men
were too old and stayed at home for that reason; and
boys do not hunt seals until they are nearly grown.

Around mid-winter we have on a clear day in Coronation Gulf about six hours of hunting light.  At that

time of year the hunters must arise before dawn, have their breakfast of seal meat and start out on the ice with the earliest light. When I had my first lesson in the mauttok hunt the conditions did not differ except that it was spring with daylight at night—or with no night, if you prefer to put it that way. Each man took with him a dog in leash and our trails led away from the village in all directions like the spokes of a wheel. The experienced hunters went singly, each with a dog, but I accompanied my host for I knew the hunting method only from description and before trying it I wanted to see how it was actually carried out.

Salt ice is sticky. On a lake there may be patches of bare ice where the wind has swept the snow away, but this can scarcely occur on the ocean for a certain amount of snow must adhere to the sticky surface of the ice. As a matter of fact, there was a fairly uniform layer of snow everywhere. It varied from something like six inches in most places to a depth of several feet if drifts had been piling up in the lee of a snag of ice where a fracture of the surface had taken place in some autumn gale. We walked slowly as if strolling at leisure. Our dog was mildly excited for he knew there was food to be secured. He would, therefore, tug on his leading string and walk ahead of his master, pulling him this way and that. Now and then he would stop and sniff at the snow. I thought then that this was the result of his special training, but I know now that any dog of keen scent will do about as he did. I should imagine that a spaniel or bloodhound from a southern country would make a good sealing dog the very first day.

We had gone about a mile when the dog stopped to sniff carefully on a drift about two feet in depth. This meant he might have found a seal hole and with a cane we poked around in the snow for a while. The scent proved false, for all we found were signs that a fox had been there earlier in the winter.

The first indication having proved worthless, we continued our zigzag stroll. Half a mile further on the dog stopped again to sniff and his master probed into the snowdrift with his cane. After a dozen or two stabs, each of which met the solid ice below, the cane went deeper than before. It had struck the seal's breathing hole and slipped through into the water beneath.

This snowdrift was comparatively soft. The hunter now put his foot upon the snow just where he had discovered the seal's hole and pressed down the snow firmly. He then took from his hunting kit an ivory rod about as big round as a knitting needle and twice as long. This rod had a little disc on one end of it the size of a ten-cent piece, or smaller. At the other end of the rod was an eyelet through which was threaded a string about a foot long fastened to a sort of ivory pin. Through the hole made by his cane the hunter now stuck down his ivory probe so that the end with the disc on it was a few inches below the surface of the water in the seal's hole. Then he packed enough loose snow around the probe so that it did not slip in further. He then stuck the pin into the snow about a foot away. This precaution was taken so that the hunting contrivance should not be lost when it came to spearing the seal.

It is now time to explain how the seal happened to be living just here under the ice. The preceding autumn had found him and all the other seals of the neighborhood swimming around freely in open water. Then the first frosts had come and young ice had formed one night.

First this ice was so weak that the seal could come up whenever he liked and break it by bumping his head against it.  He had to do this several times an hour, for a seal has to breath the free air occasionally.  He is not a fish with gills that can take oxygen from the water, but a mammal that breathes through nostrils like a dog.

The fresh water ice with which most of us are familiar is transparent like window glass and almost as hard, but the thinnest sea ice is never transparent.  In appearance it is more like ground glass which lets the light through although you cannot see through it.  Another difference is that fresh ice is so strong that a big man can walk around safely on a pond covered by an inch of it.  An inch of salt ice would not support a puppy, and children cannot play safely on three inches of it.  Where lake ice is like glass, sea ice is like ice cream until it finally hardens and toughens with increasing thickness.  We do not consider it safe to travel with a dog team and loaded sledge over sea ice less than six inches in thickness.  Once we broke through and came near losing all our belongings crossing a stretch of ice five and three-quarters inches thick.  We knew the danger and had taken the risk because the strip was only a few yards wide and we thought we could hurry across in safety.  Our dogs did get across and the ice broke just as the front end of our sled touched the solid floe, so that only the back end of the sled got into the water.  We would have lost the whole load had the ice broken when the sled was two feet farther away from the floe.

This mushiness of the sea ice in the fall enables the seals to continue their travels in the ocean underneath it until a thickness of four inches has been attained.  After that they can no longer smash their way up to the air, and so they have to gnaw their way up. The teeth of a seal look like the teeth of a dog, but they are far enough forward in his jaw so he can gnaw with them almost as well as a rat can gnaw. In the manner of a rat making a hole through a board the seal now makes a hole through the ice just big enough to stick his nostrils up against to breathe. In some cases this hole is not over half an inch in diameter, although it may be an inch or more.

Now the seal is confined to this vicinity. He may dive down fifty feet or so, searching for a fish or something else to eat, but he has to come up to the hole every now and then for a breath of air.

For convenience, or possibly because he has nothing better to do, the seal will make in the vicinity half a dozen or a dozen other breathing holes exactly like the first. As the ice gradually thickens to six inches, a foot, two feet, four feet, and even six or seven feet at a maximum, the seal has to keep busy gnawing away to keep open as many of the holes as he desires. His object is to be able to press his nostrils against a little hole at the very surface of the ice. To do this, he has to make in connection with each hole a cigar-shaped vertical chamber big enough to admit his whole body. This must mean a great deal of work, but perhaps it helps him to pass the time away.

Soon after the autumn freeze-up, the snow is bound to come and cover up all the breathing holes. This is evidently what the seal wants, for in rare instances some eddy of wind, caused perhaps by an ice hummock not far away, will keep free of snow the particular spot where the seal has one of his holes. Such a hole he always abandons because the freezing is more rapid where the ice is not blanketed by snow, or else perhaps because he sees danger in the exposed nature of this breathing place.

Whether the snow covering the air hole is four inches or four feet, it is granular and porous and the seal is able to suck in air through it to breathe.

My Eskimo friend had now discovered one of these breathing holes. He knew it was only one of several. If there were only one breathing hole to each seal, the hunter would be bound to get him in a few minutes; but there are many holes and it is a matter of chance whether the seal is using just the one you have discovered. In our case, he was evidently using some other hole for we stood there half the day and nothing happened. We were both so warmly dressed that although the temperature was about 40° below zero we did not feel cold even when standing still.

I got tired of standing still, however, and my Eskimo friend said it would be all right for me to walk around if I would go a hundred yards off. He himself stood motionless on the leeward side of the hole (for the seal has a very keen sense of smell). Under his feet he had a pad of fox skin to give added protection from the cold. In his hand he held his sealing harpoon. Like all Eskimo harpoons, this had a detachable head to which there was attached a strong line—in this case braided caribou sinew, but strong leather thongs are sometimes used.

We had been there several hours waiting for our seal to rise when another Eskimo came up who had not had luck finding a breathing hole. With his dog the new-comer started searching around in about a fifty-yard circle. Finally his dog found another of our seal's breathing holes. He then took his dog and tethered him over by our dog about a hundred yards away from either hole. The newcomer then set his indicator exactly as my friend had done and now the two waited for the seal. They also encouraged me to walk around at a considerable distance from either of them, stamping on the snow here and there. The idea was to try to scare the seal away from whatever hole he might be using to one or the other of those that were now being watched.

It may have been that I scared the seal from some distant hole to the one watched by the newcomer, for all of a sudden I saw him come to alert attention. Knowing that the seal was about to come up, I approached stealthily to within about ten yards and watched. When a seal is approaching the breathing hole that contains an indicator, the wave motion in the water created by his swimming will start the indicator trembling while the animal is still some distance off. When he finally comes right into the torpedo-shaped chamber and rises straight up through the water to press his nose against the breathing hole, he touches the lower end of the rod. If it strikes him squarely on the middle of his snout he will lift it up; but if it strikes slantingly, as it nearly always does, then instead of being lifted up, the indicator slips down deeper than before. Just at that moment the hunter drives his harpoon down alongside of the indicator. If he hits the hole in the ice he hits the seal, for his nose is at that moment in the hole.

In this case the hunter made no slip and in a moment he was struggling with a powerful animal that had been harpooned in the side of the neck. The other hunter rushed up and by the braided sinew rope one of them held the animal while the other got his ice chisel and enlarged the hole until it was something over a foot in diameter, or large enough to pull the seal out. While this was going on, the dogs were watching attentively, not only because they knew that the hunt was in progress, but also because experience had taught them that their turn to help would soon come.

After killing the seal by a rap on the head the man who had caught it went over to fetch his dog. The seal hunter's dog always wears a light leather harness. This does not incommode him at all in walking. When the seal has been killed, it is fastened to the harness by a leather trace a few feet long and the dog is told to go drag it home. If we had caught our seal early in the day the dog would have gone home alone dragging the catch up to the door of his master's house, while the hunter went across the ice to some neighbor he saw watching at another seal hole to co-operate with him as our second hunter had in this case co-operated with us. But we did not get our seal until it was almost time to go home, so we followed the dog as he dragged the seal to camp.

This method of sealing is little used in most Eskimo districts and not at all in others because the winds and currents break up the ice enough so that you can get seals in the open water all winter. There are two kinds of localities where the method is the only one available. These are on one hand such enclosed bodies of water as Coronation Gulf, and on the other the stretches far away from land (one or several hundred miles) where the currents are so sluggish that the ice remains all winter in unbroken masses, hundreds of square miles in area. In my various exploratory journeys I have had little use for the mauttok method, but I have always carried it in my mind and felt about it as one feels about an accident insurance policy—it is unnecessary as long as all goes well, but a very good thing to have up your sleeve in case of hard luck.

The third method of seal hunting is the most important in the sense that most seals are killed by it, but it is so simple that it is hardly worth describing. Where the offshore ice is broken up, you simply take your station near the edge of the landfast ice early in the morning and watch the water, waiting for a seal to appear. You may see none when you first arrive at the open water, and you may see none all day. It has happened to me that I have sat at the edge of open water day after day for a week without seeing a seal. But luck will turn and eventually they will come.

It has also happened that when I came to the edge of the water in the early morning I saw dozens of seals within shooting distance and had as many as I wanted killed within a few minutes. In traveling we never want more than one at a time, but when we are spending the winter in some settled camp we like to secure enough in the fall to last all winter. We seldom succeed in doing that, however, and usually it is necessary even when living in one place to do at least a little hunting during the winter. In a way this is really best for it keeps camp life from becoming monotonous.

The only point about hunting seals in open water is that you must shoot them through the head. When spying around, the seal will often lift himself out of the water so high that you could shoot him through the heart, but if you make an opening through his body, and especially if you perforate the lungs, he is very likely to sink. At the hunting season in the fall, we estimate that of seals shot through the head nine out of ten will float. If seals are shot through the body, many of them will sink—anything from one out of four to one out of two.

There are two kinds of seals that we hunt north of Canada and north of Alaska; the ordinary seal (*phoca hispida*) and the bearded seal (*erignathus barbatus*). Even the largest of the common seals do not go much over two hundred pounds, but the bearded seals may run up to eight hundred pounds.   Both are valuable for food, but most people prefer the bearded seals.  The great difficulty about them, however, is that when killed in the water they usually sink, and when harpooned through a hole in the ice, they are so strong that they may pull the harpoon line from the hands of the hunter and swim off with it.   There are Eskimos whose hands have been cut to the bone by the rope slipping through them as the seal was getting away.

# CHAPTER III

AMONG land animals the polar bears are the most powerful of all beasts of prey. When full grown they may be three times as big as the biggest African lion. Their white color makes them difficult to see against a background of snow or ice, and few animals have more intelligence. It is important therefore that the hunter (and especially people like us who live by hunting) shall understand their nature and habits thoroughly.

Some say the Kadiak bears of southwestern Alaska are larger than polar bears. Even if this be so, they are far less dangerous, for a grizzly is chiefly vegetarian in his diet. But polar bears live exclusively by hunting seals and under certain circumstances they are likely to mistake people for seals and attack them on that basis. This makes them, in my experience at least, far more dangerous than the grizzly. I have killed thirteen grizzlies, but only for scientific purposes or else when badly in need of food. I always avoid killing grizzlies when I can. With all their strength and their splendid weapons of teeth and claws they are generally retiring and will avoid a man whenever they can. It is possible that polar bears also would avoid men if they knew what they were. But they so frequently mistake us for seals that it makes little practical difference to us what they might do if they really knew what we were.

There is wide spread a curious belief about polar bears

—that they live mainly or partly on fish. This belief probably arose from the well-known fact that black bears and grizzlies in forests and mountains frequently eat fish. The belief has been confirmed when people about to write zoölogical or geographical text-books for schools have visited zoölogical gardens and have found that polar bears in captivity eat fish. The reason why they are fed fish in captivity is primarily that fish is cheaper than meat. I have killed many dozens of polar bears and have seen hundreds of others, but I have yet to find any evidence that they eat fish or try to catch them. Neither have I met any Eskimo who believes that polar bears ever try to catch fish.

When I first lived at Tuktuyaktok in 1906, we had bear fat to eat with our fish. Two or three bears had been killed in the early fall before I arrived and their meat had been eaten immediately but some of the fat had been saved against winter. After my arrival no bears were found in that locality and I went home at the end of my first polar expedition without ever having seen a bear.

My first bear hunt came on my second expedition, the winter of 1909-10. It was not really my bear hunt but that of some Eskimos who were living on the north coast of Alaska east of Point Barrow.

The time was mid-winter, and the sun even at noon did not rise above the southern horizon. It was not far below the horizon, though, for the clouds in the south were red and yellow and other sunset colors for several hours around noon each day, and there was light enough for aiming a rifle from nine-thirty in the morning until two-thirty in the afternoon.

The Eskimos were living in a village of three houses with a total population of about twenty people. Traps were being set for foxes in the near neighborhood.  For this and other reasons the Eskimos kept their dogs tied— otherwise they were liable to go afield and get caught in the traps.  In mid-winter this would be serious, for although a dog never freezes his feet under ordinary circumstances, his foot would be frozen solid in an hour if held between the steel jaws of a trap.

The people were at breakfast when the dogs set up a great racket.  All the men rushed out with rifles in their hands.  The morning light was not yet clear but they could see the slightly yellowish figure of a polar bear against the white of the hillside.  He was standing two or three hundred yards off and apparently considering what to make of all the racket.  As the first men were coming out his mind was made up and he started off along the coast at a rolling gallop.  Some of the Eskimos rushed to where the dogs were tied and let go half a dozen of them.  Each dog as he was freed flew like an arrow in the direction in which the bear had disappeared.  A bear can run a good deal faster than a man but not nearly as fast as a dog, and inside of a mile the first dog caught up to him and bit him sharply in the heel, whereupon the bear turned around and tried to strike the dog with his fore paw.  But the agility of a dog is superior to that of a bear and if he has good footing he is certain to avoid the blows aimed at him.

The first dog was soon joined by the second and later by all the rest.  They made a howling and snapping ring round the bear.  It did not make any difference which dog he faced, there would be another dog at his heels to bite him.

Had there been but one Eskimo hunter all might have been well.  From this adventure and from several others

of the same kind, I learned that whenever possible there
should be but a single hunter at a bear hunt.  With a
party of white men it is nearly impossible to manage this,
for unless they are old hands they become daffy with
excitement whenever a bear turns up.  Eskimos are little
better, especially the youngsters who have never seen a
bear or at least have never helped kill one.  In this case,
there were eight or ten Eskimos, ranging in age from boys
of ten or twelve to the leading man of the community who
was about fifty.  As they came they shouted to each
other and to the dogs.

The polar bear evidently realized that there was more
danger from the men than the dogs, so he set off again at
a gallop.  But the dogs nipped his heels so viciously
that he did not have quite the strength of mind to continue running and turned again in an attempt to corner
one of the dogs against an ice hummock.  Several delays
of this sort eventually enabled the hunters to get within
shooting distance and a fusillade began.  The old man
begged the others not to shoot for fear of killing some
of the dogs, but most of the excited hunters paid no
attention to him.  His intention was the sensible one of
getting within ten or fifteen yards of the scrimmage and
then watching for an opportunity to fire when no dogs
were in line with the bullets.  Waiting his chance he
would have shot the bear near the heart and everything
would have been over.  But before he got near enough,
one dog had been wounded by a stray bullet and just
as the old man was about to kill the bear, a second bullet
struck another dog and killed him instantly.  The bear
already had two or three flesh wounds which he appeared
to mistake for dog bites, for each time he was hit he
made redoubled efforts to catch the dogs.  When the old

man at last got a shot in, the bear fell dead. He found on walking up that the dog killed was the leader of his team and his favorite dog. He told me himself later that he would rather have ten bears escape than lose one such dog. This was partly sentiment; but even in money one good leader dog was worth as much as the skins of two or three bears.

I have seen several other hunts where dogs were set on bears and I have read a great deal about this sort of hunting which is common in Greenland and has been employed by certain explorers who work in that locality. The more I see and the more I read, the less inclined I am to favor the method. It is too dangerous to the dogs and if you are a good bear hunter you can get the bear well enough without the use of dogs.

Although polar bears are much more dangerous than grizzly bears, the risk to men in hunting them is commonly overrated. Still, there may be danger, as the following story shows:

It was in the early spring of 1910. Our party were on their way from the Mackenzie district by sled eastward along the north coast of the mainland. We were traveling along the shore of Dolphin and Union Straits. The coastline is fairly straight and much of the land right along the coast is low, but a short distance inland there are the foothills of a range of low mountains that run roughly parallel to the coast. My three Eskimo companions with our dog team had orders to travel about fifteen miles a day eastward along the coast and to camp at any suitable locality when they estimated that the fifteen-mile distance had been traversed. Our custom was that immediately after breakfast every morning I would leave the camp and walk about three miles directly

inland. This took me about an hour, during which the
Eskimos chatted and enjoyed themselves. At the end
of the first hour I would turn eastward to walk from hilltop to hilltop parallel to the coast and approximately
three miles inland. About this time the Eskimos would
come out of the camp and commence preparing in a
leisurely way for the day's march. They would pull
down the tent, roll up the bedding, load everything on
the sled and hitch up the dogs. Designedly this was
done slowly, and by the time they were ready to start I
would be five or six miles ahead of them.

Occasionally during the day they would stop at some
promontory and with their field glasses scan the country
inland from them and ahead for sight of me or for any
signal. My custom was that if I saw game I would heap
up a pile of stones on top of some hill. This would be
a sign to the Eskimos that I would probably kill game
about abreast of this monument. They would, accordingly, camp on the coast at the point nearest to the
monument and then come inland with an empty sled to
fetch any meat I might have secured.

We had also a system of signals which could be interpreted at a distance through field glasses. In some cases
when I saw game I sat down on a hilltop and waited until
I saw through my field glasses that the Eskimos had
stopped and were surveying the country through their
glasses. As soon as they saw me, they would make a
signal which I could see, whereupon I would stand up
and make signals which they in turn could interpret in
one of half a dozen ways. The signal might mean that
they were to camp and stay in camp, or might mean that
they were to camp and then come inland for meat. Again
the meaning might be that they could proceed to the next

suitable camping place and there await my arrival. In some cases I signaled to them that the game in sight was more convenient for them to kill than for me, whereupon two of them would immediately set off in the direction I indicated while the third made camp.

On the day in question I had seen no trace of game. I had been walking rapidly and must have been about five or six miles ahead of my companions. The mountains were running so near the coast at this place that my course was less than a mile from the beach. Up to that time we had on this journey depended for our living on caribou and grizzly bears. But now there were no signs of either, so I took up my position on a conspicuous hill and decided to spend an hour or so in a careful study of the sea ice through my field glasses in the hope of discovering either a sleeping seal or possibly a polar bear.

I had been examining the ice for some time when I noticed a spot which seemed to me more yellow than ice ought to be. It was about a mile from the coast out among the rough ice. I watched this for a long time but saw no motion. That was not conclusive in itself for a polar bear, especially after a full meal of seal meat, is likely to sleep for hours and even for the larger part of a day. Accordingly, I continued sitting and studying the ice elsewhere as well as the mountains behind me, occasionally turning my glasses to the yellow spot to see if it were still there. I think I had done this three or four times and my mind was just about made up to proceed along the coast and assume that the yellow spot was nothing but ice, when on looking back I failed to see it. It was a bear then and had started traveling or else had gotten up, moved a little way and lain down again behind a hummock where it would be invisible. If the animal was traveling, I should presently see it passing over some open space. I watched for a while but saw nothing. Evidently then the bear had merely made a short move and had gone to sleep behind a hummock.

I knew that when I got down on the sea ice it would be difficult to keep my bearings. The winter storms had broken the ice badly and it was heaped up in a chaos of hummocks that had the angular outline of very rugged mountains, although the highest peaks were no more than forty or fifty feet. When you get down among such ice, it is almost as if you were in a forest. You can see the neighboring hummocks and the sky above you, but you get no good view of your surroundings. When you climb to the top of even the highest crags of ice, you get a view of the tops of all the other crags, although here and there a little ice valley may open. But the mountains are so much higher than the ice that a man out on the ice can always get a view of them by climbing on a hummock. I accordingly memorized the mountains carefully so that by glancing back at them occasionally and keeping certain peaks in line I would be able to travel straight out upon the ice in the direction where the bear had disappeared.

Once certain of having my bearings right, I put my field glasses in their case and ran as fast as I could down the slope, for it was possible the bear might get up any time and move on. When I had traveled out on the ice about the estimated distance, I climbed on a hummock and spent some time looking around but saw nothing. The campaign now was to move from hummock to hummock for, say, a quarter of a mile until I felt sure that I had passed on beyond the bear. I would then begin to circle until I came upon the animal or else upon its tracks.

I was still thinking that the bear was ahead of me and was clambering down from a high ridge when I heard behind me a noise something like the hiss of an angry goose. From this point I shall tell the story as I wrote it down many years ago in my book "My Life With the Eskimo."

My rifle was buckled in its case slung across my back, and I was slowly and cautiously clambering down the far side of a pressure ridge, when I heard behind me a noise like the spitting of a cat or the hiss of a goose. I looked back and saw, about twenty feet away and almost above me, a polar bear.

Had he come the remaining twenty feet as quietly and quickly as a bear can, the literary value of the incident would have been lost forever; for, as the Greek fable points out, a lion does not write a book. From his eye and attitude, as well as the story his trail told afterward there was no doubting his intentions: the hiss was merely his way of saying, "Watch me do it!" Or at least that is how I interpreted it; possibly the motive was chivalry, and the hiss was his way of saying *Garde!* Whichever it was, it was the fatal mistake of a game played well to that point; for no animal on earth can afford to give warning to a man with a rifle. And why should he? Has a hunter ever played fair with one of them?

Afterward the snow told plainly the short—and for one of the participants, tragic—story. I had overestimated the bear's distance from shore, and had passed the spot where he lay, going a hundred yards or two to windward; on scenting me he had come up the wind to my trail, and had then followed it, walking about ten paces to leeward of it, apparently following my tracks by smelling them from a distance. The reason I had not seen his approach was that it had not occurred to me to look back over my own trail; I was so used to hunting bears that the possibility of one of them assuming my own role and hunting me had been left out of consideration. A good hunter, like a good detective, should leave nothing out of consideration.

In 1914 we were traveling over the moving ice pack north of Alaska. The ice in that vicinity was composed of islands, most of them several miles in diameter, and some of them as much as twenty or thirty miles in diameter, although a few were no larger than a city block and others even smaller. Like real islands, these were separated by water, but they were different from ordinary islands in being in continual motion and in bunting against each other as they moved. The motion was so very slow that it was scarcely perceptible, and when the islands collided, there was no shock that would knock you off your feet but merely a quiver and a groaning, grinding noise as one island crushed and broke the edges of another. The ice that made up the islands was of varying thickness, in few places less than three or four feet, and in many places as much as fifty or a hundred feet. The fifty or hundred-foot ice is not produced by continuous freezing, as in a lake, but rather by having thinner ice broken up and one cake heaped upon another until they are piled ten, fifteen or twenty layers deep. The different ice pieces later freeze together, making solid masses of great thickness.

Traveling over such ice we usually found a place where the corner of one island touched the corner of another, giving us a chance to cross over. But in one place we found that our island was not touching any other ice ahead of us. The water lane between us and the next island was only a dozen or two yards across and seemed to us to be getting narrower. We decided, accordingly, to stop and wait to see what would happen. We could have rigged up a device we called a sled boat for ferrying our party across, but this would have been a lot of bother and did not seem necessary, for the prospect was that in a few hours the ice masses would come together and we could then keep on our journey. Expecting only a short wait, we did not unhitch our dogs and everything was in readiness to start whenever a crossing became possible.

In the open water that was delaying us the seals were numerous. We killed some, fed our dogs, and made a great bonfire of blubber to boil a pot of fresh meat.

In the winter time we keep our rifles, field glasses and other similar things outdoors at all times. If they were taken into the house, moisture would form on them and this would be injurious. In the case of a rifle, it would cause rust on the inside of the barrel and that is the most important part of the rifle. During the winter there is no appreciable rust so long as the gun is kept outdoors, but now spring was approaching and with summer weather and increasing temperature there was likely to be rust. Under such conditions, it is my custom to oil the inside of the rifle barrel immediately after it has been used. In this case I had not only oiled my rifle, but I had put it in its case and strapped it on top of one of the sleds to be ready for the start.

We were sitting around the campfire enjoying our meal of boiled seal meat, when the dogs all at once commenced a great racket. From this point I shall allow Burt Mc-Connell to tell the story. He is now one of the editors of the Literary Digest but was then the youngest member of my ice-exploring party. He had never before seen a polar bear, and so this was a great event for him.

"We had been traveling with Stefansson northward over the moving ice of the Arctic Ocean in March and April of 1914 when, on the thirteenth day out, we were halted by a narrow lead of open water. The next morning, in the hope that a crossing might be found to the westward, the Commander started out, followed by Storkerson, Andreasen, Johansen, Crawford and myself, with the sleds and dogs. We followed the edge of the ice for an hour or more, when Storkerson saw a seal suddenly poke its head out of the water. At about the same time the Commander found a huge cake of ice adrift in the open lead, which was only about fifty feet wide at that point. Here was a ferry already built, so while we were getting the teams ready to go aboard the ferry the Commander and Storkerson walked along the lead in different directions in search of seals for dog food and for our own dinner. Four were shot in the course of an hour, then Storkerson set to work to make out of an empty tin can a stove which would burn seal blubber.

"Little did we think that the odor of the burning seal blubber and cooking seal meat would bring a polar bear into our camp, but that is just what it did. We had placed the dogs on the ferry, skinned a seal, made the stove, built a fire in it, and were cooking seal meat with the blubber from the same carcass for fuel when we were brought to our feet by a great commotion among the dogs. The Commander and Storkerson, who were nearest, ran toward the dogs to stop what they thought was a fight among them, and Crawford and I followed. I did not notice any special cause for the commotion until Storkerson yelled to us, 'It's a bear!'

"Knowing that our lives depended upon our dogs, and that a polar bear could kill one with a single blow of his powerful paw, everybody now ran to the assistance of the Commander and Storkerson. There were only two rifles on the sleds, however, so there was little that we could do except restrain the dogs from dragging the sleds into the water, in their eagerness to attack the bear.

"The white, shaggy monster was only twenty-five feet from the dogs. Fortunately, he was on the opposite side of the open water. He did not appear to be in the least afraid of the dogs, which were rearing, plunging and barking in their eagerness to be at him. But he completely ignored them, and merely stood facing them, with his head hanging downward and swinging slowly from side to side. Then he would peer into the water for a moment, as if trying to make up his mind to plunge in and swim across.

"Never in his life, it may safely be said, had this bear seen a dog. In fact, the only animals he had seen were foxes and seals, and he knew himself to be master of these. Perhaps these barking creatures were another species of fox. Well, he would plunge in, swim across, climb out on the other side with the aid of his powerful forelegs, and find out. By this time the Commander and Storkerson had arrived at the sleds which were separated from the bear by only a few feet of water, but the bear gave no heed to them or to the dogs, which by this time were in a perfect frenzy. He merely stood at the very edge of the ice, looking into the water, swaying from one side to the other like a polar bear in the zoo on a summer day, and swinging his ponderous head.

"Storkerson was the first to reach his rifle, which was lying loose on top of the sled that was farthest from the bear. Just as it appeared that the bear had made up his mind to swim over and kill our dogs, Storkerson took aim quickly and fired. The bullet, a .30-.30, hit the bear in the right foreleg, and knocked that member from under him, so that he turned a complete somersault into the water. It was at this juncture that I snapped a picture, but it was not a success. When the bear came to the surface all thought of visiting us had vanished; his only idea now was to escape.

"By this time, however, the Commander had unstrapped his rifle case and reached his rifle, which he had oiled and put away an hour before. The bear was wounded, and, while it might never menace our dogs again, it would be better to end its misery. So the Commander fired with his hard-shooting Gibbs-Mannlicher rifle as the now thoroughly frightened King of the Arctic clambered out upon the ice and started to limp away. This bullet knocked him over, but he got up again and in spite of a second hit from Storkerson's rifle, he disappeared behind a pressure ridge and was lost to view, leaving a broad trail of blood.

"During the excitement, as we now noticed, the lead had narrowed so much that Crawford and I with the .30-.30 rifle and the camera, were able to cross with the aid of a pair of skis and a long pole. We followed the trail of blood at a run, expecting at every turn to come upon the wounded animal, but we had proceeded almost half a mile before we saw him staggering along, holding his right foot clear of the ice. When he realized that he was being followed, he plunged into the first water he came to. It would be a simpler matter—so I thought—for Crawford to place a bullet in a vital place when the bear came to the surface. Three hasty shots inflicted only flesh wounds, however, and Crawford found that he had no more cartridges. I was about to run back to camp for more when the Commander appeared, bringing his Mannlicher. Although this rifle is of smaller caliber—.256—one bullet in the bear's heart killed him instantly as he clambered out upon the ice.

"In a sense, this misfortune to the bear was his own fault. The smell of the burning seal blubber and cooking seal-meat had attracted him from five miles away, as we later learned by studying his trail. On cutting him up, we saw he had not been hungry. Had he had the sense to study us from a distance of a hundred yards or even twenty-five yards, we should not have fired at him, for we had plenty of seal meat. But we had seen him first only a few feet away from our dogs and apparently hesitating only momentarily before plunging in to swim the narrow water lane that separated him from them. We fired the first shot to protect our dogs, and the others merely to put a wounded animal out of misery."

The last bear story of this book will be told by Harold Noice. Noice was born in Kansas City but brought up in Seattle. He was a boy fresh out of high school when he went to the Arctic Ocean on the whaling ship *Polar Bear*. The summer of 1915 we met the *Polar Bear* and purchased her to take the place of a ship our expedition had lost. Some of the crew of the *Polar Bear* stayed with the ship and joined our expedition. One of these was Noice. He accompanied us on two of our longest sledge journeys. He enjoyed the Arctic so much that when we sailed south in 1918 he asked to be allowed to remain behind, and spent four more years there studying the Eskimos of Coronation Gulf—till the fall of 1921. The story he tells here happened the spring of 1916 when we had discovered Meighen Island and were on our way back south to the base camp of our expedition in Banks Island. The spot where the story happened was on the sea ice twenty or thirty miles away from land and about seven hundred miles north of the arctic circle.

"Of all my hunting experiences extending over a period of six and a half years spent within the arctic circle, the most exciting was an encounter with a polar bear. Outside of parks and zoölogical gardens, it was the first I had ever seen at close range. The incident happened on one of my journeys with Stefansson. We had discovered new land in Latitude 80°N., Longitude 100°W., and were returning over the ice to our base camp some four hundred and fifty miles to the southward.

"One night just after we had pitched our tent fifteen yards from an open lead and after the Commander and I had gone inside, Charlie Andersen, the third member of our party, was about to follow us when he noticed something white moving in the water of the lead about two hundred yards from our tent. He thought at first that it was a piece of drifting ice; but when it began to move too rapidly for that, he picked up his binoculars to see what it really was. As he was focusing them upon the object it disappeared beneath the surface of the water, reappearing a little nearer to our camp. Charlie now saw that it was no chunk of ice but the head of a swimming polar bear.

"When Charlie called to us that a bear was swimming in the lead about two hundred yards away, I rushed out instantly. But the Commander was used to polar bears and did not get so excited. He put on his boots in a leisurely way before coming out and then stationed himself at the stern of our sled, telling me to take up my position at the bow.

"The sled was broadside to the lead. Charlie stood behind us where the dogs were tied, ready to quell any disturbance they might make when they caught sight of the bear.

"We waited patiently for the bear to come opposite. It is difficult to drag a heavy bear out of the water after he is shot, so we thought we could wait until he climbed out upon the ice before shooting him.

"Evidently the bear had seen the dogs sleeping in a row on the ice and had taken them to be seals. For at that time of the year seals like to lie on top of the ice beside their holes or beside open leads, basking in the warm sunshine. Polar bears make their living by sneaking up to these basking seals unawares, so it was not strange he should mistake the dogs for seals. The sled and tent looming up black against the white background resembled dirty ice, but as bears are used to seeing dirty ice he did not pay any particular attention to this.

"Thinking no doubt that he was soon to have a feed of fine fat seal meat, the bear took great pains in stalking the dogs. He would swim slowly back and forth across the lead, occasionally lifting his head a little above the level of the ice to see if the (supposed) seals had noticed him. The dogs were tired from their day's work and were lying stretched out comfortably asleep on the ice and suspecting no danger.

"Finally the bear reached a spot nearly opposite us. Stealthily he raised his massive forepaws upon the ice. Then quickly but without a sound, he lifted himself out of the water and in an instant this ferocious beast with its wicked pig-like eyes and yellow-fanged snarling muzzle, was nearly on top of us. Stefansson and I were crouched down behind the sled about three yards apart with only our heads showing. The bear was headed directly for Stefansson, giving me a quartering view. He was coming so fast that he had covered more than half the distance to us when I fired. At the report of my rifle the bear rolled over, turning a somersault towards us before he stopped, for he was going so fast. Stefansson told me to fire again, for our now frantically barking dogs were in danger should the wounded bear turn towards where they were tied. I pulled on the trigger, but it would not budge—my gun was jammed. The Commander then used his Mannlicher-Schoenauer and finished the job. I found later that sand had become lodged under the rim of my cartridge and had prevented it from slipping all the way into the chamber. The Winchester safety device had therefore prevented the hammer from falling when I pulled on the trigger—otherwise the gun would have back-fired and I might not have been able to write this story.

"After the bear had been killed, Charlie started to laugh at me for getting 'buck-fever' and hitting the bear in the leg. Now this was the first bear I had ever shot at, and as our Commander had shot dozens during his many years of hunting in the North, he had said I might kill this one. It might seem you could not miss so huge an animal as a bear coming almost straight at you, but you must remember I was pretty excited. The muzzle of my gun was probably describing wobbly curves when I was about to fire, for my heart was thumping about one hundred to the minute. It was therefore largely a matter of luck whether my bullet hit the bear's head or his feet, or missed him entirely. I knew this, but still

I felt sure it was I that had brought the bear down, until the Commander remarked that he also had fired at him. The two guns had gone off so nearly together that neither Charlie nor I knew that he had fired.

"Now the question arose, Who killed the bear? He had been hit in the forepaw and also in the shoulder. As I had never shot at a bear, Charlie insisted it was my bullet that had struck him in the paw. But I feel pretty strongly I could not have missed that badly. The Commander improved things a good deal by suggesting that when an animal is charging and when you are low down, its paws may well be in a straight line with its heart. It was even possible the same bullet might have passed through the paw and later lodged in the shoulder. His final verdict was that for purposes of record it might as well be considered my bear—he had killed enough of them before. I like to feel he missed that bear, but I must admit that (if so) it was the only poor shot I ever knew him to make at a charging polar bear, or indeed at any animal he needed to kill. I have since seen a number of polar bears but none of them have seemed to me so large or so ferocious as this one—none of them ever had the 'wicked pig-like eyes' and 'snarling yellow-fanged muzzle' of my first bear—which, when dead, presented an entirely different appearance. It turned out to be a rather small two-year-old.

"Since returning to civilization I have heard some of my friends who hunt in Alaska or Africa tell thrilling and hair-raising stories of their adventures with grizzlies and lions. I have heard them describe the lion charging with wide-open mouth and terrifying roars into the very arms of the cool, level-headed amateur hunters. Perhaps I am giving them less credit than they deserve but I just

can't help judging other people's lions by my first polar
bear.  Although I know my friends to be truthful in
everyday matters, I usually take their most thrilling
stories with just a grain of salt."

**E N D**

This map is intended primarily to illustrate the narrative of Stefansson's journeys during the time covered by this book (1906-7), but an attempt is also made to indicate graphically some of the results of his later expeditions—those of 1908-12 and 1913-18.

The dotted land areas are islands the existence of which was not previously known—islands both discovered and explored. Heavy black shading shows features previously known to exist but where Stefansson's work has resulted in fundamental changes in the maps. The barred areas at sea extend 25 miles each way from Stefansson's routes on journeys where he traversed previously unexplored regions (on the 1913-18 expedition).

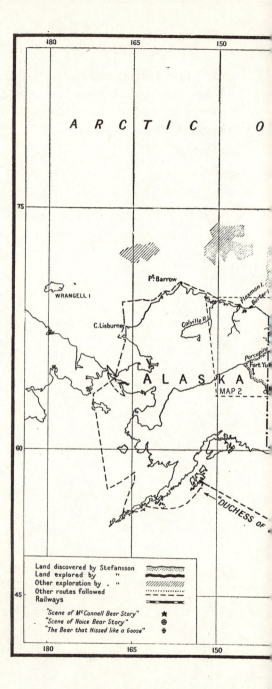

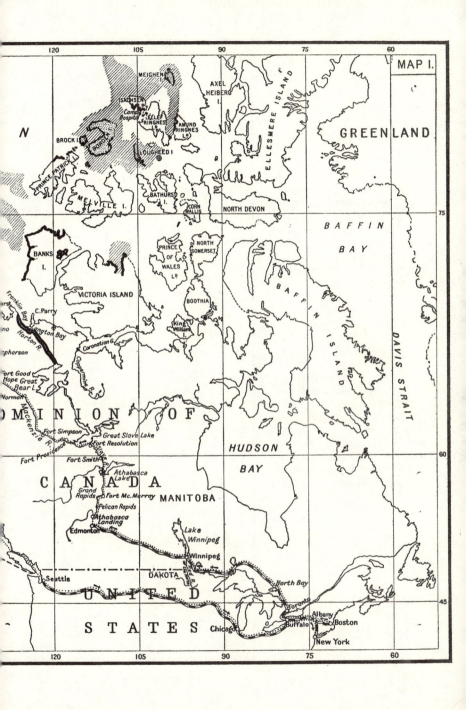

This map shows the territory covered by the narrative of this book between July, 1906, and September, 1907. More than half of the country north of the arctic circle is a spruce forest, but there are extensive prairies along the arctic coast. The prairie is narrowest on the eastern margin of the Mackenzie delta (20 or 30 miles wide) and broadest near the Colville River in Alaska (150 or 200 miles). Although the map is as correct as our present knowledge, there are uncertainties, and authorities differ on many points. For the north coast of Alaska we have followed Leffingwell's surveys and for the Eskimo Lakes those of Harrison. These are much the best sources available.

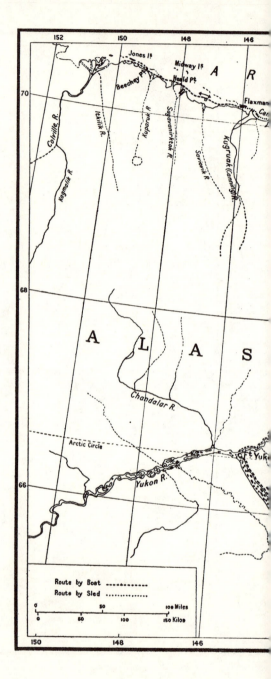

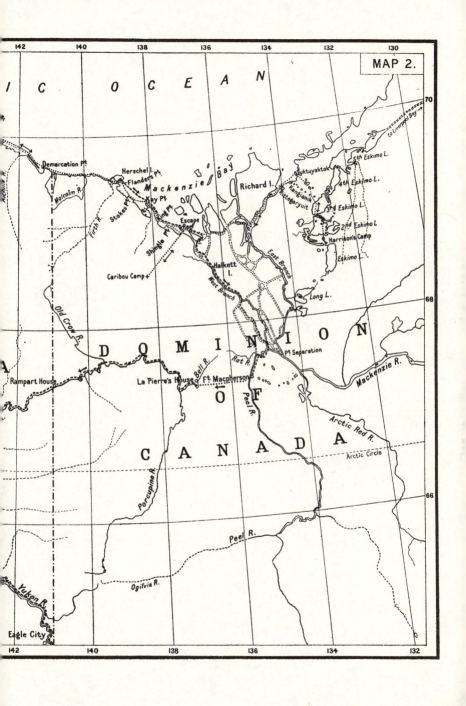